# SEARCHING
# FOR
# YOUR ANCESTORS

## Completely Updated and Revised Fifth Edition

*For everyone who wants to find his or her roots,
SEARCHING FOR YOUR ANCESTORS provides every-
thing you need to know to begin, and to follow where your
ancestors' paths may lead.*
- *Sample charts to organize your family tree*
- *Ways to obtain the facts—and to avoid false leads*
- *Specific information for over 35 ethnic groups*
- *Lists out-of-the-way sources*
- *Suggests further reading*

*The authors' advice is based on years of experience in
tracing family histories and is illustrated by specific
examples and anecdotes.*

*"Undoubtedly the most popular, authoritative and readable
guidebook for amateur genealogists and libraries."*
     —*The Maryland and Delaware Genealogist*

*"Still the most encouraging introduction for a beginner,
and the most enjoyable for anyone."*
     —*The New York Genealogical and Biographical Record*

# SEARCHING
# FOR
# YOUR ANCESTORS

*The How and Why of Genealogy*

GILBERT H. DOANE, **F.A.S.G.**

and

JAMES B. BELL, **F.S.A.**
*Director, New England Historic Genealogical Society*

## FIFTH EDITION

**BANTAM BOOKS**
TORONTO · NEW YORK · LONDON · SYDNEY

*"Think not that the nobilitie of your Ancestors doth free you to doe all that you list, contrarywise, it bindeth you more to followe vertue."*

PIERRE ERONDELL

This low-priced Bantam Book
contains the complete text of the
original hard-cover edition.
NOT ONE WORD HAS BEEN OMITTED.

SEARCHING FOR YOUR ANCESTORS:
THE HOW AND WHY OF GENEALOGY
*A Bantam Book / published by arrangement with
University of Minnesota Press*

PRINTING HISTORY
*First published 1937 by Whittlesey House (2 printings)
Revised edition published 1948 by University of Minnesota Press (3 printings)
Third edition published 1960 (5 printings)
Fourth edition published 1973
Fifth edition published 1980*

*First Bantam edition / January 1974
Revised Bantam edition / November 1982*

ISBN 0-553-20199-9

*Published simultaneously in the United States and Canada*

PRINTED IN THE UNITED STATES OF AMERICA

O   0 9 8 7 6 5 4 3 2 1

# Preface

More than four decades ago, on the Great Plains of Nebraska, in Lincoln, I took pen to paper and wrote the first edition of this book. At that time there seemed to me to be few people interested in the study of their family's past, and I wrote, at least I thought so, for a rather small and special sort of group of historians. But all of that has changed during the intervening forty and more years, and the audience of a few has increased to a multitude: a multitude of men and women, young and old, rich and poor, from every kind of national and ethnic background. The renewal of interest in genealogy is indeed stirring to my heart and imagination: I never dreamed there would be such broad interest in searching for ancestors.

You have much company in your search for your ancestors, since there has been an explosion of interest in family history during recent years. The bicentennial celebration throughout the country helped trigger a renewed interest in family history, as did the centenary jubilee in 1875 and 1876. Of course, Alex Haley's book *Roots* and the television series popularized in a dramatic and powerful way one man's lonely but persistent pursuit to know his family's history.

Interest in family history has sparked the introduction of courses on local history and families at colleges and universities, at high schools and grade schools, in centers for adult education from Maine to Hawaii. For students at every rung of education's ladder, the study of one's family history is really the study of the great themes and rhythms of history through a microscope. Every family has its immigrant ancestors: from England, or Ireland, or Germany, or Italy, or Poland, or from some other country to the United States. They may have arrived on one of the first ships in the early seventeenth century or on one of the flying-boats in the twentieth century. It makes no matter: the important fact is to identify the members of your family who boldly moved from the Old World to the New. We want to know as much about them as we are able to gather from numerous sources: their names, the dates of their arrival in the United States, and where they lived and worked.

Every family has encountered war, say, the Revolutionary War or Civil War, World Wars I or II, or the Viet Nam War. Perhaps a father, husband, or brother, a cousin, loved one, or ancestor served in one or another of these wars, and although we hope they returned safely from military service, we know many did not. Some were wounded and crippled, and some died serving their country and lie buried in cemeteries near and distant.

Every family has experienced fear and loss during economic depressions and unemployment not only in the 1930s but in earlier decades and the past fifty years, too.

Today when we visit our family doctor for an annual checkup, we are frequently asked about the medical histories and ailments of our parents, grandparents, brothers, and sisters. A medical profile of our ancestors' sicknesses is a vital reference tool for physicians in diagnosing and treating our complaints.

It is fascinating to learn, too, the sort of work our forebears followed: were they sailors or farmers, joiners or coopers, preachers or merchants? We want to know where our ancestors worked and lived. We want to identify the town, village, or farm in which they lived and determine whether or not their house is still standing.

Someone asked me recently, "Why do you think there is such an explosive interest in family history today?" It is an interesting question, and I offer my observations for whatever they may be worth. First, as I noted earlier, I think the recent bicentennial ceremonies triggered a renewed interest in our country's history as well as that of local communities and of families. Second, Alex Haley's important book has stirred up a desire among people of every national and ethnic background to search for their ancestors. Third, we have lived through some difficult and turbulent times: the assassinations of prominent political leaders, a far-off and little understood war, the damaging twin assaults of economic recessions and run-away inflation, and the uncertainty of nuclear warfare. The uncertainties of the present day seem tempered and steadied by the study of the past, of our family's history, a sort of anchor on the fast moving, ever changing time-line of history. The rhythms and events of the present day take on a new hue and understanding with an appreciation of the past.

This book is intended to be an introduction to the method of searching for elusive and forgotten ancestors. It has been prepared and written especially for the person who always thought that he or she would look up the family tree, but has never gotten around to it. The average person never does get around to it, mainly because he or she does not know how to start and feels a bit uneasy, perhaps, about asking a librarian for directions. This book is designed also for librarians in public libraries so that they may have something to put into the hands of patrons who have decided to look up their ancestors and come to librarians for advice.

A word of warning to prospective searchers for ancestors: do your own digging, at least at the beginning or until you have found out enough about your family or have definite problems you want to solve. When you have done as much as you think you can or seem to have struck a ledge of rock in your digging, then consult with or take your problem to a genealogist of good repute. But beware of circular letters that come to you unsolicited through the mails offering to supply a complete history of your family on receipt of your check. Do not waste your money on widely advertised genealogical services that appear to promise you your lineage back to the emigrant ancestor. If you fall for their subtle appeal to pride, you are likely to receive a pamphlet containing a few paragraphs on the origin of your surname, a few statements about the most prominent people of that name (which appeals, of course, to your vanity by implying that you are definitely connected with them), and a record, which may or may not be authentic, of the first few generations of the family in America. Proof of your own connection with the emigrants probably will not be given, and in the end you will in all likelihood find yourself with your same old problem and minus the money you have remitted.

There are reputable and reliable genealogists, many of them. As a rule they advertise very little and generally in genealogical magazines only, such as *The New England Historical and Genealogical Register* or *The American Genealogist*. But there are other ways and means of getting in touch with them. If the librarian of your public library or local historical society does not know any locally, the curators of the genealogical collections in the larger cities may have a list. Or write to the Board for the Certification of Genealogists, sponsored by the American Society of Genealogists, for an up-to-date list of certified genealogists, American lineage specialists, and genealogical record searchers. The address is 1307 New Hampshire Avenue, N.W., Washington, D.C. 20036. You should remember that a capable genealogist, like any other competent professional man or woman, has spent a great deal of time and money acquiring competency to solve difficult problems. So do not be surprised if a genealogist's fee seems rather stiff. As a matter of fact, it is extremely difficult to fix an equitable charge for any professional service — try to figure out what your own experience in your own line of work is really worth.

When you pay a physician, a lawyer, an architect, you are paying for accumulated wisdom and expert knowledge. The same is true when you pay an experienced genealogist. Further, you must realize that no one can guarantee you a solution to your problem.

In the interest of accuracy, from the very start beware of using books that are made up of pedigrees and biographical sketches contributed by those who subscribe to the books, sometimes called "mug" books — many reproduce photographs of the biographees. Some of these are good and some of them are bad, but all have to be checked against original records if possible. Until you have done this, you cannot be sure of their reliability. Some of the contributors to such volumes have undoubtedly been very careful in what they supplied, but others have pieced together their pedigrees from unauthentic sources or guessed at the connecting links. During the last hundred years a great many books of this kind have been published; they are to be found in every genealogical library. As you become familiar with the methods of genealogical research, you will learn to pick the flaws in them and to use them with discretion.

In this fifth edition of *Searching for Your Ancestors*, I have been joined, at my request, with my good friend, Dr. James B. Bell, Director of the New England Historic Genealogical Society. We have worked well together on a number of projects over the last several years, and his expertise and editorial hand have been brought to the tasks necessarily set for a new edition of this book. Every line of the earlier edition has been reviewed and revised when out of date and corrected when inaccurate. To reflect the extraordinary interest in the search for ancestors today I have broadened the scope of the book a bit, added new material, in hopes of providing information and assistance to persons studying their family's genealogy in the United States and across the seas.

I do want to record again my thanks to my wife Susan and to my children. They have observed and supported the preparation, writing, and revisions of this book since its birth on the plains of Nebraska a few years ago. I thank too James B. Bell, not only for his attention to details, but also for his ever ready help in preparing this edition for the printer's bench. We have many common interests, not least of which is the search for a "really good dish of ice cream." We have, on several occasions, nearly found it!

To those of you who read this book and are led into the pursuit of your ancestors, Dr. Bell and I owe you both congratulations and condolences: condolences because we know that you will never be able to rid yourselves of the desire to search one more family line, and congratulations because we know that you will have found an absorbing hobby which will enrich you in many ways.

G.H.D.
Newton, Mass.
J.B.B.
Boston, Mass.

# Contents

# PART ONE

## How to Search for Your Ancestors

# CHAPTER 1

# Jaunts and Jollities
# among Ancestors

"Who was your great-grandmother? What was her maiden name? Where did she live?"

If in the last census the enumerator had asked these questions of everyone and the results had been tabulated, the percentage of people who could give the answers would probably have been small indeed.

Yet an eighth of the blood flowing in your veins came from your great-grandmother, and possibly a much larger proportion of your individual traits: your sweet winning ways or your irascible disposition. Despite loose talk concerning the importance of heredity, we do "take after" people. A woman who lived in one of the New England states during the first half of the nineteenth century was noted for her temper and strength of will. By her first husband she had an only child, a son, who married and fathered a large family. Among his children two of the brothers fell into a dispute over some property and lived in the same small village for twenty years afterward without speaking to each other; two of the sisters "got mad" over something or other and refused to recognize each other again. When one of them died, thirty-five years later, the other deliberately mopped her own front porch while the deceased sister's funeral procession was passing! The same pertinacity cropped out in two of that same woman's grandchildren (brothers again) by her second husband.

Do you have a full quota of 1024 great-great-great-great-great-great-great-grandparents in the tenth generation back, or are you, like most of us, a cousin of your own a few times? Are you one of those really rare individuals who can trace descent from every one of the fifty passengers on the *Mayflower* in 1620 from whom a blood descent has been proved, or merely one of the thousands living today who can trace a line back to one or two of that little band? Can you follow your ancestry to an old Cavalier family in Virginia, or are you stymied by one of your forefathers who dropped, apparently from heaven, into southern Ohio about 1820? Did this man quarrel with his older brother over the distribution of their father's estate, go west in a huff, change his patronymic, and never mention his rightful name again? Or possibly your ancestor arrived in one of America's port cities, Boston, New York, Philadelphia, or Baltimore during the waves of immigration during the nineteenth century from Ireland, Italy, Germany, Poland, Russia, and other European nations.

Have you ever tried to verify the traditions that have been handed down from generation to generation in your family, say that of the seven brothers who came from England in the *Lion's Whelp*? If your name happens to be Allen and your father told you that his father said that he was a descendant of the famous and impetuous Green Mountain Boy, Ethan Allen, have you ever attempted to confirm that statement from the records? Do you know that this particular Ethan Allen had but one living male descendant of the surname Allen in 1900, and hence descent is possible in the female line only? Or did your father say that his father told him that he *thought* the family was related to the Vermont hero?

The centennial celebrations in 1876 awakened an interest in the part played in the American Revolution and the establishment of the United States by the grandparents and great-grandparents of those whose awareness of history was thereby stimulated. This, in turn, sparked the founding of numerous patriotic and hereditary societies such as the Society of Mayflower Descendants, the Daughters of the American Revolution, and the Society of Colonial Wars. Their expanding membership created a continuing interest in family history and tracing descents from more remote progenitors. Hence the development of genealogy as a discipline in this country. Since World War II, the establishment of the five-day week, the expansion of Social Security and pension benefits, and enforced retirement soon after the "prime of life" is presumed to have waned have created a new leisure class. Many in that category have turned to the study of family history as something more than a hobby; it becomes an engrossing occupation, a new vocation for an active and inquisitive mind. There are some who, having acquired competence through the years of pursuit when it was an avocation, have been able to eke out inadequate annuities by capitalizing on the expertise they have gained.

## We Learn the Story of Our Families

Digging for lost ancestors is far more than simply collecting the names of your ascendants. It sometimes takes you into strange places, and in the course of your excavations a considerable amount of history, geography, psychology, and law very likely will be added to your store of knowledge. You don't dig merely to accumulate a lot of dry bones, as it were. Or to change the metaphor, you simply cannot back-trail your progenitors without becoming interested in the times in which they lived and in the various phases of their lives and activities. Suppose you are a midwesterner and are tracing your line of ascent back to the emigrant. You find that your grandfather came to Kansas or Nebraska as a homesteader. If you are not apathetic to the past, you cannot help delving into the history of the famous Homestead Act and learning its effect on the migration to the Great Plains after the Civil War. You go back further and find that your great-grandfather came to Ohio from "York State" and you wonder how they traveled in those days. You dig into the history of the great westward movement which followed the War of 1812 and the building of the Erie Canal, and perhaps you reread *Rome Haul* or *Drums along the Mohawk* with excited interest because now you know that that was the life which your own people lived and knew, or you see some of the historical movies or "documentaries" with greater interest, picturing your own ancestors in them. Then you go back another generation or so and learn that another ancestor took part in the capture of Ticonderoga in 1776 and was one of the Green Mountain Boys. Suddenly all the glamour of that exploit of Ethan Allen's assumes an intimate meaning for you, for a man of your blood was with him and may even have heard the actual words that he used as he demanded the surrender of the fort from the British officer who was nervously clutching his trousers in the dim, cold morning light — a remark probably much more profane than the reputed "Open in the name of the Great Jehovah and the Continental Congress!" It isn't so difficult to visualize such events when you know that your own people took part in them. And incidentally you'll probably observe that in the wake of every war in our history there has developed a restlessness and dissatisfaction with life as it had been before the war, and that a great movement of people has resulted in each case.

Thus, step by step, generation by generation, you trace the blood back into the past, ultimately reaching the seaboard and the emigrant ancestor. You may be one of those fortunate enough to find records which take the line across the ocean to the "old country." Such a discovery, or the effort to make it, frequently results in a clearer understanding of the problems in the Europe of that time, or at least stimulates a desire to know more about it.

### The Kinds of Jobs

In riding this hobby you can easily see what fascinating byways there are, lanes that look so inviting you cannot proceed without investigating them a bit. Consequently, you turn your hobby horse's head away from the main trail and explore a little, knowing that you can always come back again and continue along the main road. Let us suppose that one of your ancestors was a cloth manufacturer in central New York. Doesn't the history of that trade interest you, and aren't you keen to find out what economic conditions caused the family to give up and move westward? Or, again, maybe one of them was a potter and helped to make what is known as Bennington pottery. Now that funny-looking old brown china dog, which Grandmother insisted on lugging out to Iowa with her, comes to mean something, and perhaps you delve into John Spargo's book, *The Potters and Potteries of Bennington*, to learn about its manufacture.

Or what if you come upon the rather unsavory fact that your great-great-grandfather was killed by a revenue officer in a raid on the smugglers on Lake Champlain? Are you going to give up digging because you've struck such a rock? Or are you going to look into the history of smuggling in northern Vermont around 1800? If you decide to take up the spade again you will find that many of those people on the border — then truly frontier — had the courage to earn the best living they could and to sell their produce where it would bring them the best return. You'll find that they had many admirable qualities and were people to be proud of, in spite of their apparent lawlessness.

## Migration Routes

All this and more will fascinate you. The Cumberland Gap will become more than a railway pass through the Allegheny range if your people came through it before the Baltimore and Ohio Railroad was built. The "State of Frankland" will be more than a mere phrase in a schoolbook if your people chanced to settle in Tennessee about 1780. "Natchez Trace" will cease to be a mysterious term when you follow your ancestors in their migration from the Carolinas to Louisiana and Texas. History will become part and parcel of your blood.

## Religion

Even religion may assume a new aspect, or your respect
for it may be increased. Suppose you find that you are
descended from Mary Dyer, the "Quaker Martyr," who
was hanged in Boston, 1 June 1660. Wouldn't you want
to know the reason for her fate? There is a saying among
her descendants that they are all close-mouthed because
she talked too much and got herself hanged. If you find
that your family moved from Dartmouth, Mass., to Nine
Partners, Dutchess County, N.Y., won't you want to
know why there was a migration across Connecticut
about 1735, and, moreover, why any town should have
been called "Nine Partners"? You'll find that a large
group of people who had become Quakers wanted to
get away from the rather severe and unpleasant ostra-
cism of the predominating religious element in Massachusetts and have a place of their own, where they
could worship as they pleased (and, perhaps, enforce
their own ideas of religious belief). You'll learn the history of the grants in Dutchess County and perhaps find
your family located in that curiously named area, the
Oblong, no longer on the map. You may learn of the rise
of the Hicksites, a group of Quakers who seceded from
the main body of that faith and followed Elias Hicks,
many of them moving westward into Kentucky and
southern Ohio. You will run into a hundred and one
other sects, each centered around some picturesque
leader, such as Mother Ann.

Possibly your people became Mormons and followed
Joseph Smith to Nauvoo, Ill., and later accompanied
Brigham Young across the Plains to found Salt Lake City
and the Mormon empire beyond the Rockies. After a
visit to Salt Lake and to what is perhaps the most mag-
nificent location for a city in the entire United States,
admiration for the vision of the great Mormon leader
grows apace.

Your interest in economic conditions in the past will
develop amazingly as you explore. If you have a strain
of Irish blood, you will find yourself investigating the

great potato famine in Ireland in the 1840s, or going further back and delving into life in Ireland in the seventeenth century, for there was a migration from Ireland to America as early as that. You begin to understand the difference between Ulster and "Ireland," the north and the south of the Emerald Isle, the Orangemen and the wearers of the green.

If your people are of Pennsylvania German ancestry, you may want to dig into the history of the Palatinate in the eighteenth century and find out why there was a great migration from Germany to Pennsylvania in the first half of that period. Then you will discover along what paths those people moved on, southward into Maryland and Virginia, and later westward over the mountains and through the Ohio Valley.

Perhaps you have a Huguenot line of descent. What was the history of that famous persecution? What were the conditions in France that caused a whole body of people to flee, first to England, and afterward to America? Where did they settle?

How long have there been Jews resident in America? Do you know about Judah Touro, that fine old patriarch whose remains lie in a wistaria-draped cemetery on Touro Street in Newport, R.I.? Does the name Abraham Redwood mean anything to you, and are you aware that the oldest library building in America, Redwood Library in Newport, was founded by him in 1752? This library, still a "subscription library," is located on Bellevue Avenue, one of the most noted streets in America, on which are to be found the summer villas of the Vanderbilts, Astors, and Whitneys. In front of it stands the first fern beech to be transplanted from Switzerland to America, a truly beautiful tree, well worth traveling to see in its lacy beauty on a bright summer day.

These are but a few of the fascinating byways of genealogy. Scoffers do not realize that digging for ancestors means far more than merely accumulating names. They think of it as "dry as dust" and even less interesting. They do not understand that it is a stimulating, living study, well worth pursuing, and that from it we may learn not only the history of our own family but also a great deal about the history of our country in which our own people have played a part and also a great deal about ourselves.

## Tools and Sources

Genealogical research doesn't call for a lot of expensive equipment — just a notebook, a few pencils, an inquisitive mind, and a willingness to ask questions and dig for facts. To assist beginning genealogists, Dr. Bell has compiled a companion to *Searching for Your Ancestors*, called the *Family History Record Book* (published by the University of Minnesota Press, 2037 University Ave. S.E., Minneapolis, MN 55414). The record book contains useful charts and forms for family research and provides a substantial introduction and practical advice about how to obtain and record information efficiently.

Gather what you can from relatives; the older they are, the better. But all that comes to you from Great-Aunt Hettie, or garrulous Uncle Abijah, must not be accepted as the truth. The memories of some old folks are less reliable than those of others. Some like to make a good story out of a fact; some do not realize how much they have forgotten and how much they have added to the story in telling it. Your job is to note the details as best you can and check them later.

Once the memory of your older relatives is exhausted, you begin to dig in official records: vital records, probate records, church records, and the like. Each yields its quota of amusement, as well as information, as does the following from the East Haddam, Conn., land records.

John the sone of John Warner and of Mahittabel his wife was borne December ye: 18th: 1716

Daniell ye sone of John Warnor and of Mahittabell his wife was borne May ye: 6th: 1717

To this the editor of the printed records has added the pertinent comment, "Quick work!"

Cemeteries, too, contain many things both puzzling and droll. Dr. Doane found a stone in a northern Vermont cemetery on which the inscription had been completely defaced. What is the story behind that vandalism? In the same cemetery he found the inscription:

> Sacred to the Memory of Inestimable Worth to Unrivaled Excellence and Virtue, Miss Cynthia Page, Whose Remains are Deposited here and Whose Ethereal Part Became a Seraph on the 4th of March 1824 — Aged 20 Years.

Nearby lies:

> Diah Sherwood, Died April 24, 1853, in his 90th Year. A Soldier of the Revolution

and beside him:

> Jayhannah, wife of Dyer Sherwood, Died May 22, 1833, in Her 67th Year

What a task Dr. Doane had identifying "Diah" or "Dyer!" Alas for the New Englander's propensity for attaching "r" to words ending in a vowel sound. After several years of searching he finally discovered that "Dyer" (as his name was spelled in most of the land records pertaining to him) was identical with Jedediah Sherwood, who migrated from Connecticut to Vermont about 1790, later moved to Ohio, and finally returned to Vermont, where he died.

Wills, too, are more than records of bequests and disposals. In a certain probate court there is a pre-Revolutionary will in which the testator specified the actual rooms in his house that each of his two daughters and his widow were to have after his death. Each was to have right of way through the central hallway and across the garden to the well. It is easy to picture the family: a thrice-married man who at death was survived by a daughter of each of his first two wives and by his third wife. With each of the three women jealous of the other two, the old man was wise enough to know that there would be an unholy scramble, once he was gone, unless he made explicit terms in his bequest.

Sometimes the digger for ancestors is fortunate enough to find a printed genealogy of the family into which he or she has traced his line of ascent. These records must always be checked for accuracy, and not followed blindly. Occasionally humorous elements are found in them — another proof of our contention that genealogy is not dry. In the Dewey genealogy one comes across this amazing collection of names in one family:

Armenius Philadelphus
Almira Melpomena
Pleiades Arastarcus
Victor Millenius
Octavia Ammonia

and last of all:

Encyclopedia Britannica

The last-named, the compiler states, was living unmarried at the age of 84. It is not surprising that she was a spinster. What man would want to marry an encyclopedia?

What a record is found on page 62 of *The Daniel Shed Genealogy*! There it is stated that Ebenezer Richardson, born in Billerica, Mass., 2 October 1724, married, first, Elizabeth Shed, who bore him ten children and died about 1763. He married, secondly, in October 1764, Mary Crosby, who died before 1770, for in December of that year he married, thirdly, Mrs. Lydia Danforth. She died, and he married, fourthly, in December 1776, Mrs. Catherine Wyman. She succumbed, and he married, fifthly, in May 1783, Elizabeth Bacon. She died, and he married, sixthly, Mrs. Susanne Davis, who died. In October 1799, he married, seventhly, Mrs. Keziah Wyman. As the compiler states, "after a long life, rich in marital experience, he succumbed in 1808 to the fell destroyer that had bereft him of so many wives."

The pension records of the survivors of the Revolutionary War not only yield a great store of genealogical data and military records, but present problems as well. In one such record there was found an affidavit stating that the soldier had married in Paris, Me., and removed to "Thunderstood," Vt. No atlas of Vermont ever noted such a place. It proved to be an old lady's mispronunciation and phonetic spelling of Hungerford, now Sheldon, Vt.

Incidentally, the early census takers were marvels when it came to spelling, for in the first federal census, of 1790, we find the surname Reynolds spelled in thirty-four different ways, ranging from Ranals through Renholds, Reynull, and a few other spellings to Runnels and Rynolds. They managed to spell even Brown in seven ways: Bronn, Broons, Broun, Broune, Brown, Browne, and Brownes! Possibly some of this misspelling in the printed transcript is due to difficulty in reading the old handwriting, for it is hard to read, especially if the paper has become time-stained or the ink has been exposed to the light.

## Surnames

Speaking of surnames, here is another absorbing byway of genealogical study: the history and development of names. When William the Conqueror established himself in England, surnames were almost unknown, even among noble, baronial families. They were not generally adopted until the thirteenth century or later. Most English surnames are derived from names of places or occupations, and a few from some peculiar trait or nickname. For example, the surname Atwood is derived from Atte Wood, that is, John Atte Wood, or John who lived at, or by, the wood, to distinguish him from John Atte Lea (now Atleigh, or more simply Lee), John who lived by the meadow. From these examples it is easy to see how the spelling has gradually simplified until the names have assumed the form with which we are familiar today. Sherman is an occupational name, meaning "shear man," one who sheared cloth. Chandler derives from candlemaker; Thatcher from roof-thatcher. Names derived from places generally had the French preposition *de* inserted between the given name and the surname. For instance, the earliest occurrence of the name Hungerford applied to an individual is that of Everard de Hungerford, who lived at Hungerford in Berkshire in the twelfth century. By 1500 the *de* had been dropped and the Hungerford family was well established. Seymour is a phonetic spelling of Saint Maur, with a few elisions, thus "de Saint Maur" became Seymour in the course of a few generations. Powell is a corruption of Ap Howell, a Welsh name signifying "son of Howell." Price was originally Ap Rhys, "son of Rhys," a common Welsh given name. Thistlethwaite comes from two words: thistle and thwaite, the last an Anglo-Saxon word meaning "parcel of land" (thistle patch, as we might say). Smith, the most common name, is occupational in origin — William the Smith, to distinguish him from William the Thatcher.

Thus it is easy to see that families of the same surname are not necessarily of the same common stock or origin. Smiths were common throughout England, hence the name had its origin in almost any hamlet in England. But occasionally a name is so unusual that you are justified in assuming that all people of that name living today are related in some degree. However, this is not invariably true, for such a name as Cobleigh when analyzed yields two words "cob" and "leigh," that is, a "roundish lump" and a "meadow." Many a parish might have a field in which there is a rise of ground, and hence that name might originate in several different parts of England. (See Chapter 13 for a further note on names.)

There may be some who still persist in wanting to know: "Now, why all this fuss about genealogy? Of what use is it?" One might as well ask: "Of what use postage stamps, Sandwich glass, Currier and Ives prints, baseball cards?" In the first place, it can be a hobby, an avocation. Psychologists tell us that it is good for people to have a hobby on which to spend spare time, something to study, something in the pursuit of which they can broaden their knowledge of the world and its ways. Genealogy is the study of family origins and the ways of individuals; individuals and families help to make history. The late Dr. LeRoy Crummer used to insist that "every man should study the past in order to understand the present and anticipate the future." The doctor applied that maxim to the study of medical history, but it is equally applicable to any other field. Also, individuals make up towns, towns make up counties and states, states make up nations, and nations make up the world and play an important part in its affairs. Thus, in the first or the last analysis, the individual counts.

All in all, you cannot escape the fact that your ascendants were human beings, not merely names that have survived in musty old records. They lived and breathed, had their joys and pleasures, their trials and tribulations, their work and play, however different these may have been from yours. Moreover, you will find that they, obscurely or prominently, took their part in the affairs of their times and contributed in some way to the development of civilization. By learning more about them and their times, you'll be the wiser in knowing "how we got this way."

# CHAPTER 2

# How to Search among the Relatives

IF YOU really want to dig for your ancestors and have determined to learn something about your progenitors and ascendants, the material equipment is very slight. You needn't buy a lot of tools — spades, fishing tackle, clubs — or a horse. As we have said, all you'll need is a good notebook, preferably loose-leaf, of a size convenient to carry. Don't make the mistake of getting one that is too small, or one that holds only a few sheets of paper. We think you will find it best to have a page at least five and a half by eight and a half inches (we like the size taking a standard sheet of typewriter paper, eight and a half by eleven), the format of the *Family History Record Book*. We recommend, also, one that opens like a book rather than one that opens at the end. If your notebook is hinged along the side, you can extend your pedigree charts across two pages, and thus be able to see a whole "line" without turning a page. We prefer the larger size notebook, also, because we can put into it letters and other typewritten papers by simply punching the proper holes and inserting the sheets wherever we want them. A supplementary working notebook of pocket size is useful when you begin to take trips. Indeed, some genealogists always carry about with them such a notebook in which they keep notes of the details wanted on specific problems.

## Using a Chart

Before beginning to question one's relatives, it is well to prepare an ancestral chart or skeleton outline of your ancestry. Such a chart can be made easily with a pencil and ruler on a sheet of your notebook paper — at least that is the way we usually make them for working purposes; see Form 1 (below) or the chart in the *Family History Record Book*. A similar one, printed on standard size typewriter paper, can be obtained from the New England Historic Genealogical Society, 101 Newbury

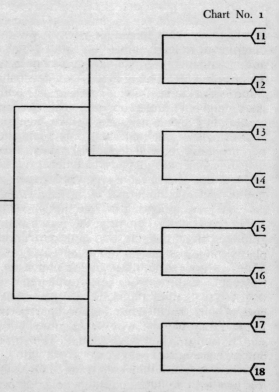

Chart No. 1

11
12
13
14
15
16
17
18

FORM 1. Skeletal Ancestral Chart.

Street, Boston, MA 02116, or other firms dealing in genealogical supplies. You can begin with your own name — if you propose to work out both paternal and maternal ancestry — on the single line of the left-hand side of this chart. On the upper of the next two horizontal lines, write your father's full name (start out right and never use an initial when you can get the full name), and immediately below it enter the place and date of his birth, the place and date of his marriage, and the place and date of his death (if he is not living). On the lower enter your mother's full maiden name. In the next column you will note that there are four horizontal lines, on and under which should be recorded the same data for your grandparents. Always record the wives under their maiden names, for in the next generation those become the names of the lines you are tracing. In the fourth column are spaces for your eight great-grandparents. Thus, on a single chart, when all the spaces are filled out, you will have the data on four generations, including yourself, if you have started with your own name.

You will notice the legend "Chart No. 1" in the upper right-hand corner of Form 1. If you look carefully, you will see that a two-digit number follows each of the eight "great-grandparent" spaces. This number refers to the chart on which that individual's line is carried along. To continue this line, let us say your paternal grandmother's paternal line, you start another chart, placing on the single line at the left-hand side the name of that great-grandfather; just as you have filled out Chart 1, you fill out his ancestry on this new chart, which gets its number, 13, from the number following his name on Chart 1. Thus this new chart becomes Chart 13. You may wonder why the numbers 2 to 10, inclusive, have been skipped. It is a little difficult to explain, but we'll try to make it clear.

If the charts are numbered consecutively, 1, 2, 3, etc., it is necessary to figure out the whole number of charts that will be needed when a particular ancestry is complete. But because it is seldom possible to work out all the lines immediately, it is easier to use a system that allows you to insert new charts at any place at any time. So, after renumbering charts many times, we hit upon this system of numbering. Calling the first outline Chart 1, we then take that number and add it to the digit representing whichever great-grandparent is carried forward. Thus one's father's mother's father comes on the third line in the right-hand column, and his chart gets the number 1 plus the digit 3, or 13. If one carries out this great-grandfather's paternal line, that is, his great-grandfather's line, the next chart gets the number 131, that is, 13 plus 1, representing the first line at the right of that chart. If, at a later date, the mother's mother's line is worked out the new chart has the number 17 and is inserted in the loose-leaf notebook following Chart 13.

Another type of chart showing a skeleton of a complete ancestry, called the radial or semicircular chart, is illustrated in Form 2. It may be drawn in full circle, one-half for paternal and one-half for maternal ancestry. This type, too, can be either purchased or drawn by hand with compass and ruler.

At the foot, or on the back, of each chart you should record the sources of your information for each generation because if you or any of your descendants ever want to join a patriotic society, or any other organization in which one qualification for membership is based on heredity, you will need those references. As a matter of fact, since genealogy is a type of history, the history of an individual family, and since history should always be documented with references to sources, you should get into the habit of noting references so that you may easily recheck your data should the occasion demand it.

Another simple type of skeleton chart or record is the pedigree, shown as Form 3 on page 57, which gives only one line of descent. The angled rules show the "blood line" from the earliest known progenitor of the senior author of this book in his patrilineal line. This same type may be used to indicate the line of descent

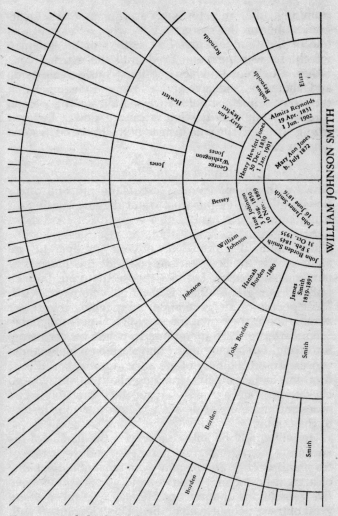

Reynold

Joshua Reynolds

Eliza

Hewlett

Mary Ann Hewlett

Almira Reynolds
19 Apr. 1831
1 Jun. 1902

Jones

George Washington Jones

Henry Hewlett Jones
30 Dec. 1830
1 Jan. 1901

Mary Ann Jones
b. July 1872

Betsey

Jane Johnson
3 Aug. 1859
10 Nov. 1889

John James Smith
16 June 1876

William Johnson

John Borden Smith
3 Feb. 1845
31 Oct. 1935

Johnson

Hannah Borden
-1880

James Smith
1819-1891

John Borden

Smith

Borden

Smith

Borden

WILLIAM JOHNSON SMITH

FORM 2. Radial Chart Showing Spaces for Six Generations of Ancestors.

from any other ancestor, such as your mother's great-grandfather on her mother's side, who, let us say, was one of the founders and first settlers of the town in which she was born and lived until she married your father, a descent in which she took considerable pride and, therefore, she gave you his name. Remember that the "blood line" should always indicate the person through whom the descent is carried down; hence it may go through the wife instead of the husband in some generations.

## Interviewing the Relatives

Now, with this preliminary excursion into dull directions ended, let us push on to our digging. With your trusty notebook in hand, and a pocketful of good sharp pencils, begin the rounds of the relatives who live within calling distance. If any of your grandparents are alive, that is the best starting point for this journey of family relationships. Let us suppose that your father's father, your grandfather, is the first whom you visit. Most people of his generation enjoy telling a younger person about their own times, which almost invariably seem better to them than those in which we are living! So, it ought to be easy to get him started on his reminiscences. The machinery of memory may creak a little at first, but as he gets into thinking about it, and you go back to see him again and again, he'll probably recall more and more of the details you need for your history of the family.

He will surely be able to give you the names of his parents — your great-grandparents — and the names of his grandparents, and he may even remember the name of a great-grandparent or two; and you will thus have five generations of ancestors. He may remember where most of these people lived or died. Don't let him off with providing simply given names or nicknames if he can possibly remember full names and proper names. If he says that his mother's name was Patty, try to find out whether it was actually Patty, or really Martha, Patience, or Patricia (Patty is used as a nickname, or diminutive, for all three). To illustrate this point: a friend had a difficult time determining the parentage of one of her great-grandmothers whose name was reported to her as Patty Cobb. The name proved to be Martha Cobb in the birth record, although she had always been called "Patty." Thus, for further search, in the event that your grandfather doesn't recall his grandmother's parentage, it is essential to know just what her full name was, as well as what she was familiarly called. Nicknames, or "pet" names, are sometimes given in parentheses or square brackets, so you can have the record of both.

## Names, Places, and Dates

Try to get your grandfather to remember and tell you as many dates and names of places as he can. Although at first you may be interested in tracing your paternal line only, you will become interested, undoubtedly, in all lines sooner or later, so it is just as well to make note of everything Grandfather tells you. Thus, if he knows the names of his mother's parents, get them while you can. Dr. Doane recalls that when he was questioning his grandfather about his mother's people — for he started on that line rather than on any of his paternal lines, in response to a query from a genealogist who was compiling a history of that family — just out of politeness (or perhaps in response to some subconscious hunch), he asked him to tell him the names of the parents of his father, and what his grandmother's maiden name was. He told Dr. Doane that he thought she was born in Sherwood (she had died several years before he was born). It was a fortunate question, for after his death a year or two later, that slight clue was all Dr. Doane had as a starting point from which to work out that line, since he could not find in the official town records any mention of his great-great-grandfather's marriage.

Dr. Doane's experience in this matter indicates how important it is to get as much information as you can from old people while you are talking with them. They have a positive genius for dying just before you decide to go back to them for further information. Had he waited until he became interested in tracing his entire ancestry, the only source of information about a starting point on this particular line would have passed beyond his reach. "Gather ye rosebuds while ye may" is a good motto for an ancestor hunter. It is infinitely better to have too much information than not enough.

### Do Take Notes

Always take notes as you talk with your relatives. Otherwise little details, which are frequently of importance to you in your pursuit of the elusive ancestor, may escape you, and you'll find yourself wishing that you had made more careful notes. If you are not sure of a point, ask about it again, or put a question mark after your note so that you may verify it more completely later.

Let us suppose that Grandfather says that his father was born in Postville, Ill., 2 July 1863, and tells you that his grandfather was fighting at the Battle of Gettysburg on that day and did not know his eldest son was born until several weeks later, because the letter giving the news did not reach him, owing to the movement of the troops. Moreover, since his grandfather was at war, his grandmother was living with her parents. This is all interesting and may furnish you with some facts that shed light on the history of the family. As he talks, he tells you that his grandparents had a pretty hard time financially after his grandfather returned from the war and that his father was four years old when the next child, his sister, was born in a covered wagon as they were crossing Iowa. Following up this lead, you question him further about the reason for the move and learn that his grandfather, as a soldier, located a homestead in Nebraska under the Homestead Act, which Congress passed in 1862.

As Grandfather has been talking you have filled in

some of the spaces on your working chart, and the blank pages following it have been filling up with notes that you can later expand into a narrative account of the family. Now you might get him to tell you the names of his brothers and sisters and give you their birth dates or, at least, the order of their births and the names of the places where they were born. Perhaps he will remember the names of paternal or maternal uncles and aunts, and some details of their lives. These data aren't essential to you, but they help to complete the picture of the family (and may enable you later to help some cousin work out a line). If he says that his Uncle Harry disappeared and that the last the family heard of him he was with Custer in the Sioux Wars, record that fact, and later, if you wish, look up the history of Custer's campaign and the famous battle of Little Big Horn River.

Perhaps Grandfather's father lost his life in the great blizzard of 12 January 1888, in Nebraska, and about 1893 his mother married again, say a widower on a neighboring farm. His stepfather's name and any details about possible half brothers and sisters will help to make the story more interesting and complete.

As a matter of fact, while you are talking with older relatives, it is always wise to get the names of brothers and sisters (whole or half) as well as aunts and uncles, and names of their children. Sometimes recollections are handed down or remembered in one branch of the family that have been forgotten (if ever known) in another. One of our correspondents remembered that his grandfather had a brother. The official death record of the grandfather did not show the names of his parents and gave only New York as his place of birth; that of his great-uncle gave all their names and the town, which enabled him to trace his paternal ancestry back to the immigrant three centuries ago.

The chances are that there are interesting anecdotes about the various migrations of the family, if they moved about at all. One of our friends told us that her grandfather was a baby when the family moved from western New York to Ohio and, as they were traveling to Buffalo to get the boat on which they were to go up Lake Erie to their new home, he, sleeping in the end of the bobsled in which they were traveling, rolled off and wasn't missed for a mile or so!

Possibly the story is entirely different and your grandfather was a bound boy and came from Michigan. In that case, urge him to recall as much as possible about himself: whether he came out of an orphanage or was bound out by his mother because his father was killed in the Civil War and she couldn't take care of him. Such a case presents a difficult problem but not necessarily an insoluble one. Local records of the community in which his foster parents lived may show something, if he remembers where they lived and who they were. Their blood descendants may recall details that he has forgotten. Orphanage records may show where he came from or who his parents were. Ask him to characterize his parents and tell you any traditions about his family. Although you yourself may not belong to any church or be of a religious turn of mind, don't forget that church records are a source of valuable information. He should also tell you to what church his family belonged; you can later try to find its records.

All such details should be noted down. But a word of caution about these questions: don't try to get too much information at any one time. Remember that old folks tire easily. Cultivate them and let them do most of the talking, and don't attempt to confine them to any one line of talk. One detail leads to another. As they turn over in their minds the incidents of their lives, more and more comes back to them. A forgotten detail is sometimes recalled the next day or later. An elderly man was repeatedly asked for information regarding his grandfather in the hope that a clue to his identity and occupation might be obtained. Finally, one day, a chance remark "rang a bell" and brought out the whole story with a wealth of detail.

## Exchanging Letters

If there are any other relatives alive, get their addresses and begin a correspondence with them. Check the details received from one against those from another. Note the discrepancies, as well as the coincidences, and try to sift the facts as you go along. It is sometimes very difficult to reconcile statements made by different members of the family, but generally there is an element of truth somewhere. What an old person recalls about one member of the family may properly apply to someone else, only the names have been mixed.

Sometimes old friends of the family, living in the community from which they came, can supply the missing data. One very interesting case has come to our attention. A friend was trying to prove his wife's descent from a passenger on the *Mayflower* to secure for her membership in the Society of Mayflower Descendants. Although she knew her grandmother's parentage, they could not find a single record to prove it. They knew that this woman's father had lived in a certain town in Connecticut, but that she had actually been born in Vermont or New Hampshire and raised by her mother's relatives, since her mother died soon after her birth. The records of Canterbury, Conn., indicate that her father died unmarried. That was a hard hurdle to take. But, by going back to Connecticut and talking with the old men in that town, they found one who had been the lifelong chum of this great-grandfather — a very old man fortunately possessing a clear mind and memory. He said that he was about the only person who knew that Septus Ensworth had gone away as a young man, that he had met a girl and married her, and that she had died at the birth of their child a year later. Brokenhearted, he left his baby daughter with his wife's family in Vermont and returned to his native town in Connecticut, where he died at an advanced age without ever seeing his daughter again. He never remarried, and, in order not to be reminded of his sorrow, hadn't talked about his early marriage except to this one very close friend. The old man, whom our friends had found, made an affidavit about these details before a notary public. With this as documentation, the line of descent was accepted and our friend's wife was admitted to the society. Two years later they went back again to see the old man, but he had died very suddenly just a month after they had met him!

This incident again shows that you must dig while the weather is good or the circumstances permit, and leave no stone unturned.

Whenever possible, it is best to talk with old people in person, for they find it difficult to write letters, especially if there are many details. In talking person to person, one question leads to another, or a chance remark leads to further queries and brings out information that they wouldn't think of writing down. Alert for facts, you can seize upon a slight clue and get them to elaborate it in conversation, but this is difficult to do in correspondence. Sometimes, however, geographical distance prevents a personal interview. In this case, make your questions as specific and clear as possible when you are writing. It is helpful to write out questions on a separate sheet of paper, leaving spaces for the answers, so they can be filled in on the same sheet, which is to be returned to you and inserted in your notebook. It is always a mark of courtesy, if nothing more, to enclose with your sheet of questions a self-addressed and stamped envelope: this makes it simpler for your correspondent to answer and helps to ensure a reply. Old people find it a task to write letters, and so they have a tendency to put off doing it — sometimes until it is too late — so it is best to do all that you can to lighten the task for them.

Dr. Doane recalls that, in the early days of his genealogical experience, he wrote to a great-aunt and asked her to give him the names of the descendants of her grandfather and tell him all she knew about them. Although she was a good correspondent and loved to

write letters, she was a little slow in answering this one.
Finally, however, Dr. Doane received a reply. She
began to enumerate the grandfather's children and tell
about their marriages. After she had listed about four of
them (he had twelve, this hardy old pioneer!), she
wrote: "Oh, this is too much to write, I'll tell you about
them sometime." It *was* too much, for when Dr. Doane
finally completed the records of all these descendants,
there were about three hundred of them! Later, when he
was able to visit her, she told him much that she did not
have the patience to write.

## Visiting Cemeteries

If you can persuade your grandfather, or another older
relative, to go to the cemetery with you and explain the
relationship that existed between those buried in the
family lot or near it, you will often save much time and
trouble. Sometimes different generations of the family
are buried in different cemeteries. For example, Dr.
Doane's grandparents, great-grandparents, and great-
great-grandparents are buried in different cemeteries in
the same town. If he hadn't had his great-aunt go the
round of those cemeteries with him, and point out the
graves of these ancestors, he would have had a great
deal of trouble finding them and securing the data from
their gravestones; for there are ten graveyards in that
town and over three thousand stones in those yards —
he has since copied the inscriptions.

## Practice Diplomacy

Tact and diplomacy are very necessary in digging
among the relatives. We know of one instance in which
a problem is practically insoluble without the Bible
records that are in the possession of a distant relative of
the person interested. The latter has in some manner
offended her relative cousin and now is at a standstill in
her search, because the possessor of the records ignores
her letters. Moreover, that relative is now suspicious of
anyone else who tries to gain access to the Bible!

When personal relations are uncertain, it is not polit
to demand access to a record, of course, but more di
lomatic to play upon the owner's sympathy or to di
cover some roundabout method of obtaining the info
mation. If you haven't ever "gotten along with" Cous
Emma, why not persuade George, her favorite, to cop
those records or get the information you want? Don
risk a brusque refusal, and at the same time arouse h
suspicion that everyone else who may approach her
working at your request. This art of getting along wi
irascible people is one of the things you can learn
genealogical work, if you haven't acquired it already.

Another thing that must be handled with tact is th
matter of private scandal. You should know all fami
scandal — not as dirt for dirt's sake, but rather because
is often necessary to the proper carrying on of the inve
tigation. While Dr. Doane was gathering material for
genealogy of his mother's maternal family, he went to
much older cousin for data about her aunts and uncle
She was very reluctant to talk about them, didn't eve
remember their names! He was surprised, for he ha
never before detected in her a failing memory. Later, h
asked his mother why she wouldn't talk and was tol
that one of the aunts had been divorced and later sent
a state mental hospital. So the genealogy was publishe
without a complete record of that branch of the family
When this cousin read it and saw that Dr. Doane did n
mention the cause of the divorce she recalled — when
was too late to use them — all the details for which h
had asked the year before. If he had known this "scan
dal" before going to her, he probably would have bee
able to indicate more clearly the reason for his inquis
tiveness and assure her of his discretion in using wh,
she told him. There is no need of raking up too muc
past scandal, but one should know enough of it to b
able to handle such situations tactfully. Moreover, wh,
seemed scandalous fifty years ago is now accepte
without batting an eyelash, at least in many circles.

# CHAPTER 3

# *What about Those Family Traditions?*

As WE have suggested, don't accept as gospel truth all that your Great-Aunt Hettie, or Uncle Abijah, tells you about the history of the family. Older people do not always realize that they have confused two different episodes and telescoped them into one; and sometimes they do not discriminate between fact and fiction. Some are natural-born storytellers and quite unconsciously embroider the facts a little here and there to make the tale more dramatic, all the while really believing that they are relating the details as they heard them from their grandfather. Others, who give every evidence of a remarkably retentive memory, tell a clear and straightforward account of the family as they received it from an older generation without realizing that the tradition may have been distorted before they heard it.

## *You Are a Detective*

So listen carefully and attentively to what your elderly relatives pass on to you. Remember, many old people talk more or less at random, skipping back and forth as the wheels of memory begin to turn more easily, or they remember more clearly some detail and go back, without warning, to correct it or add to it. Sometimes they will tell the same story twice, having recollected something they have left out. It is really quite difficult sometimes to follow the thread of their story, so you may

31

have to ask for the connection with what you have already heard.

Make an effort to remember the details as faithfully as you can, especially if you have to trust to your own memory rather than take notes. Your pencil and pad may disconcert an older person as you try to write down details or even key points in the story. Moreover, unless you have had stenographic training, or have learned speedwriting, it is virtually impossible to write fast enough to get down on paper the full story while they are reciting it. If you own a tape recorder, take it along with you. Uncle 'Bijah may be willing to talk into it, and, when you play back some of it, enjoy listening to his own voice.

Later, the sooner the better, while it is still fresh in your mind, write down what you have heard, or transcribe your notes or your tapes, so you can sort out the details and will not have to depend on your own memory to put in the connecting links.

When you have got all that Aunt Hettie told you arranged in some sort of order, you may want to go back and ask her to tell you more about one point or another. This has a double advantage: your own recollection may be clarified, or she may, by that time, remember names and facts that she left out in her earlier account of it. Names and even dates do sometimes "come to you" hours later — a fact which, as we have discovered in ourselves with the advancing years, happens quite frequently! Moreover, with the family saga somewhat organized in your own mind, you may well try to get another version of it from Uncle 'Bijah, or at least give him an opportunity to verify it. It is always an advantage if you can get two independent accounts and check to see if they tally. One cousin, aunt, or uncle may remember what another doesn't recall. The mind of one may retain details that didn't interest the other and were not remembered. By comparing and piecing together two or three independent recollections of the details, you may be able to put together a better history.

Even if accounts do not differ significantly, you must check the details as best you can against such sources as you can find, preferring public records, such as those discussed in another chapter, or any written or printed evidence you may find. This is especially important before you accept as true what your narrators have told you about an episode that happened before their own time. What a person does not know from his or her own participation in, or recollection of, a given event is hearsay, not bona fide evidence. Hearsay may be distorted or inaccurate. A mother may tell her daughter the date on which she married that daughter's father, the names of her parents and her husband's parents, as well as the date the daughter was born. Presumably such information is true, but you should make an effort to verify it if possible. When the mother tells her daughter what her father told her about his grandparents or great-grandparents, she is passing on tradition, which may be true, or distorted, or erroneous.

Speaking of differences in memory, Dr. Doane's father, fifty years ago when he first quizzed him about his mother's family, could tell him very little about that side of the house. At first, he couldn't recall even the maiden name of his grandmother, his mother's mother, who, to be sure, died when he was a boy; later, having learned her name from his sister, his father remembered some details about his cousins. Fortunately, Dr. Doane's father's only sister, fifteen months younger than he, remembered much more about her mother's people (his grandmother lived with his aunt during the last twenty years of her life, so his aunt had much more opportunity to hear those relatives mentioned). From her he got the names of her grandparents, a great-grandfather, several cousins, aunts, and uncles, and a couple of great-aunts, and great-uncles, so he could construct quite a pedigree of that family which he verified from gravestones and public records. From one of the second cousins, a "remove" or two from him, whom he discovered almost by chance, he gleaned even more about their common progenitors. The cousin was, in truth, quite a bit older than his aunt so he remembered some people whom his aunt never mentioned. From his recollections, Dr. Doane learned two interesting and significant details: one, that the great-grandfather of his grandmother, having come from Canada into northern Vermont, spoke French Canadian patòis, the language of his childhood, fluently, but quite broken English; and, second, that there was Indian blood in the family. When Dr. Doane expressed interest in the latter, his cousin became confidential, apparently having decided to trust him, and told him quite a gruesome story about a great-great uncle which was really something! When he got the progenitor's pension record from the National Archives — he served in the Revolutionary War — and noted that his birthplace was given as Saint Ours In Lower Canada (now Quebec), the French-speaking tradition seemed verified, at least circumstantially. It wasn't until he found his will in a Vermont probate office that he learned his father's name. Going to Saint Ours, he found no record, civil or ecclesiastical, of either him or his father. He has yet to verify, after half a century of searching, the Indian blood, although the temperaments of some of his grandmother's relations whom he knows, if not their physical characteristics, seem to suggest it. The gruesome story is confirmed by an account of religious fanaticism and cruelty found in Crocker's *History of the Baptists in Vermont*, which lends credence to the strain of Indian blood said to have been in the family — at least, he is willing to accept the tradition in the hope that he may yet find more convincing evidence.

This leads us to summarize the experience of a friend who successfully tracked down a similar tradition in his family. He grew up believing the tradition that was current in his father's family. When he wanted to know the facts, his father told him that his grandmother, Rachel Rice, brought Indian blood into the Perin family. Whenever he had leisure, he studied the family history and began to compile and verify the facts. He tried to study the physiognomy of as many of Rachel's descendants as he could, noting the texture of the hair, the bone structure of the features of uncles, aunts, and cousins of one degree or another. According to Mendel's law, a percentage of them should have had one or more typical Indian traits and characteristics, if the tradition was true. When he found no trace of any Indian features or even a hint of one, he concluded that there was no truth in the tradition, but he still wanted to know how it came about that his father and grandfather believed that there was Indian blood. So he continued his search for the progenitors of Rachel Rice, his great-grandmother. One of his cousins gave him his first clue, which she found in a history of Tompkins County, N.Y. This mentioned the migration of his great-grandparents, John and Rachel Perin, from western Massachusetts to that county. In reading over the chapter, he found that a family with which he had a possible connection was said to have come from Charlemont, Berkshire County, Mass., so he centered his search there. He soon discovered that Captain Moses Rice was living there when he was killed by the Indians, and his grandson Asa was carried away captive. Asa lived with his captors for about six or seven years before he was redeemed at the age of fifteen; therefore, it seemed quite unlikely that he had taken an Indian girl as a mate. Continuing his search, our friend learned that Asa married, not once but twice, white women, and fathered quite a family, among them Rachel, whom he named as Rachel Perin in his will. Thus the tradition of Indian blood was disproved, and in its place our friend found that he had a great-great-grandfather who, in his youth, was a captive among the Indians for several years. If you are sufficiently interested in how our friend followed step by step the clues that he picked up along the trail into the past, you will find the full story and the surprising happenstance by which the final, conclusive evidence was found in the *New England Historical and Genealogical Register* (Vol. 121, January 1967, pp. 29–36).

The author is Stanley E. Perin; the title, "A Tradition in Search of Its Origin." It is not only an exciting story; it is also an excellent example of first-class genealogical research.

## Beware of Fantasy

So much for one type of tradition. Now we want to discuss the fanciful type.

If the basic fact in the tradition in Mr. Perin's family became distorted in three generations, consider the following letter, which another friend of Dr. Doane's asked him to read about forty years ago. He had written to one of his distant cousins asking her to talk with her aged grandmother about the history of the family and where they had lived before moving to the West. (Note: Dr. Doane no longer has access to the original letter, which he copied verbatim changing only the names, as his friend requested.) It read:

> Here is all Grandma can think of about the fore fathers.
> Lord John Whiting, Great Grandfather, was born in 1735 near London. He came to America on the May Flower in 1776 soon after the Revolutionary War, bringing his two daughters, Lady Jane and Mabel (Not sure of the name). She, Mabel, went back to England with her father.
> Lord Whiting bought some land in Connecticut and gave it to Lady Jane for a wedding present when she married grandfather James Dupey (he was a French nobleman) in 1796 or 1798. James Dupey was Captain of the May Flower Ten sons were born to them.

We cite this fantastic account simply to point out some of the incongruities which, we trust, will strike you immediately. In fact, you might stop at this point and test your skill in spotting the anachronisms before you read on. Surely most of the school histories of our country still contain an account of the historic voyage of the *Mayflower* overloaded with 102 passengers and all the alleged heirlooms, the date of its arrival, and the horrors of that first winter, 1620–21. Most high-school students know that the Revolutionary War was not over until the surrender of Cornwallis at Yorktown in 1781, and that the independence of the United States was not formally recognized until the signing of the Treaty of Paris in 1783. These facts are sufficient to give warning that this story must have been told by an elderly person whose memory was no longer accurate. Consequently, it is of almost no value to one searching for ancestors and trying to discover something about the history of his or her family. The only clue of immediate value lies in the mention of Connecticut as the place of settlement, and there research should be centered once the trail has been followed back to New England. You may be interested to know that Dr. Doane's friend found that this was true. Following up some of the distaff families he discovered a line of descent from one of the passengers on the historic *Mayflower*, although the name was not that mentioned by Grandma, and another from a Huguenot who fled from France after the revocation of the Edict of Nantes in 1685 and settled in Connecticut.

In these two examples of family traditions, the one had on the face of it the semblance of truth, but, after careful examination, followed by tracing the pedigree of the great-grandmother involved, proved to be a distortion of fact; the other, which seemed to be a figment of the imagination, or at most the tale of one whose mind, perhaps weakened by illness and age, wandered from one vague recollection to another in strange fancy, did have, deeply buried in its fantasy, some basic facts.

## Oral History

There was, however, in the history of our progenitors, a time when oral tradition was remarkably clear and accurate. Pedigrees were memorized and handed on from generation to generation, with appropriate additions in each. There were uncounted examples of such oral pedigrees among the ancient Scandinavians, the Irish, the Welsh, the Scots, the Icelanders, the Maoris in New Zealand, and the native tribes of Africa. In Ireland, for example, for many centuries, the *filid*, or the hereditary historians of the clan, or sept, were trained to memorize and recite, without error or omission, the descent from the "founder" or progenitor, not only of the main stem of the family, but also its agnate branches. In Iceland, there were handed down from generation to generation lines of descent from the first settlers who came across the sea from Scandinavia in the ninth century to colonize that uninhabited island. These pedigrees were not written down until the twelfth century when Ari Thorgilsson compiled the *Landnamabok* in which they were entered. In New Zealand it took a Maori chieftain three days to recite, before a government land commission, the descent of his people for thirty-four generations in order to justify their claim to certain territory. From generation to generation he gave the names, not only in the direct male line, but in the agnate branches stemming from each generation. Many Welsh pedigrees, traced back to the early kings of both North and South Wales, were handed on by trained bards for many generations before they were finally written down. Historical scholarship has found the documentary proof that substantiates the authenticity and accuracy of many of those ancient pedigrees, so their reliability should not be too hastily denied.

There is at least one famous black family in the United States whose history has been faithfully and accurately memorized and handed on from generation to generation, beginning with the progenitor who was brought from Africa on a slave ship in the eighteenth century. Probably there are many others.

The story of this one family has been so poignantly told by one of the descendants, Alex Haley, in his book *Roots* that we cannot refrain from abridging and paraphrasing it as an example of what may be done to verify a family tradition such as his. As a boy in western Tennessee, he squatted beside his grandmother's chair and listened while she and her visiting sisters and cousins talked about their forefathers and their traditional lineage, which made a deep impression on him.

In maturity, Mr. Haley remembered that his grandmother always referred to her progenitor as "the African" who came to "Naplis," whom she sometimes called Kintay, and that she said he was cutting down a tree to make a drum when he was captured. Also, she used words that were strange to the boy, often enough to impress them upon his memory, words like *ko* for a banjo and *Kamby Bolongo*, which meant a large river, and others, some of which she repeated to herself while working about the house. She talked also about the successive generations from the African, using the names of each individual, what he or she did, and where he or she lived. Then, one day in 1965, when he was walking by the National Archives in Washington, he suddenly remembered his grandmother's account of the family history. On impulse, he went in and asked if there were census records of Alamance County, N.C., where her people had lived about 1860–70. In these records he found the first confirmation of the accuracy of his grandmother's recollections: her grandfather and his family were listed! Another step was to identify the language or dialect to which those strange words that she used belonged. At the University of Wisconsin he found Dr. Vansina, an African professor of linguistics, who, listening intently to Mr. Haley's repetition of them, told him that the dialect was known as Mandinka in which the word for river was *Bolong*, which, combined with *Kamby*, undoubtedly referred to the Gambia River in West Africa. With this knowledge, Mr. Haley went to Bathurst, at the mouth of the Gambia, where he learned the location of the tribe which spoke that dialect; but he had to return to America before he could organize a safari. Finally, months later, the officials in Bathurst wrote him that they had learned that a *griot* (very old man) who could recite the history of the Kinte tribe was living at Juffure, miles away up the river in the interior and invited him to return to Africa, which he did. From the *griot* he heard the history of the Kinte tribe and was told that a young man of the village, named Kinte, went into the forest one day to cut a tree and make a drum — the very tradition Mr. Haley had heard his grandmother repeat. Kinte was captured and was never seen again. The *griot* also told him about the tribe from the time it left Old Mali and migrated to Mauretania, whence, later, Kairaba Junta Kinte, a Muslim Marabout (holy man), came into Gambia and settled in Juffure. This man was the grandfather of Kinte, "the African" who came to 'Naplis (Annapolis, Md.) in 1767.

# CHAPTER 4

# Out of the Family Papers

WHILE YOU are talking with Grandfather and the other older relatives, try to find out if they have any written records of the family. Sometimes, as we have said, this requires tact, for the owners may be perversely inclined to think that you want to run off with some document; at other times, you can ask outright to see the family Bible and other papers and easily obtain permission to make a copy of the records they contain, so you have to play it by ear. If Grandfather happens to be in the right mood, he may even give you the Bible, but beware lest by accepting it you are going to offend Aunt Mamie. A timely refusal may win her eternal good will and perhaps, later, even the Bible itself.

If you are at a distance from these older relatives and have to seek by correspondence any records they may have, be sure to tell them that you are compiling a history of the family (promise them a copy, if need be), for sometimes they may suspect, however far it may be from the truth, that you are getting ready to claim some mythical "estate." It is truly amazing how many people have a notion that their family is entitled to some great estate overseas. They have heard of the "Drake estate," or the "Buchanan estate," or the "Edwards estate"; or they have read in the newspapers about the litigation over the Wendell estate and seen printed lists of the great number of claimants. Colonel Green, the famous

Hetty's son, hadn't been dead a month when three women came into the genealogical library in the city where we live, to attempt to find records proving that they were among the rightful heirs to the Green and Howland millions. The old estates, so frequently dangled before the eyes of the susceptible, have long since been outlawed; those recently in the courts are of such a nature that very explicit proof must be established by any claimant. So be careful to avoid suspicion that you are going to steal evidence that will enable you to claim property.

## Bible Records

Sometimes old letters, diaries, and other family papers exist. One or two old letters, in faded handwriting, badly worn along the creases, may contain clues to places of residence or details of family history that would otherwise be completely lost in the obscurity of the past. Sometimes a dull old diary will contain, interspersed among accounts of the weather, notes of baptisms, weddings, and funerals. Old family account books are another source of information, perhaps meager, but sometimes very illuminating. Even the framed sampler, worked by Great-Great-Aunt Hannah at the age of eleven, may prove to be of value. Don't overlook such items, for everything is grist to the genealogist's mill.

Let us take a look first at the family Bible. If other evidence is lacking, Bible records can be most useful. But the genealogist should use them with care. Occasionally someone has tampered with a Bible record, attempted to change a date or erase an entry altogether, although generally any alteration that has been made can be easily detected. An instance of such tampering comes to mind. Dr. Doane was gathering data for a history of the family and wanted the record of the immediate family of a double cousin of his, a woman of his grandfather's age (he was then in his eighties). She was inclined to be a bit vain and couldn't "remember" her own age! So he finally persuaded her to let him see her husband's family Bible — it was his second or third visit. When he came to the entry of her birth (her husband's father had meticulously entered the birth dates of the husbands and wives of his several children), he found that the year had been scratched out, although the month and day were there. He always carries a magnifying glass in his pocket for use in deciphering old handwriting and faded records. So, with a pretense of being unable to read some of the writing, which really was faded, he looked at the date she thought she had eradicated and, catching a faint residue of the ink, was able to make out "1831." Later, he verified this through his grandfather (she was his first cousin), who remembered that she was just about two years younger than he was. Really, there is little that can be done to a written record that cannot be detected upon careful examination.

The genealogist may puzzle for hours and perhaps worry for months over certain problems connected with the use of Bible records. Some such records are remarkably full; others, unusually scant and inadequate. In one old Bible with which we are familiar (the volume was printed in 1609), the records begin about 1650 and give the name, the exact hour and minute of birth, and the sign of the zodiac under which each child was born (in those days astrology and the casting of horoscopes were taken seriously, so it was considered important to know these details). We have seen some eighteenth- and early nineteenth-century Bibles containing this same sort of meticulous record. Other Bibles have such exasperatingly meager data as "My wife was delivered of a son at six o'clock p.m. November the 12th, 1785" — with no name given.

Often one comes across a Bible with a record beginning like this:

Grandfather David Richardson, born 1700, died August 1770
Remember Richardson, born 1703, died August 1760

followed by a list of their children, with dates of birth and death given. Such a record is obviously not a contemporary record, and was made many, many years after "Grandfather" was born, for David Richardson would never have called himself "grandfather." On the face of it, it looks as though David Richardson had married Remember Richardson (indeed, the present owner of this very Bible had interpreted the record in that way); but one should be suspicious of such a record, for, although occasionally cousins of the same surname did marry, it was not a very common practice. Further search in this particular case disclosed the fact that David Richardson's wife was Remember Ward. The granddaughter who made this record knew her only as Remember Richardson and, therefore, entered that name in the Bible.

Very few Bibles contain records dated before the eighteenth century, and most of the many we have examined, commence with records dated in the 1780s and 1790s. Most of the older Bibles have disappeared, although once in a while they do turn up in unexpected places. For example, the Greene family Bible, containing records dating from early in the seventeenth century, turned up in the possession of a descendant of an entirely different surname out in Nebraska, sixteen hundred miles away from Rhode Island, where the first record was entered in it. So, however remote the possibility, don't entirely give up hope of finding one you are looking for. It may turn up in the possession of a third or fourth cousin, or even in a bookshop.

One of the first things to do when examining a Bible is to determine when the book was printed. If the title page has the date 1817 on it, or the preface or translator's note is signed 1817, you know at once that any records dated before that year were entered from memory (or, perhaps, copied from some older Bible). In this event, these records should be carefully verified, if possible, from other sources — gravestones, town or church records. Records of births, marriages, and deaths occurring after that date were probably entered soon after they occurred. If, on the other hand, the Bible was published in 1609, and that printed date is found on its title page or on the half titles that mark the beginnings of the Old and New Testaments, and if the *handwriting in which the records were written* is of several different periods, then you may be reasonably certain that you have a genuine old record, containing, perhaps, several generations of the family births, marriages, and deaths.

Occasionally a son was sufficiently interested in his family, when he was married and was about to start his own family life, to copy from the original Bible, kept by his father, the data it contained. But this rarely happened, for, we regret to say, our ancestors were not always of a genealogical turn of mind, and generally did not think of doing such a thing. Young people are always more interested in the future, as they should be, than in the past, however much they can learn from it.

Generally speaking, late in the eighteenth century and early in the nineteenth, a young couple, newly married and just starting out in life, either received a brand-new Bible as a gift from parents or well-wishers, or bought one with their first spare cash. It was a period during which "respectable people" still belonged to a church and read the Bible regularly. Sometimes they would enter their family names, but more frequently they were content to enter only the dates of their own births, that of their marriage, and then, from time to time as the children came along, the records of their progeny. Fortunately, in many nineteenth-century Bibles parents entered the name of the place as well as the date of birth. This was a century of great movement, as families by the thousands were migrating westward, staying but a few years in one place and then moving on as they heard of richer lands.

Not infrequently there is a question about the authenticity of the dates of the records in the family Bible. If the handwriting in which the records are made gives evidence of contemporary entry, there can be little ques-

tion, however. You all know that your handwriting ha
varied from year to year as you have grown older. Jus
compare your diary of ten years ago with that writte
last month, if you want an example. So, if the handwrit
ing of these old records varies from entry to entry, if th
ink seems to be of a different quality in each of them
you may be certain that the data were entered as eac
child came along. But if there is a "copperplate" even
ness about the handwriting, then, if the records do no
tally with others you have found, you will have to prov
the correctness of one record or the other. For instance
there may be a difference between the record of you
grandmother's birth as it is given in the Bible and tha
which you have found in the official records of the tow
in which she was born. Perhaps the baptismal record or
the church books may settle the question, if it is th
matter of the correct year, and sometimes the grave
stone will determine it, although gravestone inscription
are quite likely to have been made from Bible records
Sometimes it is impossible to settle the question. In tha
event you should carefully give both of the dates yo
have found, one in parentheses following the other, in
dicating, of course, which is which, thus:

Sarah Richardson, born in Newton, Mass., 14 April 177
(Newton records; her Bible record gives the date 1773); die
23 January 1848, "aged 74" (according to an obituary notice)

Generally, in the case of such a discrepancy, the tow
records should be accepted as more reliable. In this par
ticular case, Sarah (Richardson) Clough wrote up he
Bible record when she was well along in years and ma
have made an error of a year in her age (although people
are generally given credit for knowing their own age). I
she was born in 1773, as her Bible states, she would no
have been seventy-five until three months after he
death, and therefore the newspaper obituary was cor
rect in stating that she was "aged 74" at the time of he
death. But sometimes, when the birthday is approach
ing, the age on that birthday is given in such a notice

and even on the gravestone. Generally, we have noted that, in such a case, the person concerned was within a few weeks of the birthday — not as many as three months. The genealogist, however, to protect himself or herself against the accusation of inaccuracy, should always note such a discrepancy, give both of the dates found, and perhaps also explain the reason for accepting either one or the other.

Sometimes a Bible record was begun by a young married couple in this way:

Luther Whitney, born 23 February 1781
Hannah Whitney, born 27 December 1777

This type of record, unlike the one of identical surnames in the Richardson family Bible quoted above, offers no hint that Whitney may not have been the maiden name of the wife. Ostensibly Luther Whitney married Hannah Whitney (the date and place of the marriage were not entered in the Bible), but we are always skeptical when we come across such a Bible record, especially when no other record verifies the wife's name. We feel reasonably certain, in this case, that Hannah's maiden name was not Whitney because it has been impossible to establish her in any of the Whitney families in or around Adams, Mass., where their first two children were born. It is, of course, possible that she was a cousin, or belonging to some other Whitney family; the name is not uncommon.

If you cannot get possession of the Bible record that is important to you, get either a certified copy, sworn to before a notary public, or a photocopy or photostat of the record for your notebook. Moreover, if you cannot have the Bible to keep, it is always wise to make a careful note of the full name and address of the person who owns the Bible and the date on which you made the copy. Then, if you ever need to use that record for legal purposes or as a basis for membership in one of the hereditary or patriotic societies, you have certified evidence of this link in your ancestry, for you can submit your copy of this record to the society, with the name and address of its owner, and their genealogist can probably gain access to it for verification if desired.

## Diaries

Another sort of family record unfortunately much less common in occurrence than a Bible, but very valuable when it is found, is an old diary. Some diaries are exceedingly interesting, not only because they contain a wealth of genealogical details, but also because they were written by keen observers and display considerable evidence of the writer's personality. Unfortunately, sometimes the keeper of the diary was more interested in the affairs that were going on about him or her than in the details for which the genealogist is looking. In that case, however interesting it may be, the diary is a disappointment; it should be carefully read, nevertheless, for there may be some important clues buried in it.

One mid-nineteenth-century diary, which we happen to know, is almost purely a business record. The author was a miller in a small town, so he recorded each day just how many bushels of corn, wheat, and oats he ground in his mill, and how many feet of lumber were sawed. But he generally noted also the name of the individual for whom he ground or sawed. This has made the diary valuable to us in helping others trace their ancestry, and has enabled us to determine when some of the houses in the town were built. But this diarist also recorded which members of his family went to church each Sunday, so, in the absence of other records, we have been able to determine just when his sons and daughters moved away from home. When he mentioned a funeral, he was exasperatingly brief and made such statements as "Went to Florence's funeral." No clue to Florence's identity. One entry puzzled us a long time: "Went to Aunt Debbie's funeral." We knew of no Aunt Debbie or Deborah in the family. She proved to be a local character of such kindliness that she was "aunt" to everyone who knew her. Another exasperating entry was "Thomas started back West." Finally we learned that this Thomas was his cousin, the only son of his only uncle, who had moved west to Illinois. That is the last record we have been able to find about Thomas, for this branch of the family appears never to have heard of him again.

Tantalizing as such diaries are, they must be carefully studied, for the alert mind will find much of use in them. It is a good plan to make careful notes of any names mentioned in them, for sometimes such names may prove to be of importance to you. In this same diary we noted that the diarist went to "Thomas Morse's funeral" on a given date. This entry, although it was of no immediate use to us, later enabled us to help a correspondent who was searching for the date of her great-grandfather's death. The town records did not contain the required information, and it was not until some time later that we found his gravestone in a forgotten cemetery.

While we are on the subject of diaries, let us note that there are many invaluable colonial diaries which have been found and printed. These very old diaries frequently enable a genealogist to prove a line of descent, and sometimes they make very good reading, furnishing a picture of the times in which their authors lived. Samuel Sewall's *Diary* (published by the Massachusetts Historical Society) is one of the most important documents that we have, for he loved functions and attended every christening, wedding, and burial that came to his notice. He tells also just what dowry he had to give each of his several wives. It is amusing to note that they came cheaper as he and the prospective spouse got older (perhaps the ladies had less chance of getting a husband as their ages increased). The judge, for he was a judge and even sat on the famous witchcraft trials, lived in Boston, so his diary was concerned with that vicinity. He kept a diary during the latter half of his life, which covered the period from 1674 to 1729. An even older diary, the years including 1653 to 1684, is that of Thomas

Minor, born in England, who became one of the first settlers of Stonington, Conn. It is replete with information regarding those who lived there during the pioneer days of the settlement and was published in 1899 by one of his descendants. Joshua Hempstead's diary, covering thirty-seven years between 1711 and 1748, does much the same thing for New London, Conn. John Winthrop's *Journal*, which has never been published in its entirety, is another invaluable source for Massachusetts and Connecticut families. He was a physician of a sort and made detailed records of many of his cases.

## Family Letters

Family letters are likewise worth reading. Not unlike diaries, they frequently present a wealth of detail, although surnames are seldom mentioned in them, and they may shed considerable light on the character and personality of the writer. The one surviving letter written by Dr. Doane's great-great-grandmother gives a vivid picture of her personality and amplifies and confirms the family tradition concerning her characteristics in pecuniary matters. This particular letter was written to her son in Michigan about a month after her mother's death in 1839. She baldly states the fact that "Mother has been dead nearly a month and I haven't gotten my share of her things yet!" Even without the tradition that she quarreled with her husband because he loaned some of her money without her consent, and that she refused to speak to him again until it was repaid (about seven years later), we get from this single sentence in her letter an unforgettable picture of the redoubtable old lady and her determination that no one should do her out of what was rightfully hers.

Another old letter among the family papers set Dr. Doane on the right road to determining the descendants of a different branch of the family. This was written in a fine schoolgirlish hand on dainty paper such as, about a hundred years ago, could be found only in cities. In it were mentioned all such parties and visits as a young girl loves, and a number of names of cousins of whose existence he had been unaware. Another such letter, written in the 1840s and full of news about widely scattered relatives, enabled its finder to trace her family back several generations because it gave her the necessary clues to the places they had lived.

## Other Family Record Sources

Family account books also help considerably. Once, while attending a country auction in a Vermont hamlet, Dr. Doane pulled out of a basket of trash which was set aside to be burned (not even put up for auction) a long, narrow daybook. The entries dated from about 1803 to 1825 and contained many names of individuals and places. Through it he was able to establish the locality from which the migration was made. Aside from such details, of importance in a family history, this old account book sheds light on the prices of labor and materials at that time, especially in a rural community.

An account book, or ledger, in the possession of a gentleman in New York, proves to be practically a census of a small community in Dutchess County, for it was kept by a storekeeper. It contains evidence of the approximate dates of marriages, deaths, and removals, as the accounts are opened and closed or as the names of the customers are changed. From it he was able to prove almost to a month the date of the migration of his own family from that Dutchess County village to northern Vermont, for he noted the date on which the account was closed and marked "Paid in full." By comparing that date with those of some deeds in Vermont, he could set the date of migration. R. E. Dale, of Lincoln, Neb., edited this old account book of Dunkin's Store, Dover Furnace (Pawling Precinct), N.Y., and published it in the genealogical department of the *Boston Evening Transcript*, June 28, July 10, and July 18, 1935, as note 2751.

Although you may never have examined very closely the sampler hanging in its frame on the wall, it may contain data for your history. Sometimes a young seamstress, doing her cross-stitching, worked into the sampler a list of her brothers and sisters and their ages. If she dated the sampler (many samplers are dated), you know approximately when each of the relatives was born. Sometime, if you are interested, get Edith Standwood Bolton's *American Samplers* from the library and examine it. Not only a fascinating account, it is a genealogical source book as well, for Mrs. Bolton has illustrated a number of samplers and given the family data from many more.

Another type of needlework which is of value to the ancestor hunter is the so-called "friendship" quilt and its variations. About a hundred and fifty years ago it was the vogue to work quilts made up of pieces on which were embroidered or signed in indelible ink the names of the maker's close friends and relatives. Sometimes the girls who inscribed their names even embroidered the pieces themselves and presented them to the maker, who put them together. One quilt of this kind, in the possession of a descendant of the Standish family, contains the names and dates of all the members of the family, including aunts and cousins.

Another coverlet enabled one ancestor hunter to trace her family back across half a dozen states to the locality from which her ancestors came. It was embroidered by a great-grandmother for her hope chest. Taking a justifiable pride in her skill, she worked into one panel of the "spread" her maiden name, the date, and the name of the town in Maine in which she was then living.

Even old family silver may prove useful to the genealogist. Although very old silver is uncommon, an occasional piece has survived and been preserved as an heirloom. An old spoon engraved thus:

A B
C

has its clue, for initials placed in this manner on really old silver generally mean that the piece belonged to a husband and wife jointly. In this case, let us say Abijah and Betsy Cole. It may have been a wedding gift. Old tankards and silver mugs are frequently engraved in the same manner. Sometimes it is difficult to identify such initials, but they do serve as a clue that may put you on the right track. Recently, reading the will of Captain Lawrence Clarke, of Newport and Middletown, R.I., instead of depending upon the published abstract of it, we noted that he bequeathed to his son Lawrence "the silver cup marked L T which belonged to my grandfather." Captain Clarke's mother's maiden name had not been known hitherto; his own given name is not found in any of the earlier generations of his father's family. There was a Lawrence Turner living in Newport in the seventeenth century, but, as far as the town records show, no other man with the initials L T. Was Margaret, the second wife of the Reverend Joseph Clarke, the daughter of Lawrence Turner? We think so. One other slight bit of circumstantial evidence seems to confirm this assumption: Lawrence Turner was called a brick maker in one document; Lawrence Clarke, when he was not much over sixteen, was granted permission by the town council to dig clay for bricks. This indicates that he may have been apprenticed to his grandfather, whose silver cup he later possessed.

Thus you see an important adjunct to the family memories is any record that may exist in the family archives or possession. You should always try to locate such records and with their aid get the older relatives to explain as much about the family as possible. Sometimes the sight of an old letter or a bit of silver recalls to an aging mind the story back of it or relationships that have been forgotten and might not otherwise come to mind. In digging for ancestors, no stone is too small or too insignificant to be left unturned.

CHAPTER 5

# *Digging in Books and Libraries*

By THE time you have talked to or had correspondence with the older relatives and perhaps the older friends of the family, and have dug what you can out of the old family papers and records, you will probably have gathered sufficient data in your notebook and on your chart to begin searching in printed material. Perhaps you are lucky enough to live near a library containing a genealogical collection, say in Boston, New York, Washington, Chicago, Seattle, San Francisco, or Los Angeles, to mention only a few of the larger cities in which there are well-known genealogical collections. This material may be found in public libraries or other libraries, such as the New England Historic Genealogical Society Library in Boston, the Newberry Library in Chicago, the great collection of the Genealogical Society in Salt Lake City, Utah, or the Library of Congress in Washington. Even though your public library may not contain a special collection of genealogical material, the librarian should know where such collections can be found.

If you do not live near a genealogical library, large or small, perhaps you can plan your vacation to include a visit to a city in which there is a good collection. One of our friends, whose family likes an annual trip to some city, always manages to go to a place like Chicago, San Francisco, or New York for his vacation. While his family enjoys the shops and city sights during the day, he, with his notebook and the problems on which he is working, spends the time in the library, digging for his ancestors. Each year he comes back with a problem or two solved and a sheaf of notes which keep him busy through many of the long winter evenings.

If you have never used a genealogical collection before, the first thing to do is to have a good talk with the curator or assistant in charge who, from long experience in serving genealogists, knows how to help a beginner get started right. He or she knows the collection and can efficiently direct your use of it. The curator will explain its arrangement to you and show you any special indexes that have been made for it.

## Printed Genealogies

Once you have exlained your problem to the curator, he or she will get out for you any printed genealogies of the family or families in which you are interested that are available in this collection. You may be fortunate enough to have such a genealogy put into your hands immediately and to find in it your line of descent — once you have become familiar with the system on which it is arranged. (A certain amount of study is required in order to pick up any genealogy and use it intelligently, for the system of arrangement varies a great deal from one volume to another.) In the event that you have such good fortune, you can either copy the complete line of your descent from the book before you or plan to buy a copy of it from one of the booksellers who handle genealogical books, such as Goodspeed's Book Shop in Boston, the Genealogical Publishing Co. in Baltimore, Md., or the Chas. R. Tuttle Co., Rutland, Vt. Sometimes the volume is rare, for genealogies are almost always printed in small editions; hence a copy may be very difficult to find and very expensive when found. But even if you are fortunate enough to be able to afford to buy a copy, you will want to make a working pedigree from the copy in the library as a basis for running back the female lines. No one printed volume will be likely to contain all your ancestry; otherwise you would know about it and probably not be reading this book.

Such a working pedigree looks something like the illustration on page 57. You will note that we have given, at the top of the column at the left-hand side of the page, the exact title of the volume used, and in that column, opposite each generation, the references to the pages on which the data for each generation were found. It is essential that you take such references as you go along. Otherwise you will have to check back through the volume to get them and use more valuable time later. Many a genealogist who started out without these references has cursed himself or herself for the oversight when they were needed later, especially if the book is in a distant library.

This pedigree is based on what Dr. Doane happened to find in first consulting the book entitled *The Doane Family*, by Alfred Adler Doane (Boston, 1902), in the New York State Library in Albany many years ago. Harry Harvey Doane, listed on page 298 of this book, was Dr. Doane's father, so here he found his complete Doane line back to the immigrant John Doane (or Done, as the name was then spelled), who appeared in Plymouth, Mass., about 1630. As you will note on this working pedigree, when Dr. Doane found this line he discovered his descent from the Bangs, Hamblen, Bearse, Higgins, Howe, and Randall families as well, and so he began to dig for the ancestors in those lines and work those pedigrees back to the immigrants, and, in one or two cases, across the Atlantic into England, and for two or three generations there. He found printed genealogies for the Hamblen (that is, Hamlin) and Higgins families but he had to do a lot of digging for the rest. He has not yet found Azubah Doane, his great-great-grandmother!

Now, even though you find such a line in print, you must be very careful about accepting it as correct in every detail. Not everything that glitters is gold, and not

THE DOANE FAMILY by A.A. DOANE

pp. 1-18    **DEAC. JOHN DOANE =**
Plymouth, ca. 1630
Died Eastham 21 Feb.
1685, ae. 95 yrs.

*30 April 1662*

pp. 21-26    **JOHN DOANE, JR. = HANNAH BANGS,** dau.
Born Plymouth    of Edward Bangs
ca. 1635; died    born ca. 1644, liv. 1677
Eastham 15 Mar. 1708
ae. 73 yrs.

*3 Dec. 1696*

p. 45    **SAMUEL DOANE = MARTHA³ HAMBLEN**
Born Eastham 2 Mar. 1673    dau. of John² (James¹) and Sarah
Died Eastham 15 Aug. 1756    (Bearse) Hamblen. Born Barnstable
   3 Dec. 1696, living in 1734

*1 Oct. 1730*

p. 68    **SIMEON DOANE = APPHIA HIGGINS**
Born Eastham 1 Dec. 1708
Died Eastham 4 Dec. 1789

pp. 98-99    **BENJAMIN DOANE = RUTH**
Died North Brookfield, Mass.    Died at Eastham
Born Eastham, ca. 1738    16 Aug. 1778 ae. 39
3 Jan. 1824, ae. 86 yrs.

pp. 165-166    **BENJAMIN DOANE = AZUBAH DOANE**
Born Eastham 29 Aug. 1772    Born 27 Sept. 1772
Died Bakersfield, Vt.    Died Bakersfield 27 June 1845
27 Aug. 1846    (Her ancestry not given
   in Doane genealogy)

*1 Dec. 1829*

p. 298    **JAMES HARVEY DOANE = PERSIS HOWE**
Born Bakersfield, 20 Sept. 1802    Born 4 Nov. 1807
Died Bakersfield, 18 June 1847    Died 30 Sept. 1873

*15 Feb. 1870*

p. 298    **BRADLEY JOHN DOANE = ELLEN H. RANDALL**
Born Bakersfield, 9 Aug. 1846
Died Bakersfield, 22 June 1901

p. 298    **HARRY HARVEY DOANE**
Born Bakersfield 1 July 1873

FORM 3. The Doane Pedigree.

everything that is printed is true, in spite of the popular belief. Genealogies are compiled and published, sometimes at great expense, by all sorts of people. Some of these records are reliable and trustworthy; some of them are filled with glaring errors. A beautifully printed genealogy, elaborately bound in tooled leather, may be full of mistakes and almost worthless, or even worse than that, grossly misleading. Another family history, printed on cheap paper from worn type, may prove to be notable for its accuracy. You cannot tell from the outward appearance and the physical makeup, although as a general rule a book breeds confidence if it is carefully printed on good paper and substantially and tastefully bound in cloth. By studying the contents of a volume you can form a pretty good idea of the intelligence, acumen, and accuracy of the author or compiler.

If there are discrepancies in dates, for instance, you should be suspicious and check carefully. Suppose you find that John Jones, who emigrated to America in 1630 and died in Dorchester, Mass., in 1685, aged eighty years, is stated, in the book before you, to have been the son of Sir William Jones, of Buxton, Herts., England. In reading the chapter on the English origin of the family, you note that Sir William, reputed father of John, the emigrant, died in 1600 and was buried in Buxton. If you stop to figure John's possible birth date, you will see that there is obviously something wrong, for no man who died in 1600 could be the father of a child born in 1605. This sounds ridiculous, doesn't it? Yet, we have known unheeding ancestor hunters to accept such a statement "because they found it in print." Obviously, anyone who would allow such an error to be printed is careless; therefore, anything you find in a genealogy compiled by such an author should be carefully checked — by the original records, if possible.

Sometimes the genealogist or compiler of the book does not actually make such a statement, but the person using it makes a careless assumption from the documents that the compiler has printed in the genealogy.

For instance, many of the descendants of Deacon John Doane of Plymouth and Eastham, Mass., who have used A. A. Doane's book have assumed that the Deacon's wife was named Abigail. This assumption is based on the will that Mr. Doane copied from the Registry of Probate at Barnstable, Mass. John Doane, in his will, dated in 1678 (misprinted 1768 in the book), bequeathed his dwelling house and a certain "upland and meadow" about it to his "loving wife." Since Abigail Doane certified to the truthfulness of the inventory of his estate in 1686, it has been assumed that she was his widow and the mother of his children. Now Mr. Doane also printed a verbatim copy of a deed, dated in 1681, in which John Doane conveyed this same dwelling house and "upland and meadow" about it to his daughter Abigail. Obviously his wife had died between 18 May 1678, the date of his will, and 2 December 1681, the date of this deed. Hence, the Abigail Doane who certified the inventory must have been his daughter, to whom he had deeded the house originally intended for his widow if she survived him. Later research by another genealogist indicates that Deacon John Doane had a wife named Ann in 1648 when they both signed a conveyance, who was dead before 1659 when he and his wife Lydia conveyed some land in Eastham (see Mary Walton Ferris's *The Dawes-Gates Ancestral Lines*, Chicago, 1931, 1943, Vol. 2, pp. 304–5).

We doubt if there is a genealogy that does not contain a typographical error or misprint, and there are very few in which there are not some mistakes made by the compiler in interpreting the records at his or her disposal. You should be alert to catch these, and, whenever you see one, try to check it against the original records. Not infrequently you may find that a genealogist has killed off the child from whom you know you are descended, because he did not find that child mentioned in its father's will, or for some other such reason. In a case of this kind, you must be careful to supply ample proof of your ancestor's life and connection with the parents.

## Indexes

Failing a published genealogy of the family in which you are interested, the curator of the collection in which you are working will show you how to find any genealogies of the family that have been printed in periodicals as well as genealogies of other families with which yours is connected, and local histories. Or the curator will show you how to get at these "buried" genealogies through such indexes as Jacobus's, Durrie's, and Munsell's (for a list of such indexes see Appendix A). These indexes vary in completeness. Some are limited but thorough in covering the ground they are supposed to cover. (Always read the preface and see what the compiler's intentions were.) Others, although they are supposed to be adequate, are very much out of date. Some libraries have compiled indexes to their genealogical collections. For example, the Newberry Library, Chicago, indexed family sketches in all local histories it acquired until about 1917. This index, *The Genealogical Index of the Newberry Library* (Boston, 1960, 4 vols.), has been reproduced by offset printing and is available in several of the large libraries. *The American Genealogical Index*, conceived by Fremont J. Rider, of Middletown, Conn., is another valuable tool, for it combines in one alphabetical order all the names in a considerable number of genealogies, thus making it short work to locate a given name (watch, however, for variant spellings). A second series, *The American Genealogical-Biographical Index*, is now being published; it includes all names in the Genealogical Department of the *Boston Evening Transcript*, 1906–41 (see page 228), the many lists of Revolutionary War soldiers, and several more genealogies.

Frequently such an index will be very useful to you. Although the library in which you are working may not have the volumes to which it refers, if you can get the names of the authors and the titles of such books, you can make a note to use them in some other library where they are to be found or, perhaps, ask some friend to consult them for you.

## Local Histories

you do not find a reference to the family in which you
re interested, the next thing to do is to locate a history
f the town or county in which you know they lived.
ven though your family may have been too obscure to
arrant a genealogy of it in the history of that town, you
ay find a valuable clue there. For instance, by studying
e history of the town of Fairfield in Abby Maria
emenway's *Vermont Historical Gazetteer*, we found that
any of the settlers of that town came from Connec-
cut, mainly from Litchfield and Fairfield counties, or
om Dutchess County, N.Y., which borders Connec-
cut. We noted that many of the grantees of Fairfield,
t., were from New Fairfield, Conn., and later discov-
red that New Fairfield was settled by families from
round Fairfield, Conn. The very names of the towns
re indicative of these facts. This led us, first, to Mrs.
lizabeth Hubbell Schenck's *History of Fairfield, Connec-
cut*, where Dr. Doane found the clues for his Gilbert
ne and those cognate to it; and later to Donald Lines
acobus's *History and Genealogy of the Families of Old
airfield*, where they were given more accurately and
ompletely.

There is, unfortunately, no comprehensive and up-
-date bibliography of local history, although bibliog-
aphies of varying completeness exist for some of the
tates. A very helpful tool to start your search for books
n local history is the five volume *United States Local
istories in the Library of Congress, A Bibliography* (Balti-
nore, 1975) which includes state and local histories for
very state in the union. A word of caution: it does not
nclude a list of all the histories published for a state or
own so you will want to inquire for further information
rom the local library or historical society in the commu-
ity of your interest. The New York State Library has
ublished bibliographies for Maine, Connecticut, and
Jew York, which are now sadly out of date, but still
ery useful for material published years ago. Hammond
as compiled a bibliography of local histories of New

Hampshire towns. Recently three important state bibliographies have been published under the auspices of the Committee for a New England Bibliography. The volumes are a first-class bibliographic model, and it is hoped that other states and regions of the United States will follow this example. The volumes which have appeared are: *Massachusetts: A Bibliography of Its History* (Boston, 1976); *Maine: A Bibliography of Its History* (Boston, 1977); and *New Hampshire: A Bibliography of Its History* (Boston, 1979). In preparation are bibliographic volumes for Vermont, Rhode Island, and Connecticut. There are now genealogical guides to many more states. Such bibliographies, when they exist, enable you to learn very quickly whether or not there are any printed records about the locality in which your family lived. Once you have the reference, you can generally obtain access to it and examine it or have it examined for you.

If your library has no such bibliography and is too small to have a genealogical collection, you should secure a copy of the *Catalogue of Genealogies and Local Histories*, which is issued at intervals of two or three years by Goodspeed's Book Shop, 18 Beacon Street, Boston, Mass. 02108. There is a small charge for handling and mailing. Although it lists only the books that Goodspeed's has for sale, it is invaluable to the genealogist, for Goodspeed's stock is large and makes a specialty of genealogical books. Other bookshops deal in genealogies, and two, Chas. E. Tuttle, Rutland, Vt. 05701, and the Genealogical Publishing Co., Inc., 111 Water St., Baltimore, Md. 21202, publish catalogs. These catalogs are almost the only inexpensive bibliographies of genealogies and local histories available.

You should become familiar, however, with two extensive printed lists of genealogies, which are arranged under family names. One of these is, to give its exact title, *Genealogies in the Library of Congress* (Baltimore, 1976) and a *Supplement* listing materials received by the library between 1972 and 1976 (Baltimore, 1977), which is of great value. Noted are genealogies in a variety of formats, printed, typescripts and handwritten, which are in the library's collections. Here you will find genealogies from around the world and in many languages: American, English, Canadian, Irish, Welsh, Scottish, Australian, Latin American, Polish, German, Dutch, Scandinavian, French, Spanish, Portuguese, Italian, and Asian. This list has cross-references, so it frequently furnishes a clue to a "buried" genealogy. Another list is that published by the Long Island Historical Society, of Brooklyn, N.Y., in 1935. It is called *Catalogue of American Genealogies in the Library of the Long Island Historical Society*; it lists over eight thousand books dealing with genealogy, as well as about eight hundred and fifty manuscripts, typescripts, and photostat copies of original wills, etc. By looking up your family in either or both of these volumes, you can quickly determine whether or not a genealogy of interest to you has been published. You may find one and you may not. If you do, you may find in it what you want; or you may have considerable digging to do before you can connect your line with those given in it.

## Journals

In addition to the printed genealogies and local histories, the curator of a genealogical collection will give you an introduction to the genealogical magazines covering the part or parts of the country in which you are interested. The oldest and most comprehensive periodical devoted to genealogy is the *New England Historical and Genealogical Register*, familiarly known as the *Register*, the first number of which was published in January 1847, under the aegis of the New England Historic Genealogical Society. Consolidated indexes to Vols. 1–50 and 51–112 have been published. The latter was privately printed; it is not a complete index of all names, but rather a subject index. Genealogies of a great many families have been published in it, so you should not allow the local nature of its title to keep you from looking through its indexes for any material for which you may be looking. Quite naturally the preponderance of the material is about New England families, but many of these families are now scattered throughout the United States. In addition to genealogies, this journal contains many transcripts and abstracts of local records, such as town records, probate records, church records, and copies of cemetery inscriptions from many New England towns. For years the society has maintained a Committee on English Research, and published the results of careful and painstaking research on the English origin of American families. Another committee of this society has been compiling a record of American families possessing authentic coats of arms. Nine parts of this roll have been published, carefully illustrated with drawings of the arms. The first two parts were published in the *Register*, Vol. 82 (April 1928), pp. 146–68, and Vol. 86 (July 1932), pp. 258–86, and later were issued as reprints. All parts have appeared in pamphlet form. The committee has registered several hundred coats as authentic and rightfully borne or used by their respective families. Undoubtedly additional parts will be published as more coats of arms are authenticated and the roll grows.

The *New York Genealogical and Biographical Record* is another important periodical for the genealogist. As the title indicates, this is devoted mainly to records pertaining to New York. In it have been published transcripts of the 1800 census for several of the counties in that state, as well as genealogies, cemetery inscriptions, abstracts of wills and deeds, and other valuable contributions. The *American Genealogist* (formerly the *New Haven Genealogical Magazine*) is yet another excellent periodical and is devoted exclusively to New England records before 1800 and to studies of genealogical problems rather than long detailed genealogies. *Tyler's Genealogical Quarterly*, the *William and Mary Quarterly*, and the *Virginia Magazine of Biography and History* are all devoted mainly to Virginia genealogy. The *Pennsylvania Magazine* contains a great deal of genealogy. The *Na-*

*tional Genealogical Society Quarterly*, published in
Washington, D.C., has reprinted some of its more general articles in a series entitled "Special Publications"
which are very useful. There are many other genealogical magazines (most of them much newer than those
mentioned) which are devoted to the interests of special
parts of the country or to special fields of research. A
complete list of these would be too detailed for our purpose, but you can easily find their names if you begin
poking about in a library. There are over a hundred of
them!

In addition to the magazines now being published,
there are many that were comparatively short-lived, but
that contain material of great importance to the ancestor
hunter. Such a magazine as the *Old Northwest Genealogical Quarterly*, which was published between 1898 and
1912, is very valuable, for it contains many records of
interest to those who trace their ancestry through the
region known as the Old Northwest, particularly the
Western Reserve in Ohio. The series of magazines
edited by the late Eben Putnam, of Salem, Mass., a capable genealogist, is another valuable lot. The *Newport
Historical Magazine* (later called the *Rhode Island Historical
Magazine*) is another, for it contains transcripts of many
early records of that locality.

Most of these magazines, as well as several which are
not mentioned here, have been indexed in Jacobus's
*Index to Genealogical Periodicals*. It should be remembered
that Mr. Jacobus indexed articles (that is, contributions
pertaining to families) and local histories only and did
not include in his index all the specific names of individuals mentioned in these periodicals. If he had included these, the cost of compiling and publishing such
an index would have been prohibitive. Mr. Jacobus included in Vol. III (1953) his "Own Index" to genealogies
that are "buried" in certain selected books containing
ancestral lines and compiled by able genealogists. There
is published yearly a useful *Genealogical Periodical Annual
Index*, compiled and published by Laird Towle, of

Bowie, Maryland. He indexes about a hundred journals.

The late William Wade Hinshaw, of Washington, D.C., devoted the later part of his life to the publication of Quaker records. He compiled the first six large volumes of the *Encyclopedia of American Quaker Genealogy*. Vol. 1 covers the North Carolina meetings (remember that many New England Quakers moved to Pennsylvania and thence southward along the Appalachian valleys to North Carolina, then over the mountains and up through Tennessee and Kentucky to southern Ohio and Indiana); Vol. 2 includes four Philadelphia meetings; Vol. 3, New York City and Long Island meetings; Vols. 4 and 5, the Ohio meetings; and Vol. 6, the Virginia meetings. Vol. 7 contains the records of the Indiana meetings, compiled by Willard Heiss. Others may yet be published. These should never be overlooked, even though you may not be aware that your family once had Quaker affiliations. They may save you hours of searching, a long trip, and many dollars as well.

In all genealogical libraries worthy of the name you will find many other sources of genealogical material — manuscripts that have been deposited there, collections of clippings and other scattered material, and so forth. One of the most important of these supplementary sources is the printed transcript of the 1790 census of the United States, taken in 1790 and 1791 and printed in 1909 by the Bureau of the Census. In a later chapter we shall have more to say about this valuable set of books and the census itself.

## Newspapers

While we are discussing printed material, mention must be made of the *Boston Evening Transcript* and its genealogical department. Back in 1876, at the suggestion of Oliver Wendell Holmes, the *Transcript* began a department of "Notes and Queries." By 1894 the genealogical queries had become so numerous that a separate department was devoted to them. As long as the *Transcript* was published (that is, until 1941) this department appeared, sometimes twice a week, at other times daily. A wealth of genealogical material was printed in this newspaper: queries from ancestor hunters, answers from others who had been successful in their quest; copies of gravestone inscriptions from forgotten and overgrown cemeteries (mainly in New England, to be sure), abstracts of probate records and deed books, carefully worked out genealogies, and so forth. Many notable genealogists contributed to the *Transcript* columns, and many arguments over disputed points were included. Much of the material was of a high standard of excellence, and, though some of it was pure guesswork and must be used with caution, it is worth looking at. Rider's *American Genealogical-Biographical Index*, as noted above (see page 60), is including all names that appeared in the *Transcript's* columns between 1906 and 1941 (note that the earlier years are still unindexed). Since the pages containing the Genealogical Department have been reproduced on microcards and are usually available in the larger libraries having genealogical collections, this vast storehouse of data, much of it unavailable elsewhere, is now being opened for general use. You may find in it the very records for which you are searching.

The *Hartford Times* had a Genealogical Department in its Saturday issue for many years, beginning in 1933. Alas, this too has been given up.

Fortunately, in 1968 the Connecticut Society of Genealogists was organized and commenced the *Connecticut Nutmegger*. About half of this quarterly is given over to queries. Only members of the society may submit them, but each is allowed five in any one issue. Answers are not published and are mailed directly to the querist. Many members have reported excellent results, so membership seems worthwhile. Write to the Secretary, P.O. Box 435, Glastonbury, Conn. 06033, for more information.

Another query medium of national scope was *Genealogy & History*, a magazine devoted entirely to queries and answers, which was published by Adrian Ely Mount.

The Everton Publishers, P.O. Box 368, Logan, Utah 84321, publish the *Genealogical Helper*, which has several special issues each year devoted to directories of libraries, genealogists, etc.

Libraries as a general rule will not lend genealogical books, either by mail or locally. They are too much in demand in the library. Moreover, most of them are extremely difficult to replace if they are inadvertently lost or destroyed or otherwise fail to get back to their home base. So do not ask if you may take them home, and do not request your local librarian to borrow them on interlibrary loan for your use.

The New England Historic Genealogical Society, however, does lend duplicates from its great collection of books to its members under certain conditions. If you want to do much digging at home, even though you may live a thousand miles or more away from "the home of the bean and the cod," it may be worth your while to apply for membership in that society. The address of the society is 101 Newbury Street, Boston, Mass. 02116, and the dues are forty dollars a year. Members receive the *New England Historical and Genealogical Register*, a quarterly of which we've already spoken, and may borrow duplicate books from the society's library.

While on the subject of societies, we should tell you that there are many of them. "N.E.," as many old hands call the one we've just mentioned, is the oldest and most distinguished. Many others are more or less active and flourishing, and a large number of them publish magazines of some sort. They range from purely local organizations which are, sometimes, nothing more than clubs, to state-wide groups that meet once a year. The *Genealogical Helper*, mentioned above, has a list of them. The American Association for State and Local History publishes a *Directory of Historical Societies and Agencies in the United States and Canada*, which is useful in locating local historical societies.

In using libraries, particularly by mail, you must remember that none has the staff to do extensive research for you, and most have a rule limiting the amount of time that may be spent in answering your questions. If it is obvious that much time will be required, you will probably be sent a list of local genealogists so you can make your arrangements directly with one of them. In considering their fees, you must remember that you will be paying for experienced and even expert assistance which is more efficient than ordinary labor.

We shall not attempt to list all the genealogical libraries in the country because there is a special issue of the *Genealogical Helper* that lists them all every other year or so. This can be purchased for a small sum from the publishers in Logan, Utah.

CHAPTER **6**

# Blowing the Dust
## Off the Town Records

WHEN YOU have tried to connect the lines that you have
worked out from your family papers with those that you
find in the books at the library, and perhaps have prod-
ded the memories of your relatives a bit more in the
process, you may find that you still lack a generation or
two or must have more information before you can
definitely establish your pedigree. Then you will want
to get at the records of the town in which your people
lived and find out what data can be had there. If you
happen to live in the same community in which several
generations of your family have lived, you will have
many pleasant afternoons examining the records in the
office of the town clerk or whatever the keeper of
records happens to be called in your locality.

### Town Records Offices

Take your chart and your notebook under your arm and
make an expedition to that person's office, use your
most ingratiating manner (the one most suited to the
person who has charge of the records), and ask if you
can see the records covering the period in which you are
digging or, if the clerk seems so inclined, actually to
help you find the information that you want.

In some states laws have recently been enacted pro-
hibiting unrestricted use of vital records by anyone
other than genealogists or members of historical

societies, so it is wise to find out what the law is before you ask for such records. Granted such laws may have been enacted to prevent scandalmongers from verifying (or using illegally) records of bastardy, bigamy, illegal marriages, etc., this precautionary measure works a hardship on those who have a valid right to see the records of their own people.

Even though in most states public records are public property, and you have a right to use them, some of the officials who keep those records may be very jealous of them and guard them from "alien hands." Others are more than helpful to those who are sufficiently interested in what they contain to take the time to study them and use them. Some town clerks are crotchety and cranky and grumble a lot about the trouble of getting down the big ledgers — we have rarely seen town records kept in a volume that is light weight and easy to handle! Others appear to be annoyed, when they are really delightful old bears who grumble a bit merely to maintain their dignity but who really enjoy the diversion that you create by coming to them for information. Some insist on a fee (the law in some states provides that a fee shall be paid for copies of old records), and others wave a hand and say "Come again!" It is up to you to size up the person and handle him or her with tact and consideration.

Sometimes such records are actually kept neatly in repair. Once we had occasion to stop in Belchertown, Mass., and look at the vital records of that town, which we found carefully preserved between layers of Japanese silk and in excellent condition. They were, as well, in the custody of a fine gentleman to whom it was a pleasure to talk. But more frequently the old ledgers are covered with dust and dog-eared, loose in their bindings and falling to pieces. Sometimes they have been thoroughly indexed, but more frequently there may be no index or, what is really worse, a poorly made, inaccurate, and inadequate one. Sometimes they have been carefully kept and are fairly complete, including much more than one would expect. Dr. Doane stopped one time in the town of Bridport, Vt., to get some records for a case on which he was working, and found a wonderful set of records that included not only the births, deaths, and marriages as they had been entered throughout the century and more of the town's existence, but also a complete transcript of all the cemetery inscriptions in town.

Only in rare instances are the early vital records of a town kept in special volumes devoted exclusively to that purpose. Generally they are interspersed among other records, those of the business affairs and transactions of the town, land records, tax lists, and town accounts. The town clerk should know in which volumes there are to be found vital records, but many times it pays to go poking about yourself, if what you are handed does not contain the records you are searching for — provided, of course, you have gained the clerk's confidence and thus secured permission to enter the sanctum in which the records are kept. After you have been digging a very long time, you will have developed an instinct that seems to telegraph from your subconscious the message: "That's the volume you want!" You begin to have hunches; and when you do, you should play them.

In many towns the records have been destroyed by fire — hard luck in such a case. In others they have been lost. Occasionally lost records are restored, and sometimes records turn up after their existence has been completely forgotten. A few years ago in a certain town where we had done considerable searching, there was a change in the town clerkship, and the offices were cleaned up. We mean really cleaned, not merely swept. The great safe in which the volumes of town records were stored was actually moved out from the wall — for the first time in fifty years, probably. Behind it was the thin, large, flat folio volume containing the mid-nineteenth-century records of births, marriages, and deaths. It had slipped down there many years before and had never been missed. What problems it solved, and how eagerly we began to check carefully through it!

Although the date varies in the several states, there were practically no general laws requiring the registration of births, marriages, and deaths before 1850; and in the states in which there were such laws, they were frequently ignored or rather carelessly observed by the town officials. (In some cases they were ignored even after 1850 and up until the twentieth century.) So, you can never be sure that you will find the record you are searching for.

However, we are going on the supposition that the records exist and that you have gained access to them. Let us suppose that you have your chart complete through your Grandfather Merrick, that you have gone to the library and found a Merrick genealogy that does not "come down" to him, and that, therefore, you must work the line back another generation or two before you can make the "connection." Let us suppose that his name was Joseph Merrick and that you know he was born in Derby, N.H., about 1834. You have gone to the town clerk's office and have in your hands the volume covering that period. You begin to search for Merrick records. You find "Joseph, son of Jeremiah and Hannah Merrick, born 24 March 1833." Make a note of it and the page and number of the volume on which it was found — the date is near enough that of your Joseph to warrant an investigation of the record — and continue your search. Now, we'll grant you that your Joseph is the only one in whom you are interested, but for the purposes of proof and identification the names of his brothers and sisters are useful and sometimes essential. So, if you are wise, you will take down the records of the other children of Jeremiah and Hannah Merrick, because someone may remember that Grandfather Merrick had a sister Hannah and a brother Jerry, or you may find a will at the probate court in which Jeremiah Merrick, Jr., directs that his property be divided between his brother Joseph and his sister Hannah, thus proving that your Joseph was identical with the son of Jeremiah and Hannah Merrick of that name.

## Births

But let us assume that in proceeding through the volume you find another Joseph Merrick, born there 2 June 1835, son of John and Mary Merrick; and perhaps even a third Joseph Merrick, son of Henry and Jane, born there 31 May 1834.

Now you have a problem. Which of these three Joseph Merricks was your grandfather? How are you going to prove one of them to be your grandfather? The name seems to be a common one in the Merrick family, and it is quite possible that all three Josephs were the grandsons or great-grandsons of a progenitor named Joseph Merrick.

## Marriages

One method of identification is that of eliminating the Josephs who could not have been your grandfather. Perhaps on further search you find that Joseph, son of Henry and Jane Merrick, died in 1835. Thus one of them is eliminated. And possibly, still further on, in another volume of records, you find the marriage of Joseph Merrick and Sarah Jones on 25 December 1857. From your family records you have already learned that your grandfather, Joseph Merrick, married Almira Buck, 30 June 1856. Obviously, this isn't the marriage record of your grandfather, but you still don't know which Joseph Merrick was yours, especially since there was no indication in this record of the parentage of the groom. You seem to be up against a blank wall in your attempt to determine whether Jeremiah or John Merrick was your great-grandfather.

## Deaths

The next thing to do is to take a look at the death record of your grandfather. As vital records came to be kept systematically, and, especially, in the later part of the nineteenth century when special ledgers were provided for them, the parentage of the deceased was noted in his death record (and in marriage records the parentage of both the contracting parties). So, in looking at the official town record of the death of your grandfather you may find his parentage given.

But sometimes these details were overlooked by a careless clerk or by the physician reporting the death. Sometimes a man was so old that he was living with grandchildren who did not know his parents' names and the record was never turned in. For the sake of our problem, let us suppose that this was the case and the death record of your Joseph Merrick gives no indication of his parentage. Thus you are forced to continue your search and must work your problem out by using other records and even circumstantial evidence. That is why we advised taking a complete list of the brothers and sisters of each Joseph, as you came across them.

## Probate

The easiest step to take next is to go to the probate office, generally in the county seat, although occasionally the probate district is not identical with the county and the probate office is in another town.

But before you take that journey, look back still further in the vital records while you have access to them. Suppose that you find the marriage record of "Jeremiah Merrick and Hannah Lyon, 21 May 1828." Suppose that your grandfather named his eldest daughter Hannah Lyon Merrick, and perhaps one of his sons James Lyon Merrick, possibly your father. Here is circumstantial evidence that your grandfather was connected with the Lyon family in some way — otherwise why his or his wife's insistence that the name "Lyon" be carried on by at least two of his children? It certainly looks reasonable that he named his eldest daughter after his mother, and perhaps his son after his grandfather Lyon — the case is even sounder if you find a record stating that James and Hannah Lyon had a daughter named Hannah, born, say

21 August 1807 (thus old enough to be the Hannah Lyon who married Jeremiah Merrick in 1828).

Pending further proof from the probate records, or possibly the cemetery inscriptions, you may acccept as probable this parentage of your grandfather, Joseph Merrick, and continue your search for another generation of the Merrick line, the parentage of Jeremiah Merrick, your hypothetical great-grandfather. If he married in 1828, he was probably at least twenty years old and, therefore, was born in 1808 or before, for few men married before they were twenty (it is more common to find a young woman marrying before that age than it is to find a young man doing so). But your search through the earlier volumes of records does not produce the birth record of Jeremiah Merrick. He may have been born in another, perhaps a neighboring, town; or possibly his birth was not recorded. You should, however, make note of any other Merricks born during this period. Say you find a single Merrick record, that of the birth of a son to Joseph and Mary Merrick in 1805, no name given. This is tantalizing, for the unnamed son may have been your Jeremiah (or, of course, Henry or John). You find nothing more, on further search, not even the marriage of Joseph and Mary.

## Land Records

Now ask to see the land records, for they are very valuable to the genealogist. As we get further back into the history of the country and vital records become more and more sketchy, these land records assume paramount importance. Even into the nineteenth century many land records are teeming with genealogical details. A husband and wife may deed land jointly — in many states this was required if the land came into the family through the wife's inheritance. Sometimes a father would transfer land to his son "for love"; sometimes the heirs of an estate would give a joint deed, signed by all of them and even the wives and husbands of those who happened to be married — we found one such deed that was signed by nineteen people, all of them descendants of the man who had owned that house and lot when he died; sometimes residence in other localities was indicated (for instance, John Merrick, of Malone, N.Y., might deed land in Derby, N.H., thus indicating a residence in Derby before he removed to Malone). Sometimes people went back to their original home to spend their old age, and you will find a deed indicating this — let us say that you find a deed in which Joseph Merrick, of Hannah, Mass., transfers his land in Derby. Sometimes, of course, a man was speculating in land and bought a lot of it in a town to which he never went — a link in Dr. Doane's own ancestry is established by such a deed, for Samuel Hungerford, of New Fairfield, Conn., deeded land in Fairfield, Vt., to his daughter, Eunice Soule, and her husband, Joseph Soule, "for love."

To return to the case of the parentage of your great-grandfather, Jeremiah Merrick: suppose you find a deed in which Joseph Merrick, of Hannah, Mass., conveys his land in Derby to his son, Jeremiah, in 1830. Here you have pretty definite information that your Jeremiah was identical with the son of Joseph. You can picture the young man, married two years, making a go of it and receiving the farm on which he was living from his father who had removed to Hannah, Mass., by 1830. You still lack the birth record of Jeremiah, and perhaps his death record, but you are on the trail and no longer digging blindly. You still have probate records and cemetery records to help you establish your case.

## Location of Public Records

About twenty-five years before Social Security made a central repository of vital records important to many people, most of the states had passed laws creating such an office and requiring that copies of all vital records be filed in a specified state office — sometimes the Health Department, sometimes the Department of Vital Records. In many of the older states all vital records contained on the town books have been copied and sent to this central state office. These transcripts are made on cards, one for each individual record. The cards are generally filed in alphabetical order under the surname. In the *New England Historical and Genealogical Register*, Vol. 90 (January 1936), pp. 9–31, there is an article on the various state methods of keeping vital records, arranged by states. A digest of that article is to be found in Appendix B of this book.

In some states the law was made sufficiently inclusive to require that all cemetery records be included with the vital records from the town books (although in Vermont we find that this law has not been fully observed); and occasionally the law has directed that a transcript of church records as well be made.

By writing to the state office of vital records you can obtain all the information that is on file for, let us say, Jeremiah Merrick. For the official title and address of the appropriate office in each of the several states, get a copy of *Where to Write for Birth and Death Records* (DHEW-HRA 75-1142), *Where to Write for Marriage Records* (DHEW-HRA 74-1144), and *Where to Write for Divorce Records* (DHEW-HRA 75-1145) from the Superintendent of Documents, United States Government Printing Office, Washington, D.C. 20402. The price is 35 cents, but do not send stamps. These useful pamphlets will indicate how early the records in each state begin, give you the price for ordinary and certified copies, or, in certain instances, direct you to city or county offices for such records. No state office can be expected to supply an unlimited number of records — say you want all Merrick entries, births, marriages, and deaths — but will usually send you a list of local searchers. You select one and write for an estimate which is generally based on the time involved. Some searchers, from sad experiences, ask for payment in advance, others may rely on your honesty.

In a few states some of the vital records of the various towns have been printed. Massachusetts has taken the lead in this matter, thanks to the impetus given to the movement by individuals and privately endowed societies interested in genealogical and historical matters. The vital records down to 1850 of most of the towns in eastern Massachusetts, and many of those in the western part of the state, have been printed and are to be found in most genealogical libraries. The records of a few of the towns in Connecticut and Maine have been printed also. The vital records of scattered towns in other states have been printed in magazines, as appendixes to local histories, and occasionally at the personal expense of some interested individual or society.

The early land records of Suffolk County, Mass., have been printed and, in their black binding labeled "Suffolk Deeds," are familiar to many genealogists. Others have been abstracted and printed in whole or in part. The colonial documents of New York, Rhode Island, Plymouth Colony, and Massachusetts Bay Colony, and the Providence, R.I., and Hartford, Conn., land records have been printed, to mention but a few. Most libraries having genealogical or historical collections own these volumes.

## Mortgage Records

To return to the town offices, don't overlook the mortgage records, which, although they are not so frequently useful, do sometimes contain valuable clues.

## Tax Lists

Then there are tax lists, which provide a sort of census of the town, in that all taxpayers are listed. Since the federal census is taken every ten years, these tax lists frequently serve as an intermediate census, and from them you can determine just when your people moved away from the town, or ceased to pay taxes, at least. You can figure out the size of their farms or how much land they owned and the value of it. Aside from definitely locating your people in that town, they help you to paint a picture of your family's standing and interests.

## School Censuses

In some localities in the 1870s there were school censuses taken. In these were records of the heads of families and the names of children of school age in each family. If the vital records were poorly kept, these school censuses are valuable, because the age of each child was specified, and sometimes these records are more accessible to the searcher than the federal census records. They may or may not be valuable to you, but at least they are worth knowing about.

You may think that these various kinds of town records are as dry as the dust that so frequently covers them. But if you are on the watch for anything humorous, you will find many a funny thing in them. After all, these people were human, as even the dry old records show. There is one Connecticut marriage record, solemnly and seriously entered on the books and duly printed in a transcript, in which one John Boughton marries "I Dono Who"! Now it is quite obvious that the clerk did not know the name of the bride, perhaps forgot to ask it or had actually forgotten it when he came to make the entry on the books. Anyhow, we suspect that many a descendant of this couple has laughed off irritation over this funny entry and searched elsewhere for the bride's name. Sometimes the clerk was not sufficiently interested to ask for such details. Sometimes he entered merely the sex of a child, as "a son" or "a daughter," whose birth he was recording, or the clergyman who performed the baptism forgot to write it down. Sometimes the spelling is quite phonetic, and you get curious names like "Febe" for Phoebe and "Kerrence" for Concurrence (we have once seen this spelled "Kurrants"). Alys and Ellis have been known for Alice. Joll has been used for Joel. Misspellings of surnames are even worse. Apostrophes were almost unknown, so sometimes an "s" was added to a name: for instance, Soule became Sowles, where the reference was to Soule's children or something of the sort. Sometimes the clerk didn't cross his "t" or dot his "i," and you get unintentional misspellings, such as Merrell for Merritt. The further back you go, the more precarious the art of spelling becomes, so you must be always alert to catch it and never overlook a name because it isn't spelled exactly as you spell it today.

If it is not possible for you to go to the town clerk's office — if you live too far away and find it impossible to go halfway across a continent to consult the records — you have two means of getting at them. You may write to the clerk and ask him or her to find the record that you want and send you a copy of it; or you may employ a private searcher to go and examine the records in person — a relative, perhaps, or a professional genealogist.

Many town clerks are not especially interested in genealogy (all this fuss about ancestors seems trivial to them), so any search they make is bound to be rather perfunctory and unsatisfactory. You must remember that your problem does not seem important to them and may even irritate them because it takes them from some more lucrative or pleasant occupation and makes it necessary to lift down those heavy volumes. A search by such a clerk is bound to be rather haphazard and he or she may easily overlook the record most important to you.

On the other hand, you may be fortunate in finding a clerk who is really interested in the records, has them completely and thoroughly indexed, and can give you accurate information. Such an official will frequently go out of his or her way to assist you and may refuse to accept any fee for services. However, whichever type of clerk you find, my advice is that you should never accept a statement that such and such a record doesn't exist until you have had the opportunity to check it yourself or through another's service. Sometimes one eye will see what another missed. But it doesn't pay to let the clerk know that you doubt his or her word, or to insist too much that the records be checked again. File the letter among your notes and make a mental memorandum, if not a written one, to go there sometime to take a look for yourself. But you might write again and ask whether he or she searched the land records for any evidence bearing on your problem. Generally you can tell by the tone of the reply whether the search has been very thorough. If the tone is brusque and abrupt or if the clerk says that the records "seem" to contain no evidence, you may suspect that he or she merely "seemed" to search them. If the clerk goes into details, you may have more confidence in the thoroughness of the search.

In writing for records, you should always offer to pay any fee that the clerk may charge, and you will find it a good policy to enclose a self-addressed stamped envelope for reply. The fact that you are willing to pay for data will have a good effect upon the clerk. Most people dislike those, particularly strangers, who are trying to get something for nothing, and many officials, particularly those living in small towns, object to being ordered about. Play up to them and make your need seem important to them, and impress them with the fact that you depend upon their good will and intelligence to help you solve your problem. It tickles their vanity, even though they may be shrewd enough to see through your ruse.

Moreover, in writing, always state your questions clearly and give all the information you can which will enable the clerk to make the search as easily as possible. Remember that he or she has many duties and may be very busy, without clerical help. You are more likely to be served if you state your problem clearly and ask for specific information. A demanding letter giving meager information, such as "I want the record of my great-grandfather, who lived in your town; please send it by return mail," will probably go into the wastebasket, for it contains no names, no dates (even approximate), and no indication of what the ancestor's name may have been. Nobody unfamiliar with your problem can pull such information out of thin air. How is the clerk to know even the surname of the man whose birth record you require? He or she is far too busy to take the time to figure back four generations and decide that the man in question must have lived about a hundred years ago. Your chance of success would be much better if you wrote a letter like this:

> I am searching for the record of the parentage, birth, and marriage of my great-grandfather, Jeremiah Merrick, who is supposed to have married in your town sometime before 1835, and was probably born there between 1800 and 1810. I will gladly pay any fee you may charge for a search of your records, and I enclose an envelope for your reply, which I hope to have at your convenience.

Don't be discouraged if the results of a search of the town records are very meager, for the sources of information are not exhausted, and you may yet solve your problem from other records.

For instance, there may be something in the county court records — we do not mean just the probate court, which will be discussed in Chapter 8, but those mentioned on pages 105–10. Some lawsuits involve evidence of descent from the original grantee of the property in dispute, others may include testimony from relatives distant in ties of blood as well as in locality. By chance, in the papers accompanying such a case the very data you are looking for may be found, or a locality may be named with which you have never connected any of the family, and in the town clerk's office in that place you may find the records you need to prove your descent. We know of one lawsuit involving right of burial in a cemetery lot — a man sued his second cousin for burying the remains of an aged aunt in her grandfather's lot and tried to get a court order requiring that they be removed. He based his case on the fact that the deceased's mother had married and hence could no longer be considered a member of her father's family, but belonged in her husband's family; therefore, her offspring was not entitled to space in her father's lot. In the evidence submitted there was quite a bit of genealogy of the family, and a copy of the original owner's will, lost in the file of the probate court, was produced. It all made us think of J. P. Marquand's novel *The Late George Apley* and the amusing episode of the burial of Cousin Hannah's remains — if you enjoy a chuckle, look it up and read it.

# CHAPTER 7

# Inscriptions in Cemeteries

PERHAPS NOWHERE is the transitory nature of the existence of human individuals brought home to us more vividly than in an old country graveyard which lies neglected and forgotten on a rural hillside. There are thousands of such burial grounds in the United States, each of them known only to comparatively few people, even among those living in the very town in which it is located. It frequently happens that no descendant of those whose remains are buried in such a cemetery is living near there today. In many other cases descendants living there do not care a tinker's damn about the condition of the almost forgotten graves; or, to be more charitable, they are physically or financially unable to care for them. In some places the entire character of the population has changed and the old families have either died out entirely or moved away, to be replaced by recent immigrants who have no interest in the old burial places. Sometimes brush and brambles have grown so high that not a stone is visible when you first look at the thicket that is supposed to be the cemetery lot. Even a ten-foot obelisk may stand obscured from view by the dense young forest about it. Thus has the local fame of some proud old family been blotted out by nature's luxuriant growth.

Families once prominent in the community are now forgotten, even though their position and influence has been subtly indicated by the quality of the marble or granite marking their graves. In one town in northern Vermont, Dr. Doane found the fine marble "table-slab" over the grave of the most prominent pioneer settler of the town so weathered by the rains and snows of a hundred and thirty-odd years that the long inscription, which presumably records his standing, has been obliterated beyond recall. Yet the old volume recording the affairs of the first quarter century of that town contains his name on practically every page. Only an antiquarian, like Dr. Doane, and one or two others are aware that he played an important part in the establishment of the town, and it is doubtful whether anyone besides Dr. Doane knows where he was buried. Not a person of his name lives in the town today or has lived in it for a hundred years. Probably 95 percent of today's inhabitants of that town would not recognize his name at all. *Sic transit gloria mundi!*

Such a circumstance is not peculiar to that particular town but is duplicated in hundreds of others throughout the country. We live in an age that has little respect for the past and shows no inclination to profit by the experience of those who have lived successfully and died in peace.

Part of the explanation of this neglect of the old cemeteries is that the elements making up the population of these old towns have changed radically during the last century. Old families have died out, or their descendants have moved away to the cities. New people have come in, bought up the old farms, gained control of the town affairs, and, having no active, intimate interest in the past history of the town, have allowed the burial places of the town fathers to become neglected. These, in the course of time, revert to natural growth, for Nature, always fighting her children, has her way unless there is a continual guard kept against her ruthlessness.

Gravestones sink into the ground or fall down and get broken by barbarians and vandals. The encroaching sod soon covers them and they become buried beneath grass, dead leaves, and broken twigs. Sometimes unfeeling human beings have picked up these old stones, carried them away and used them as hearthstones, as doorsteps, or as a part of the foundation of a new barn or outbuilding, or for anything else for which a flat stone may have been needed. Sometimes cows, breaking through an old rail fence surrounding a cemetery or clambering over a crumbling stone wall, have rubbed against the gravestones and knocked them over, and then trampled them into the dirt.

Years later there comes along an ancestor hunter, looking for the records that those stones contain. On many occasions he must literally dig the records of his ancestors out of the sod, and sometimes, if he has the means, he may restore the cemetery to some degree of order and have the stones reset. Or, when unable to bear the expense of restoration, he carefully copies the inscriptions and preserves them in one way or another for the use of others searching for the data recorded on them.

In searching the cemeteries for the records of your forebears, the task is made easier if you can take an older relative with you, for frequently your grandfather, your great-uncle, or an old cousin can tell you about the relationships that existed between the individuals buried there. Sitting at home, they may not recall even the names of those who died so many years ago, but, when they are confronted with a memorial stone, the little bell rings in their minds and their memory is restored.

Dr. Doane recalls trying, several years ago, to get a complete list of the children of his great-great-grandfather from his great-aunt. She knew that her father was one of twelve children, six boys and six girls. She could name eleven of them but could not recall the names of the sixth girl and her husband. They had the dates of birth from the eldest in 1791 to the youngest in 1817. Since the six older children, whom she could remember, came along in 1791, 1795, 1797, 1799, 1801, and 1803, they felt confident that the missing girl was born in 1793, because, as his great-aunt remarked, "they had 'em every two years in those days." So, one fine afternoon, Dr. Doane helped Great-Aunt Elizabeth into the car and they drove to the cemetery where most of the family were buried. They began a systematic search of the yard, picking out the stones of all women whose births were indicated as occurring in 1793. They hadn't gone very far before Dr. Doane found a stone on which this inscription stood: "Amanda, wife of Willis Northrop, died March 23rd, 1852, in her 59th yr." Sure enough, his great-aunt recalled her "Aunt Mandy" immediately, and they had the missing child!

But if you are not fortunate enough to be able to take your relatives to the cemetery and thus refresh their memory, you yourself can figure out (and later prove from other records) many of the relationships that you need for your record of the family. For instance, let us suppose that you are still trying to find the records of your great-grandfather, Jeremiah Merrick, and his wife, Hannah. You find in the cemetery their graves with stones reading like this:

Jeremiah Merrick          Hannah, Wife of
1805–1851              Jeremiah Merrick
                          1808–1878

In your search of the town records you have already found that she was Hannah Lyon. Beside her here in the cemetery, you find a stone reading:

James Lyon
1770–1841

and on the other side of James, another:

Hannah
Consort of
James Lyon
Died
May 3rd, 1838
In Her 66th Year

And perhaps beyond them, in the same lot, several children of James and Hannah Lyon, possibly two or three of them dying in maturity but apparently unmarried.

You would be justified in assuming that James and Hannah Lyon were the parents of Hannah, wife of Jeremiah Merrick. Your record of the marriage of Jeremiah Merrick to Hannah Lyon in 1828, and now the approximate date of her birth figures from her gravestone, together with the ages of James and Hannah Lyon at that time, indicate pretty clearly that they were her parents. This is further substantiated by the fact that your grandfather named a son James Lyon Merrick. Moreover, Hannah (Lyon) Merrick was obviously named for her mother, Hannah, "consort of James Lyon." James Lyon's will, or the administration of his estate, will probably prove your contention.

Perhaps in another lot, not far away or in an even older cemetery in the town, you find this inscription on an old slate stone:

> Mary S., wife of
> Joseph Merrick
> Died
> October 28th, 1805
> In The 30th Year
> Of Her Age

But you do not find beside her or in any other cemetery in the town the grave of her husband, Joseph Merrick (who, you may recall, was living in Hannah, Mass. in 1830, and may have been buried there). However, there are, in the lot with her, three small children, let us say:

| Jeremiah | Mary |
|---|---|
| Infant Son of | Daughter of |
| Joseph & Mary Merrick | Joseph & Mary Merrick |
| Died | Died |
| May 6th, 1801 | May 8th, 1801 |
| Aged 6 w'ks | Aged 2 y'rs |

> John
> Son of

Joseph & Mary Merrick
Died
May 1st, 1801
Aged 4 y'rs

Here you get a picture of what happened in that fateful
May of 1801 — an epidemic of smallpox, diphtheria, or
scarlet fever sweeping through the town and hitting the
Merrick family pretty hard, for they lost three small
children, perhaps their entire family, within a week.
Possibly the mother had it, too, and survived to die only
four years later, probably soon after the birth of your
Jeremiah, whom she named for the youngest boy that
had died. Probably the John Merrick whose son Joseph
was born in 1835 was another son, born in 1803 and
named for the John who died in 1801; and perhaps the
Henry you found was an elder son who survived the
epidemic. Families in those days frequently repeated the
names of deceased children, so anxious were they to
have those names continued in the family. We know of
four sons in one family who were given the same name,
each after an older brother who died in infancy.

## Search·Too Adjacent Town Cemeteries

Sometimes it is well to examine the cemeteries in towns
that border on the town in which your people lived.
Boundary lines have changed, and land that was once in
their town is now in another. Moreover, families marry
back and forth, regardless of boundaries. Again, in
northern Vermont, we know of four towns whose borders touch at one point. There is a graveyard in the
point of one, within a stone's throw of the other three.
In this cemetery are buried members of families who
lived in three of those towns. There Dr. Doane found,
after years of intermittent searching for his grave, the
tombstone of the first husband of his great-great-
grandmother. He died at the age of twenty-six — was
killed in an accident in the sawmill where he worked.
Dying so young and within four years after his marriage, he was buried in his father's lot in that little ceme-

tery. His widow married again, produced a large family for her second husband, and was buried beside that husband, nine miles away. You might assume from the inscription of the first husband's stone, and the absence of any wife beside him, that he died unmarried and was buried near his parents. Yet a large family developed through the only child of that early marriage. So it is not safe to assume too much from a single grave. Your genealogical intuition and your knowledge of conditions prevailing at the time in which these individuals lived must lead you to reasonable conclusions.

## Private Burial Grounds

A century ago there were many more private cemeteries than there are now. In frontier communities especially, many people were buried on their own land or at the edge of the clearings they had made and were developing. Not many years ago Dr. Doane was prowling about on the back roads of his native town, searching for small cemeteries and isolated graves. He stopped to call on an old friend of his mother's and asked him if he knew about any graveyards or private burial grounds in that part of town. He told him there was a gravestone in a small pasture near the house of his son-in-law, so they went over there and found it at the foot of a decayed apple tree which had long since passed its prime. The inscription read: "Bridget, wife of James H. Hawley, Esq., Died in August, 1791, aged 26 years & 3 months." That farm had originally been part of a large tract of land owned by Mr. Hawley, one of the pioneer settlers, who, together with another wife, was buried beneath an imposing monument in a cemetery in a neighboring town. Bridget, his first wife (she was born a Stanton), with whom he had shared the hardships of pioneering, lies forgotten beneath an old apple tree not far from the spot where they built their first cabin.

## Carefully Read the Inscriptions

When working in old cemeteries you must really study the stones. Weathered inscriptions are difficult to read.

Sometimes their legibility depends upon the light. If the sun is bright and the day is clear, the shadows may be sharp and easy to read. But if the sun's rays hit the stone at such an angle that no shadows are cast in the incisions on the stones, you must shade the stone, or the inscription, so that you can read the letters. Sometimes, especially when you are attempting to photograph a stone, it is better to trace each letter of the inscription with common white chalk; in photographs the inscription always stands out much more clearly if this is done. Follow carefully the course of the engraving with your chalk so that you may get all the lines, especially the fine lines. Sometimes it is easier to make a rubbing of the face of the stone. Take a large piece of wrapping paper, lay it flat against the stone, and rub over it with a soft lead or a piece of marking crayon, such as shippers use in marking packing cases — just as you, when a child, used to make rubbings of the front of your geography book when you were too bored in school to study.

Many different kinds of stones have been used for grave markers. These fall more or less into periods. Mrs. Harriette Merrifield Forbes's *Gravestones of Early New England and the Men Who Made Them, 1653–1800* (1927) and Allan I. Ludwig's book, *Graven Images: New England Stonecarving, 1650–1815* (1966), are interesting studies of the types of markers used before 1800. In the late eighteenth and early nineteenth centuries the stone commonly used was a soft, dark slate, which weathered easily and quickly and had a tendency to split off as the snow and ice worked on it in the wintertime or the rain soaked into its crevices in the summer. During this period the engravers used mainly a Roman letter, which is easily read if it has not weathered too much.

Between 1800 and 1850 a kind of grayish-blue slate was used. This is a harder stone than the dark slate and takes a better polish. But during this period the engravers used an Italic script for their lettering, which is sometimes very difficult to read. The heavy lines of the down strokes made by the engravers were cut deeply and have survived, but the hairlines of the cross strokes, such as most of the top of a figure 7 and the cross stroke of the elaborate 4, and sometimes the semihorizontal strokes of the 3's, 8's, and 9's, were lightly incised and on many stones these are almost or entirely weathered away. If the light isn't right, or your fingers aren't sensitive in tracing them, they are very difficult to see and read. Not infrequently a novice at reading gravestone inscriptions will misinterpret the figure 4 and read it as 11 or even 21 or 71, especially if the little horizontal stroke is obscured by a tiny bit of lichen or is not plain in the direct light of the sun, and the other figures of the date are illegible. Figures that are often confused are 8 and 3, while 9 in that script looks odd, and if the elongated tail has become obscured the figure may be mistaken for 0. The figure 1 was frequently made with an extended serif that can be read as a 7, thus throwing out calculations appreciably, and 2 is also confused with 7, especially if the lower tail is illegible. On a weathered stone 5 and 6, or 6 and 0 may be confused; and sometimes 3 and 5 are hardly distinguishable. A rubbing will sometimes solve the problem of reading.

So in reading the inscriptions on this type of stone and those of the period, 1800–50, you should be unusually careful to get an accurate transcription of the record. If you have any reason to question your interpretation of the figures, you should indicate that uncertainty with a question mark and a note of what the alternative reading might be.

About 1840 or a little later a type of hard marble came into use and with it, perhaps because of its hardness, the use of Italic script began to wane and Roman lettering came back. Late in the nineteenth century granite came into popular use, and with it raised lettering, which unfortunately is sometimes as difficult to read as incised lettering, especially if the light isn't right or if lichen has grown over the stone. Within the last few years, the art of sandblasting an inscription into the stone has come into use. By this method the wording is cut in very deep, so it bids fair to stand a great deal of weathering and survive much longer than the old, hand-chiseled inscription.

Before 1850, gravestone inscriptions rarely contained inclusive dates, but generally the date of death followed by a statement of the age of the decedent. Sometimes this was given in years, months, and days: "Aged 87 yr's, 6 m's, & 3 d's." Given such an inscription, following the old rule that you learned in arithmetic, you can figure out the exact date of birth. But if you have an inscription such as "Aged 87 Years" your problem is not so simple. Only in extremely rare cases does a person die on the anniversary of his birth; consequently, whenever you find such an inscription, you may be reasonably sure that the odd months and days of the deceased's age were omitted from the inscription. Generally such an inscription implies that the decedent had passed his eighty-seventh birthday, but he may have been within a few weeks of it. You cannot tell from the inscription. If it reads: "Died April 25th, 1841, aged 87 years," he may have been born in 1753 or 1754, for his eighty-seventh birthday may have occurred some time after 25 April 1840 and before 1 January 1841, and hence he was born in 1753; or the birthday had occurred in 1841 before 25 April, or had been about to occur, and hence he was born in 1754. If you fail to find any evidence of the exact date of birth, you should always indicate the approximate date as, in this case, 1753–54.

It is equally difficult to figure birth dates from inscriptions that read like this: "Died May 1st, 1840, in the 26th year of his age." If a man was twenty-five in April 1840, he entered his twenty-sixth year at that time, and thus was born in 1815; on the other hand, if he had his twenty-fifth birthday after 1 May 1839, he was still in his twenty-sixth year when he died, but was born in 1814. So here again, failing other data, you must record the birth as 1814–15.

In copying inscriptions from gravestones it is always wise to copy *verbatim ac litteratim*, word for word and letter for letter, including all punctuation as it is given. This eliminates some of the chances for error. If a stone reads: "consort of," copy it that way, and do not substitute "wife" for "consort." "Consort" signifies that the husband (or, in rare cases, the wife) was living at the time, whereas "wife" does not necessarily have that meaning. "Relict" always means widow (although occasionally, widower); hence, in the absence of other evidence, you know that the wife survived her husband. It is a small point, but sometimes it is very significant. Of course, the introductory phrases, "In memory of" and "Sacred to the memory of," add nothing to one's knowledge, and they can be omitted without loss; but there is a difference between "in her 57th year" and "aged 57 years."

In the event of illegible inscriptions or portions of inscriptions, it is a good plan to enclose your interpretation of the illegible part in square brackets, thus [ ], when you make your transcription. This is a device used universally to indicate an editor's substitution for the original. Thus, any experienced person reading the following transcription:

> [Sacre]d to the Memory of
> [Jere]miah Merrick
> [Wh]o Died
> [Ja]nuary 24th 1841
> [in] his 36th
> [year]

would know that the inscription was partially illegible and that the copyist had supplied the portion enclosed in the brackets, probably having made out enough of the worn letters to be reasonably sure of what they were originally.

This same device can be used to add a descriptive phrase, thus:

> Hannah, Wife of
> Jeremiah Merrick,
> died
> August 1 [remainder of
> stone broken away]

While poking about in old cemeteries, you come across many sad things and many amusing things as well. There are those, we know, who feel it is very disrespectful to the dead to find amusement in anything in a cemetery, but we hope that attitude is changing, for many of the dead enjoyed gaiety in life and probably, if they know anything about it, welcome a bit of it over their resting places. Death can be beautiful or ludicrous, as well as sad. The lugubriousness of the earlier attitude toward it is amply expressed in the first line of the following epitaph from the gravestone of Eunice, wife of Joseph Soule:

> Corruption, earth and worms
> Shall but refine this flesh
> Till my triumphant spirit comes
> To put it on afresh.

In the same cemetery, Dr. Doane found this epitaph on the stone of Lewis Leach, who died in 1841:

> This modest stone, what few vain marbles can,
> May truly say, Here lies an honest man:
> Calmly he looked on either life and here
> Saw nothing to regret or there to fear.

There are nice implications in the following verses from the marker of Clarissa Page (was she a sister of the Cynthia Page, whose epitaph we quoted in Chapter One? — they rest in different cemeteries in the same town):

> While sculptured marble speaks of fame
> And monuments o'er merit rise
> This stone shall to the world proclaim
> Tomb'd deep in earth here virtue lies.

And this in 1813, before the great Victoria was born!

Many people, some of whom are not even interested in digging for ancestors, collect epitaphs, make rubbings from seventeenth- and eighteenth-century gravestones, and plan their picnics and the spare moments of their vacations to include a cemetery, where they examine the old stones and copy what appeals to them.

In one cemetery we came across an orderly row of tombstones recording the existence of five of the wives of the patriarch who lay beyond them, with room left for the grave of the sixth, who survived him! In another we found, side by side, the graves of three sisters near those of their parents. These "Gilbert girls," as they were called, had a total age of more than 240 years and all died unmarried, carrying on their father's farm to the last. Near them were the "Olmstead girls," each of whom lived into her seventies. A telling indication of the New England tendency to spinsterhood!

Such inscriptions as these from a small remote village are not unusual. They can be duplicated in hundreds of others. Moreover, the discerning ancestor hunter can read the outline of the history of any town in its cemeteries. The changing types of names indicate the changes in the elements of the population. The rise and fall of families can be read in the simplicity and grandeur of the stones over their graves. Even the remnants of slavery can be noted, for we found in a small cemetery overlooking the Missouri River a simple marker of an old slave who was buried at the feet of a young woman whom she had nursed throughout a fatal illness.

Occasionally one finds a reminder of some very gruesome event. On a back road, in the town of Fairfield, Vt., there is a pasture in which, some hundred yards from the road, stands a small obelisk about three feet high. It is the memorial to Marrietta N. Ball, who was murdered near that spot in 1874. Sunken into it at one time was a daguerreotype portrait of Miss Ball, and below the identifying inscription was engraved a brief account of the manner in which she was killed: she was attacked while walking home from the school where she was teaching, her body was dismembered, and the torso was found on the spot where the monument stands. One other memorial stone of this kind is known to exist in the United States — somewhere in Rhode Island, we are told — but the type is more frequently found in England.

Although, as a general rule, a gravestone tells very little about the personal characteristics and history of the individual beyond the dates of the two major events in life (birth and death), occasionally a stone gives a glimpse of the person he or she was. In a roadside cemetery within a mile of the eastern shore of Lake Champlain, we found the following inscription. It is not necessary to tell in more detail the story it contains:

When true friends part
'Tis the survivor dies

. . . .

This Monument,
By a Beloved friend is
Erected to the Memory of
JOSEPH R. FAY
Who Died on The 19th of May
1803 in the 25th Year
of His Age.
Thoughtful yet Smiling

. . . .

Farewell Bright Soul! A Short Farewell
Till we shall meet in realms above
In the sweet grove, where pleasures Dwell
An Trees of Life bear Fruits of Love

. . . .

Could twin born Souls walk in hand!
Thro the dark shades of Death!
Vain Wish!

CHAPTER **8**

# Where There's a Will
# There's a Way

THERE IS scarcely any legal record, containing names of individuals, that is not of use to a genealogist. The ancestor hunter who proposes to conduct a thorough search and who wants as complete a picture of his or her ascendants as possible should by all means use all the records he or she can find. Some of them are of paramount importance in proving a descent; others are interesting only as they shed light upon the life and activities of the individual whom they concern. An excellent reference guide to the use of various sorts of legal records for genealogical research has recently been published by Noel C. Stevenson: *Genealogical Evidence: A Guide to the Standard of Proof Relating to Pedigrees, Ancestry, Heirship and Family History*. Using legal cases to instruct us in the procedures of mining genealogical information from the records, he carefully illustrates the significance of the materials for our work.

## Probate Court Records

Undoubtedly the most important evidence of the genealogy of a family is a collection of the probate court records that pertain to it. Wills are generally indisputable documents concerning the relationship of individuals, although occasionally the information they give is exasperatingly meager, and sometimes they reveal more than the wording tells. Sometimes, on the other hand, they tell too much to suit the pride of the descendants. But the wise person knows that his or her ancestors were human beings with human attributes and shortcomings, and, therefore, accepts them for what they were and tries to determine his or her heritage from them.

Each state has (and in colonial days each colony had) its own laws of probate. Our knowledge and the space at our disposal are too limited to permit us to discuss here the differences in those laws, as they vary from state to state, or to consider the changes that have been made in them during the successive periods of American history. It is up to you, as an ancestor hunter keen on a find, to study the laws that affect the communities in which your ancestors lived, not only the probate laws, but the land laws and other laws governing the conduct of individuals. Although a great deal of digging can be accomplished without studying such laws, it is more fun and nets you a broader knowledge of the world if you have acquired some such knowledge.

## Wills

There are two types of wills: the written will, signed and witnessed, and the spoken will, called the nuncupative will, generally given by the decedent on the deathbed in the presence of witnesses who are later called before the probate judge to swear to the testamentary intentions of the testator. The written will is by far the more common form today. In fact, nuncupative wills are rare in the twentieth century. But in the early colonial days, when writing material was not always at hand and a considerable proportion of the population could not write at all or wrote with difficulty even when in the best of health, nuncupative wills were much more common.

Wills have been known since pre-Christian times, and several truly ancient wills have survived, in tradition at least. The Bible (Genesis 48–49) mentions the will of Jacob, the Patriarch. Several wills are mentioned in the records of ancient Greece which have survived. But the oldest written will known to be extant today in its original form is that of Sekhenren, an Egyptian. This will, dating from about 2550 B.C., was found by the late Sir William M. F. Petrie, the well-known Egyptologist, among some papyri he excavated many years ago. It might easily have been drawn within the last century, so curiously modern is the wording. The vocabulary of the law does not change as rapidly as language in everyday use. Sekhenren settled his property upon his wife, Teta, for life, and specified that his buildings should not be destroyed, although she was empowered to give them to any of her children. He even named a guardian for his infant children. This will was witnessed in the form of which our courts approve and contained an attestation clause very much like our modern clause of this sort.

English wills dating from the time of the Norman Conquest are common, and in the case of many the parchment on which they were written has survived. An interesting study of the wills of our English progenitors and those of our ascendants on this side of the Atlantic might be made, for they shed a great deal of light not only on the ownership and transfer of land but also on the kind of possessions people have valued from time to time and from period to period in history. Old wills, English and American, frequently specified what was to be done with such things as silver and pewter, clothing, household utensils, books, and other truly personal property. Today there is little respect for personal property, but in colonial days, when "hard money" was scarce, possessions were more important. A piece of silver was greatly valued — it represented money; a gun or a sword was precious and worthy of mention in a will; a book was rare and truly treasured. Speaking of books, the identity of the second wife of one of the colonial ministers, the Reverend John Sherman, of Watertown, Mass., is solved by a clause in the will of her mother, Isabella (d'Arcy) (Launce) Simpson, who bequeathed her "great Bible" to her son-in-law in New England.

In the seventeenth and eighteenth centuries, during the period of the colonization of North America, many wills contained bequests of rings or money for the purchase of a ring — "fifteen shillings for a ring," "ten shillings for a ring," were common phrases in the wills of the well-to-do. This referred to what we call memorial rings. They were finger rings, each to be worn in memory of a deceased friend. Many of these memorial rings have survived. The late Sir Frederick Crispe made a large collection of them and published a descriptive catalogue of it. Generally such rings were engraved with the name, date of death, and age of the deceased. Sometimes they were enameled, and coffins, death's-heads, spades, crossbones, and other symbols of death were worked into the designs on them. Generally such a ring was in the form of a band, much like the old-fashioned yellow gold wedding ring, but occasionally they were more elaborate. We have seen one memorial ring, made late in the eighteenth century, in which a bit of the woven hair of the deceased was set under glass, and held in place by pearls. Izaak Walton, the famous fisherman, not only bequeathed several such rings to his friends whom he wished to have remember him, but indicated in his will the inscriptions that were to be engraved on them! Not long ago there was found in Nebraska a memorial ring of Sir Francis Nicholson, one of the colonial governors of Virginia, Maryland, and South Carolina.

This is but an indication of the byways into which you may be led by the study of wills and testamentary bequests. William Hazlitt, the nineteenth-century English essayist, wrote a delightful essay "On Will-Making," which is to be found in his volume *Table Talk, or Original Essays*. It will be well worth your time to read it, for Hazlitt, a keen observer of human foibles, points out some of the ridiculous aspects of wills and, incidentally, comments in a pithy manner on human nature.

Seriously, however, the ancestor hunter must make

n extensive use of wills as he or she digs. The best plan
s to visit in person the probate office of the region in
vhich your people lived, and read thoroughly and with
n alert mind all wills that pertain to them although
oday photocopies made by Xerox or a similar machine
ave a lot of trouble. A phrase, an apparently insig-
uificant bequest, or the mention of persons whose rela-
ionship to the legator is not specified will frequently
erve as the clue to further digging. As a general rule the
estator names his wife, his sons in the order of their
irth, and his daughters in the order of age. This is
specially true in wills made in colonial times. The very
vording of the will may indicate clearly just how he felt
oward each of them. "Cut off with a shilling" is a popu-
ar saying, but it has more than one implication in family
uistory: possibly a previous settlement upon that heir,
or a retaliation for some offense committed many years
oefore, or a distrust of the legatee's acumen or capacity
o use property wisely. Today, in America, the amount
of such a bequest is generally a dollar, or some sum that
s ridiculously small in comparison with the size of the
state or the shares of the other heirs.

Not long ago we read the will of a woman who survived her husband a great many years and managed the
property he left her with acumen and sagacity. Her es-
ate was of considerable size, and in her original will she
nentioned by name all of her surviving children and
grandchildren, bequeathing to each of them a just share
of her property. A few years after the will was written,
igned, and witnessed, she added a codicil in which she
evoked her bequest to the widow of one of her sons
and gave explicit reasons for her action. Knowing that
any money left to the children of that son (they were all
ninors) would, by hook or crook, soon be squandered
oy their mother, she cut off those children as well, and
stated that the reason for such unnatural action was the
"vile" character of their mother. Such a will arouses
wonder, especially when it is known that the testator's

reputation for a kindly disposition and a lovable character, albeit companioned by a strong, shrewd mind, has
survived her these many years.

Wills are generally considered to be a source of proof
of descent rather than of ascent, but occasionally the
parentage of the testator, even though he was an old
man, is given in the will. Several years ago Dr. Doane
was tracing a Randall line back to the immigrant. He
was "stuck" with a Joseph Randall, whose gravestone
he had found bearing the information that he "died February 22nd, 1822, aged 67 years." Dr. Doane had found
out that he was a Revolutionary soldier, and that he had
a pension for his service as such. The pension records in
Washington stated that he was born in Canada and enlisted first in 1775 from "Saint Tour" (which is Saint
Ours, near Richelieu, Quebec). They also gave the date
of his marriage to Judith Bowen in Lebanon, N.H. Finally Dr. Doane did what he should have done earlier —
went to the probate office to search for Joseph Randall's
will. To his great pleasure and astonishment, Randall
had disposed of any property that might be due him
from the estate of *his father*, Michael Randall, and im-
plied that that estate was in "Lower Canada," as
Quebec used to be called. The will was exasperating in
another aspect, however, because he mentioned none of
his children by name and left all his property to his
widow with the request that she divide "equally among
our youngest children" anything that should remain at
the time of her death.

## The Record of Distribution

Wills are not the only records or documents to be found
in a probate office that are of use to a genealogist. Next
in importance to a will is the distribution of an estate.
Such a document shows just what proportion of the
estate went to each heir, and each heir is generally
named. Frequently the relationship of the heirs to the
decedent is shown as "son John" and "daughter Jane"
are assigned their respective shares. When a person has

died intestate, that is, without leaving a will, the distribution is made in accordance with the law governing cases of the sort. In such an event, owing to the absence of a will, the record of distribution becomes a very important document to the ancestor hunter. We know of one distribution in which over twenty heirs are named and the amount given to each is specified, although the relationship is not specifically stated. The deceased died intestate without children, so his widow received one-third, and the remaining two-thirds of his estate were divided among the surviving brothers and sisters and the heirs of those who had predeceased him. By carefully adding the amounts received by the several groups of heirs it is possible, with a little trouble, to figure out which were which in relationship to the deceased and to the surviving brothers and sisters. This distribution proved to be of great value in determining the number of children of the deceased's father who grew to maturity, married, and produced offspring, and it helped Dr. Doane considerably in tracing the descendants of one branch of a family whose genealogy he was compiling. A little common sense and a little experience in using such a record will enable you to get a great many clues from a document of this sort.

## Appointment of Guardians

In the old days, a guardian for minor children — even though one parent survived — had to be selected and appointed by the judge of probate; in some states this is still true. The records of such appointments not only indicate relationships but sometimes contain a commentary on the conditions existing within the family. In colonial days, and even later, children of fourteen were allowed to signify their acceptance of the guardian chosen by the judge, or, when they reached that age, were permitted, with the consent of the court, to choose a new guardian. Hence, a widow might be appointed guardian of her young children, and one of them, say a son, upon reaching the age of fourteen might choose his uncle or even a friend as his guardian, in lieu of his mother. This frequently happened when the mother had married again.

Guardianship papers are also filed for defectives and for old people who have passed into senility and are no longer capable of managing their own property. Not a few scandals have arisen over such cases, and sometimes it is necessary to refer to the records of courts other than probate courts (orphans' courts, for instance) for more complete data in connection with them. Jurisdiction over such cases varies in the several states, so you should talk with a lawyer about the legal aspects, or you, yourself, in your search for further information, should study the law.

## Records of Lawsuits

Most amateurs, and many professional genealogists, completely overlook other types of legal court records in their search for ancestors. However, buried in the files of innumerable courts throughout the country are depositions, records of lawsuits, and other court actions that teem with clues to the identity of those who have lived in the past — your ancestors and ours. There are printed indexes to the "reports" of the several states — the long series of printed volumes of cases that have been tried in the courts and "reported" for the use of other lawyers seeking precedents for their arguments and briefs. As a general rule, the documents cited are not printed in full but merely abstracted or summed up, so from the printed reports you get just the pith of what they contain. An examination of the actual documents in the files of the court in which the case was tried will frequently give you much more information, and you may even obtain certified copies of the original records that were filed with those documents at the time the case was tried. Quite naturally, and as you would expect, lawsuits over the distribution of estates, and contests of wills, are of the most value to the ancestor hunter. But we found valuable data in a suit against an insurance company in Wisconsin and still more in a contest over the ownership of some land in central New York. The records of criminal trials, especially murder cases, frequently produce evidence of a relationship for which other records cannot be found.

These more miscellaneous types of court records should be searched in person, either by yourself or by a competent genealogist whom you have hired to do the searching for you. The clerk of such a court, unaccustomed to this use of the records in his or her custody, will hardly know how to get from them the details that you want, for, as a general rule, the clerk has no knowledge of the data that a genealogist requires.

## Clerks of Probate Courts

But probate records and transcripts or abstracts of other documents connected with the settlement of an estate can be secured by correspondence. The clerks of probate courts are all accustomed to receiving letters from all parts of the country asking for information contained in wills, inventories, and distributions. When a fee established by law is paid, it is, in many states, the duty of the probate clerk to furnish certified copies of wills or other papers pertaining to the settlement of an estate. Many probate clerks will undertake to make abstracts, especially if paid for it, but this is generally a private arrangement between you and the clerk. Usually there is someone in the probate office who is willing to augment a slender salary in this way. If you order a certified copy, it is always wise to find out in advance how much it is going to cost you — some wills are lengthy documents! Also, you should be sure that it will contain what you are looking for, since many testators have been exasperatingly reticent about their children's names. We have found that it is generally wise to word your initial query something like this: "Is there on file in your office the will of John Doe, who died about 1821? Or an agreement of his heirs? Or any other paper that mentions his daughter, Mary Jones? If so, can you supply an abstract, and how much would that cost?" Be sure to give the probate office some idea of the date of the instrument for which you are searching, for there may be two or three or more John Does, all of whom left wills. If you are not at all certain of the date of death, ask the clerk to give you the dates of the wills that are on file in the office — in the light of your other clues they may mean something to you.

Sometimes, when you are trying to determine the parentage of an ancestor, it is feasible to have the clerk examine all the wills made by persons of that surname which are on file in the office. Possibly the clerk can do this at his or her leisure and can tell you whether your ancestor, or anyone of his name, is mentioned in any of these wills. Suppose, for instance, that you know that your great-grandfather was born in Cabell County, W. Va., and have come upon a tradition that was ten years old when his father died. You could write to the probate clerk of that county, giving the clues you have, and ask if a child of his name was mentioned in the will of any of the same surname who died about 1808–10, let us say, and offer, of course, to pay for a copy or an abstract of the will in which he was mentioned. Frequently a clerk will go out of his or her way to obtain the data that you want. Once, while examining in person the records of a probate court, we found that the clerk was descended from the individual whose will we were seeking. On the slender claim of cousinship, he practically turned the place upside down in helping us and used his intimate knowledge of the records under his jurisdiction greatly to our advantage. (And, of course, to his own, for whatever he found to aid us gave him so many more data for himself. We have often wondered whether he became thoroughly inoculated with the genealogical virus and went on with his digging.)

Although the names of testators are indexed in the probate court files, the names of persons mentioned in wills are not indexed. Would that every probate court ordered such an index made! It would be of great assistance to us genealogists. Frequently we are searching for the identity of some ancestor's wife whom we know only by her given name. In innumerable cases the will of her father, could we but find it, would prove her identity. But it takes a great deal of time and patience to read through volume after volume of crabbed old handwriting in the hope of finding her mentioned in some will. If we had an index to the legatees, witnesses, and other individuals mentioned in testaments and distributions, our work would be much simpler, although perhaps not quite so thrilling.

It is a good plan to find out just what the probate court is called in the state in which you are searching, particularly if you are working by correspondence, for the names differ in some states. Most states call the repository for wills and other probate records the probate office, or probate court. But in New York, for instance, it is called the surrogate's court, because it is in the charge of a surrogate. Moreover, in some states the limits of the probate district do not correspond with the county limits, although generally they do and you will find the probate records in the county court house. There are sometimes exceptions even within states. For example, in Vermont, although many of the probate districts correspond with the counties, there are twenty probate offices and only fourteen counties. Occasionally the limits of a probate district have been changed in the course of time, so it becomes necessary to learn something about the history of the district.

Incidentally, many states issue, generally through the office of the secretary of state, a manual in which are listed all state and county officials. In many states this manual can be obtained for the asking. There certainly is no harm done in applying for it. If you do get it, you will have definite information about where and to whom to write for your data.

For instance, there is an unofficial annual publication for Vermont, first issued in 1818 as *Walton's Vermont Register*, now called *The Vermont Year Book* (published by the National Survey, Chester, Vt.). It contains, in alphabetical order, a list of all the towns, cities, and villages in the state. Under each town it gives its location, area, elevation, population, officers, manufacturers, merchants, churches, pastors, lawyers, postmaster, etc. In the introductory section the state and county officers are listed, as well as schools, colleges, and other institutions and organizations. A folded map of the state is usually included. Such a handbook is useful to the ancestor hunter and should be consulted in your search.

Incidentally, a useful book, compiled with painstaking care by Noel C. Stevenson, of Laguna Hills, Calif., a Fellow of the American Society of Genealogists, is *Search and Research* (1977), which tells you under the heading "Official Records" where the probate offices are located and gives you many other valuable addresses. It is arranged by states and is easy to use.

# CHAPTER 9

# What You Can Find in the Church Records

LONG BEFORE the earliest colonists came to America, it had become the custom in most European countries to keep records of the members of the ecclesiastical parishes. In fact, in England an Act of Parliament was passed in 1538, requiring the clerk of each parish to keep a register of all marriages, christenings, and burials that occurred within his jurisdiction. In many of the English and European parishes these records have survived from the sixteenth century to the present day, although innumerable volumes have been destroyed by fire or lost by careless custodians.

Although for a while our forebears in this country, particularly in New England, did not recognize as legal the ecclesiastical ceremony of marriage — the colonies of Plymouth and Massachusetts Bay were especially anxious to get away from the authority of the official church, to separate church and state, as it were — the hundreds of volumes of church records extant, dating from the earliest colonial days, are of inestimable value to the ancestor hunter. Buried in them are many records without which the problems would be even more serious than they are.

It is interesting to note that, religious as the Puritans are reputed to have been and were, they considered marriage not as a religious sacrament, but as a civil contract. A marriage ceremony was performed before a

111

magistrate. In fact, at one time ministers of the church were *forbidden* to perform a marriage. Hence, although you will find baptisms and burials recorded in the record books of the old churches, you will not find the early marriages entered there. But "intentions" of marriage may be found in church records since "publication of banns" in the church preceded the civil ceremony. Sometimes, however, there was a slip; the "intention" was not fulfilled and each of the parties married someone else! Study the baptismal records of the children and note the mother's name (if both parties are mentioned, as they generally were if both were members of the church). If there is a change in the mother's name between, say the fourth and fifth children, it is an indication of the death of the first wife and the remarriage of the father, even though the spacing between the children may not be more than the usual two years — in those days, when a wife was an economic necessity, they didn't always wait a "respectable" period! Young children had to be cared for, fields had to be tilled, meals had to be cooked, wool had to be carded, spun, and woven: a man could not do everything! So, be alert for any change in marriage partners.

Sometimes a man and his wife were not admitted to the church until after several children had been born — perhaps they did not settle in that town until some time after their marriage, or perhaps they did not realize what it meant to them spiritually or socially to be members of a church. Respectability in those days was closely allied to church membership and religious belief. Frequently you will find the baptismal record of a family of two adults and four or five children on a single page of the church records, perhaps following the record of the admittance of the parents to membership.

Sometimes, especially in pre-Revolutionary records, you will find children baptized "in the name of" one parent or the other. This generally means that that parent was a member of the church while the other was not, although, if the record of the admittance of both parents to membership has been found, it may simply mean that one parent was absent from church the day on which the child was presented for baptism. If, however, the record reads:

> Admitted to the Ch. Clarissa Smith and baptized for her four children, John, Seth, Sarah, and Clarissa.

you may be sure that Clarissa's husband did not become a member at that time, and perhaps never did. In rare instances, when the record of the admittance of both husband and wife to the church is given and then the baptism of a child is recorded in the name of the wife only, it may be an indication that the paternity of the child was in question.

## Difficult to Locate

Church records, unlike town records, are not always easy to locate. They were generally kept by the minister, or, more recently, by a clerk. Since few churches had offices for the minister in the church building, the record books were kept at the minister's home (or of some other individual) who had charge of them. Sometimes the pastor moved on to another charge and took the records along, perhaps through oversight. Sometimes they got back to his successor, sometimes they didn't. Many of them were destroyed by fire or flood, many of them mislaid or lost, and occasionally some were inadvertently destroyed in other ways. Occasionally they were deposited for safekeeping in some secure place and forgotten. This is especially true of churches that have gone out of existence in older communities. Dr. Doane has been looking for years for the records of a church in his native town, which was once Methodist and then Baptist and then a "union" church. Each person to whom he talks knows there are records, but no one can say just where they are. An excellent and comprehensive handbook that should be consulted before you begin your search for church records for any religious group in any state is E. Kay Kirkham's *A Survey of American Church Records*.

Sometimes the state organization of the church or religious society has gathered into its keeping the older records and those of the abandoned churches. In many cases, in the older states, state historical societies have become the custodians of the records of many of the churches, particularly those no longer active, which exist or have existed within their borders. In Connecticut, and undoubtedly in many other states, the State Library has gathered into its fireproof vaults many of the ancient church records of the state and stands always ready to accept the custody of more. In Vermont the Vermont State Historical Society has obtained possession of many such records.

Some of the church historical societies have actively collected the records of their denominations. For example, at the Colgate-Rochester Divinity School, Rochester, N.Y., the American Baptist Historical Library contains many invaluable records pertaining to the activities of the Baptist Church in North America — both manuscript and printed. Incidentally, in this connection it is valuable to know that the Baptists were organized into associations, covering several towns. These associations held annual or biennial meetings, and frequently the proceedings were published and the list of the official delegates was printed with the proceedings. These printed proceedings, collected at Rochester, are truly a source of data for the ancestor hunter — especially the list of delegates contained in them.

The Drew Theological Seminary in Madison, N.J., has a collection of historical material pertaining to the Methodist Church.

Those interested in the records of the Roman Catholic Church should consult Cora C. Curry's *Records of the Roman Catholic Church in the United States as a Source of Authentic Genealogical and Historical Material* (Washington, 1935; National Genealogical Society Publication No. 5). The records of the Episcopal Church are retained in the parishes, but the records of abandoned missions and parishes will be found in the diocesan offices. The American Jewish Archives, Cincinnati, Ohio, and the American Jewish Historical Society, Waltham, Massachusetts, have large collections of historical material.

One great difficulty in locating church records arises when the church is of the "mission" type, that is, the pastorate is supplied from a neighboring church or congregation. Sometimes there is a clerk who has charge of the records, but quite as often the records are kept by the minister who supplies the pulpit, and who carries them with him or, worse yet, makes the record of a baptism or marriage when he gets home from the service, if he happens to remember to do it.

## Ministers' Private Record Books

Some ministers kept private record books and carried them about with them as they served one charge after another. This was especially true of Methodist circuit riders, who traveled constantly from one group of communicants to another. The heirs of these ministers have sometimes preserved such record books; but more frequently, we fear, the records have been destroyed as worthless or lost during the migrations of the family. These are generally nineteenth-century records, but they cover a period that the genealogist has difficulty bridging. It is sometimes much harder to find the records of the generations between 1775 and 1850 than it is to find those covering 1620 to 1775. Moreover, the period between 1800 and 1870 was one of great migration — the West was being opened up for settlement. Pioneer settlements were not organized to keep vital records. Marriage licenses were scarcely known. The itinerant minister sometimes had several ceremonies to perform on one of his rare visits to the community. Hence, his record, if he kept one, is sometimes the only source of data — and it is very difficult to find that marriage book. Whenever you do find such a volume in private hands, you should make every effort possible to secure it for deposit in a historical or genealogical library, or should urge its owner to deposit it. Failing in this, you should attempt to secure a careful and accurate transcript or microfilm of it and publish or deposit that transcript. By doing this you can greatly help other ancestor hunters and save someone else the time you spent in your search for the records.

## Genealogical Society of Utah

One collection of genealogical records kept by a religious organization, which is of great importance (undoubtedly the largest in the world), is that at Salt Lake City, in the offices of the Church of Jesus Christ of Latter-day Saints, popularly known as the Mormon Church. The interest of Latter-day Saints in genealogy is based on their theological belief that family relationships are intended to be eternal and not limited to our earthly existence. Accordingly living members have an obligation to search out the records of their ancestors, proving carefully the connections from one generation to another, and to trace these family lines as far back into history as possible. This accounts for the presence of these records in Salt Lake City. The Genealogical Department of the Latter-day Saints maintains an important library, holding thousands of the world's family genealogies, past and present genealogical periodicals, and published and manuscript histories of many countries, states, counties, and towns.

The center of the Salt Lake City program is the microfilming project. More than one million rolls of microfilm have been gathered on such materials as vital records, church records, cemetery records, probate records, and land records. The Church has carried its microfilming program to every continent in every part of the world. Outside of Salt Lake City, the Church maintains huge vaults tunneled into a granite mountain where a negative copy of each microfilm is protected from erosion by humans and the environment. The Genealogical Department's library has available for public use over six million genealogical records of individual families which were compiled by members of the Latter-day Saints Church. Called the Family Group Records Archives, the forms in this collection record the full names of all members of a family unit, their dates of birth or christening, marriage, death or burial, and the locations where these events took place. Additional information, such as occupation of the husband, source references, and essential explanations are included too. More than thirty million index cards containing names and a variety of genealogical information on both living and deceased members of the Church are available for use at a small fee. Throughout the United States, Canada, and elsewhere the Latter-day Saints have established branch libraries generally located in their local church buildings. Each branch library gathers its own collection of basic genealogies and histories and is staffed and funded by local members of the Church. Through interlibrary loan, readers living near a branch library have access to the Salt Lake City library's microfim collection.

### Quaker Records

The records of the Quaker meetings are being published as the *Encyclopedia of American Quaker Genealogy*, which has already been mentioned (see page 66). The Friends keep very careful records of all their members, their births, marriages, and deaths, as well as transfers from one meeting to another. When using Quaker records you should remember that they use numbers to refer to months and days of the week. Generally the number representing the month is given first, the day second, and then the year of our era, thus: 1-9-1777, meaning January 9, 1777. A Friends marriage record, or certificate, will be signed by all those present; hence it has unusual value to the genealogist.

### Additional Information

Church records contain more of interest to the ancestor hunter than marriages, baptisms, and burials. Frequently the records of the transference of members, generally by "letter," to another congregation serve as valuable clues to migration; and, vice versa, the admittance of new members by "letter" from another church will enable you to trace a migrating ancestor back to his or her former residence. As an example, one church record book contains these data: "Admitted to this Ch. Lewis Gilbert, by letter from the Ch. in Cornish." This leads the digger to another state and another source of information — the town records and the church records of Cornish. Membership lists are sometimes annotated with data added in a later handwriting. Words, such as "dec'd" (for deceased) or "removed," have been written into the margins, generally by a later clerk who was revising the membership list. Dates are sometimes added to these notes, thus, possibly, giving you the date of an individual's death, for which you have found no other proof.

Once in a while you will find "excom," or some similar abbreviation, written in. To our astonishment, we found several such notes on the membership list of a certain Congregational church. We had never before known or heard that the Congregational Church sometimes excommunicated members, but as we leafed through the records of that church, we found several lengthy accounts of excommunication trials. One man and his wife were tried on several counts, back about 1819, and were finally declared excommunicated from the church for blasphemous language, failing to attend church on Sunday, and nonsupport of the church. Verbatim reports of some of the evidence made very interesting reading, and from these reports we gained a very vivid picture of the family life of this couple. The dignified and righteous old deacons reported the names they had heard each call the other, and also the opinion each had expressed of the other. Moreover, the record of this same trial gave us considerable insight into the rivalry existing at that time between the two Protestant churches in the town, for it seems there had been some proselytizing by the other church and its members had told these backsliders what they thought of the tenets of the "Society" (Congregational) to which the defendants belonged. One can imagine the gossip at afternoon tea parties on the front porches, that summer of 1819, and the sanctimonious awe with which some of the words and phrases were repeated — in quotation, of course!

Amusement aside, however, church records are far too valuable to be overlooked when you go digging for ancestors. You should make every effort to find them and use them, even if you have to go through them page by page in search of the records of your ancestors.

CHAPTER **10**

# Government Aid in the Search

MANY RECORDS to be found in the archives of the government of the United States are of great value to those who dig for ancestors. From the earliest days of its existence, even during its provisional period, the federal government has been accumulating records that quite naturally pertain to individuals. Among the earliest of this kind are the payrolls of the troops serving in the Continental Army during the Revolutionary War. These are of value to persons who wish to establish membership in the Daughters of the American Revolution, and the other organizations, called "patriotic societies," in which membership is based on a descent from a patriot of that period. Some of the later records are, however, of more general interest.

## Census Records

Probably the most important records in the National Archives in Washington are those gathered by the census takers every ten years. The first federal census was taken in 1790 and was probably ordered by Congress for the purpose of determining the possible military strength of the nation. The returns of this census were published by the Bureau of the Census in 1909, in twelve volumes known to genealogists as the 1790 census. We quote from the introduction to one of those volumes:

The First Census of the United States (1790) comprised an enumeration of the inhabitants of the present states of Connecticut, Delaware, Georgia, Kentucky, Maine, Maryland, Massachusetts, New Hampshire, New Jersey, New York, North Carolina, Pennsylvania, Rhode Island, South Carolina, Tennessee, Vermont, and Virginia. . . . A complete set of schedules for each state, with a summary for the counties, and in many cases for towns, was filed in the State Department, but unfortunately they are not now complete, the returns for the states of Delaware, Georgia, Kentucky, New Jersey, Tennessee, and Virginia having been destroyed when the British burned the Capitol at Washington during the War of 1812.

It was found, however, that partial returns for Virginia were available in the state's own enumerations (called "tax lists") of 1782, 1783, 1784, and 1785; so it was possible to reconstruct for Virginia a list comprising "most of the names of heads of families for nearly half of the state." These lists were printed in 1909 to form the Virginia volume of the set.

Thus we have printed schedules for Connecticut, Maine (originally taken as part of Massachusetts), Massachusetts, Maryland, New York, North Carolina, Pennsylvania, Rhode Island, South Carolina, Vermont, and Virginia, in which are listed the heads of families living in those states in 1790. The returns for South Carolina were not all in until March 1792, because the marshal for that state had difficulty finding enumerators who would work for the salary the government was authorized by Congress to pay. Since Vermont was not admitted until 1791, the actual census in that state was not taken until April-September 1791. For a list of schedules on file, and those missing, see Appendix C.

In addition to those volumes, the Bureau of the Census published, also in 1909, an analysis of this census, called *A Century of Population Growth from the First Census of the United States to the Twelfth, 1790–1900*, which forms a useful supplement frequently overlooked by genealogists and ancestor hunters. There are two par-

ticularly valuable features of this supplement. The firs
is the series of maps showing the development of th
country from 1790 to 1900, especially useful because
indicates the boundary lines of the various counties o
the several states and the changes that have been mad
in them from time to time. The second useful feature i
the lengthy table of names found in the census schedule
in 1790, showing which spellings were used for eac
name in the different schedules. This list, called "Tabl
111," is found on pages 227–70 of this volume, and i
worthy of careful study, for only a few names achieve
the distinction of uniform spelling in this census. Thos
are generally monosyllables like Fox, Gage, etc., whic
even a census taker could not help but spell correctly. A
complex name like Fitzgerald appears in twenty-fou
different spellings, including one as strange looking a
Fitsjerald. Even as simple a name as Smith is found i
nine different spellings.

The instructions issued to the 650 "marshals" wh
took this census directed them to list the heads o
families by name and note the number of individual
living in each of the families in the following fiv
classifications: (1) free white males, sixteen years an
older, including heads of families; (2) free white male
under sixteen years; (3) free white females, includin
heads of families; (4) all other free persons; and (5
slaves. The "all other free persons" comprised whit
people who were not considered heads of families (fo
instance, in Exeter, N.H., Joel Gill is so listed, but wa
not considered a "head of a family," although the cen
sus, following his name, noted three "free persons" –
apparently himself and two others); free colored per
sons; and possibly a few Indians.

The amateur ancestor hunter who has traced his o
her lineage back to 1800 or a little before will find thes
printed volumes of the 1790 census a mine of informa
tion and a source of clues that can be followed up i
further searching. Let us suppose you are tracing
Pangbourne line, and that Grandfather Pangbourne ha

told you that his people came from Vermont. You know
from the records he has given you that his father, whom
we will call John Pangbourne, was born about 1788–89,
presumably in Vermont. You are searching for a clue to
his parentage, so you consult the 1790 census for Vermont. Here you find that Stephen and Samuel
Pangbourn and Timothy Pengborn were heads of
families in the town of Addison, Addison County, Vt.,
in 1790 (1790 census, Vermont, p. 11); that Samuel and
Joseph Pangbone were heads of families in Ferrisburg,
Addison County, Vt. (1790 census, p. 12); and that Jesse
Pangbowen was the head of a family in Fairfield, Chit-
tenden County, Vt. (1790 census, p. 24).

The differences in the spelling of the surname should
be ignored, for two reasons. In the first place, spelling
was precarious at that time: people even signed their
own names with different spellings on different occasions; and clerks frequently spelled names as they heard
them pronounced rather than bothering to ask how to
spell them. The other reason is that these census records
were printed more than 125 years after they were written, so the paper and ink have faded, fine strokes of the
pen have worn away as the pages have rubbed against
each other in use, and the clerks, expert as they were in
reading old documents, have occasionally erred in interpreting the several handwritings in which these
records were written. Hence, although the name was
printed "Pangbowen" or "Pangbone," an examination
of the original record in Washington might show that
the name was actually written "Pangbourn" and was
misinterpreted by the clerk who prepared the copy for
the printer. Or, the marshal who made the enumeration
in Ferrisburg or the one who made it in Fairfield did not
catch the soft Vermont slur of the "r" and understood
the name as "Pangbone" or "Pangbowen."

Of these heads of families named Pangbourne (in its
several spellings) one, Jesse, can be eliminated immediately, for the time being at least, for his family consisted of but two males over sixteen, no boys and no

females. It is possible that he had left his family somewhere else and, with a man to help him, was preparing
a home in Fairfield at that time. But we will not consider
that possibility in this instance. Thus your search is nar-
rowed down to Stephen, Timothy, and Samuel in Addison, and Joseph and Samuel in Ferrisburg, each of
whom had in his family a male or males under sixteen —
your hypothetical John Pangbourne would have been in
this classification if he had been born in 1788–89.

You will note that, through the use of this census, you
have been able to narrow the field of your search to two
towns in Addison County, Vt. So you are in a position
to go ahead, searching the vital records in those towns,
the wills and other probate records in that probate district, etc., for evidence that one of these five men was
the father of your great-grandfather. In writing to the
town and probate clerks you ought to leave nothing to
chance, and, therefore, should mention the various
spellings of the name that you have found in the census
records.

Possibly the 1800 census might be of further assistance to you. The Vermont Historical Society has published that Vermont census from a photostat copy which
has been in its possession some time. From this we learn
that there were only two Pangborn families then residing in the state: Reuben Pangborn at Panton, Addison
County, with two males under ten, one male between
ten and sixteen, one male between twenty-six and
forty-five (without question Reuben himself), one
female under ten years, one between ten and sixteen,
and one between twenty-six and forty-five; and
Stephen Pangborn, still in the town of Addison, with
one male between sixteen and twenty-six, and one over
forty-five (undoubtedly Stephen himself), two females
between sixteen and twenty-six, and one female over
forty-five (probably Mrs. Stephen). Either your
hypothetical John had migrated elsewhere with his
father's family or he was the son of Reuben Pangborn.

None of the schedules for the censuses after 1790 has been printed by the government, although they are all on file in Washington (a few schedules, such as the Alabama schedule for 1800, have been lost or destroyed). In order to use them one has to have them searched in Washington. Such a search is not so very expensive, and it may produce results very useful to you. Frequently, by searching these later census records you can trace the progress of a family, either as the children mature, marry, establish families of their own, and come to be listed as heads of families, or as they disappear from the records of one town and appear in those of another. You can determine the approximate date of the death of a man as his name disappears from the census records. If he died young, frequently his widow is listed as the head of the family in the next census — not a few women appear, even in 1790, as heads of families consisting, generally, of minor children.

As an example of the use of successive censuses, let us take a bona fide case this time, in which the only records used are those obtained from the censuses themselves. John Castle (or Castel, as his name was spelled in some of the census records) was a resident of Fairfield, Vt., and first appears there as head of a family in the 1810 census, when his family consisted of one male aged between twenty-six and forty-five, two males under ten, one female between twenty-six and forty-five, and two females under ten. By using our heads and a little arithmetic we can figure out that he was born between 1765 and 1784 (if he was aged between twenty-six and forty-five in 1810); since all the children were under ten, he was probably married about 1799 or 1800, or perhaps a year later than that (allowing a year after marriage before the birth of the first child, and two years between the births of the other three). Since neither he nor any other man of the name of Castle was listed in the 1800 census of Fairfield, we know that he must have settled there some time after 1800 and probably was not married there. So we begin to get a picture of his family.

In 1820 his family, as enumerated in the census of that year, consisted of one male between twenty-six and forty-five, two males between ten and sixteen, three males under ten, one female between twenty-six and forty-five, one female between sixteen and twenty-six, one female between ten and sixteen, and two females under ten. Now we can narrow his birth date down to some time between 1775 and 1784 (he was still under forty-five in 1820); moreover, he now has nine children (unless the female between sixteen and twenty-six was a hired girl helping his wife, or some other dependent, which is unlikely in so clear-cut a case as this).

In 1830, as the census of Fairfield for that year states, his family was made up of one male between fifty and sixty, one male between twenty and thirty, one male between fifteen and twenty, two males between ten and fifteen, one male between five and ten; one female between fifty and sixty, one female between twenty and thirty, two females between ten and fifteen. Taking this additional record we can narrow still further the period in which he must have been born; that is, sometime between 1775 (as determined by the 1820 census) and 1780 (since he was over fifty in 1830) — quite different from the 1765–84 which we got from the 1810 census. The same is true of the birth date of his wife.

This John Castle was still listed as the head of a family in Fairfield in 1840, the family then consisting of one male between sixty and seventy, one female between sixty and seventy, one female between thirty and forty, and one female between twenty and thirty. It is obvious that all the boys had married and established homes of their own or had moved away or were working somewhere and that the girls had all married except two who were staying at home with the "old folks." Living in the same neighborhood we find Stanley Castle as the head of a family consisting of two males between twenty and thirty, one male under five, two females between twenty and thirty, and one female between fifteen and twenty. From this record and the proximity of the two families, we can assume that Stanley was one of the sons of John Castle, perhaps born about 1810, that he had married some time between 1835 and 1840, since he had a son under five, and possibly that he was working the original farm (his parents having perhaps moved to a smaller house up the road, let us say) or had bought himself a farm near his father's. Possibly the male of his own age in the census was one of his brothers; and possibly the extra females were his sisters, or those of his wife.

Now, using only the data that we have obtained from the successive censuses of Fairfield, Vt., we can construct a tentative account of John Castle (we should note that no person of the name of Castle appears in the 1850 census of Fairfield), something like this:

John Castle was born between 1775 and 1780; he was living in 1840. He married about 1800, and settled in Fairfield, Vt., before 1810. He appears as a head of a family there in the United States censuses of 1810 to 1840 inclusive.

He had children.

  i. A daughter, b. *ca.* 1800–4 (under 10 in 1810; 16–26 in 1820; 20–30 in 1830).
 ii. A son, b. *ca.* 1804–10 (under 10 in 1810; 10–16 in 1820; 20–30 in 1830).
iii. A daughter, b. *ca.* 1804–10 (under 10 in 1810; 10–16 in 1820); married or died before 1830, when she was no longer listed in her father's family.
 iv. A son, b. *ca.* 1804–10 (under 10 in 1810; 10–16 in 1820); away or dead in 1830, when he was no longer listed in his father's family.
  v. A son, b. *ca.* 1810–15 (under 10 in 1820; 15–20 in 1830); perhaps the Stanley Castle of the 1840 census.
 vi. A son, b. *ca.* 1815–20 (under 10 in 1820; 10–15 in 1830).
vii. A daughter, b. *ca.* 1815–20 (under 10 in 1820; 10–15 in 1830).
viii. A daughter, b. *ca.* 1815–20 (under 10 in 1820; 10–15 in 1830).

   ix. A daughter, b. *ca*. 1815–20 (under 10 in 1820; 10–15 in 1830).

   x. A son, b. *ca*. 1820 (probably the 3d male under 10 in 1820; 5–10 in 1830).

You will have noticed that only the head of the family is named in these first five censuses, 1790 to 1840, although the classification of the members of the family by age had been extended and was much more close than in the first census. Undoubtedly this increase in the number of classes within the family was due to the government's growing interest in education and the desire to ascertain how many children of school age there were in the United States. The military interest, shown in the first census, was still there, but by 1840 men of military age were more closely classified than they had been in 1790.

## The 1850 Federal Census

Beginning with the census of 1850 each individual member of the family or household was listed by name. The age in years, the occupation, the place of birth (that is, the state or the country), and the value of the real estate of each was given. Thus, for the first time it was possible, in 1850, to determine from the census records the nationalities making up the population of the United States. From the viewpoint of the genealogist, this census is very valuable because it does list each member of the family by name, and gives the age and place of birth of each. Let us take a typical record from the 1850 census of Center Township, Lake County, Ind.:

| David Hungerford, aged | 46, | farmer, | born in Conn. |
| Eunice | " | " | 44 | " | " N.Y. |
| Esther | " | " | 18 | " | " Ohio |
| Marian | " | " | 14 | " | " " |
| Busan D. | " (male) " | 12 | " | " " |
| Freeman G. | " | " | 10 | " | " " |
| Mary A. | " | " | 5 | " | " Mich. |
| Hannah A. | " | " | 2 | " | " Ind. |

From this record we get the following story about the family: David Hungerford was born in Connecticut

about 1803–4; probably he met his wife, Eunice, somewhere in Ohio and married her there about 1830; their
first four children were born in Ohio, and then, between
1840 and 1844, they moved to Michigan where they
lived but a short time; about 1846–47 they moved,
probably to Center Township, Lake County, Ind.,
where they were living in the summer of 1850. It looks
as though they might have lost a child between Esther
and Marian, and another between Freeman G. and
Mary A. It happens that after obtaining the census
record, we found a record of his family, which proved
the suppositions we had made, supplied the names of
the two children who had died, and gave the further
information that David Hungerford removed to Oak-
land, Ia., and died there in 1855.

The records of all the federal censuses from 1800 to
1900, inclusive, may be consulted in the National Archives in Washington; they are also available on microfilm and may be used also at the eleven archives
branches located in key metropolitan areas throughout
the United States. Incidentally, the 1900 census indexes
are arranged by state and by the Soundex system of
codes which uses a letter and three numbers to phoneti-
cally spell the family name. Under this system similar
family names are indexed together regardless of minor
variations in spelling. An index card, which was prepared for each household, notes for each member of the
household the following information: name; date of
birth; age; place of birth; citizenship; and for the head of
the household, the volume, enumeration district, sheet,
and line number of the census schedule. Frequently the
index card records the family's address in 1900. You can
purchase the reel of film that covers the area in which
your ancestors lived (see Appendix C); but be sure you
have a reading machine which will enable you to en-
large the microfilm copy and project it on a surface from
which you can read it. The larger libraries have such
reading machines, and those with genealogical collections have some of the microfilm copies, perhaps all of

them. The census records since 1900 (the 1890 schedules were burned in a fire) are available in the Kansas depository of the Bureau of the Census but may be used only under certain conditions, for the contents are still considered confidential. Write to the National Archives and Records Service, General Services Administration, Washington, D.C. 20408, for the earlier records. For the later ones, ask the Bureau of the Census, United States Department of Commerce, Pittsburg, Kansas 66762, for the "Application for Search of Census Records"; it lists the regulations governing their use and tells you how to obtain copies.

You should not overlook the census records as a source of information in digging for ancestors. Although those who "took" the censuses (that is, the "enumerators") were human beings and liable to error, and sometimes the person who answered the questions didn't know or didn't remember correctly, the records given in the census schedules are valuable and furnish important data which can generally be checked against other documents, such as a Bible record. In using census records, or in having them searched, try to get your ancestor pinned down to a definite locality if you possibly can. It is easier to search the records for Allegany County, New York, in 1850, even though the schedule runs to more than 700 pages, than it is to search those for the entire western end of New York State; and it saves a great deal of time if you know that your ancestor lived in Granger township!

## Other Government Records

There are many other types of records in Washington that will be of use to you in your search for ancestors. For instance, there is a great mass of land records; there are petitions to Congress for "relief" for one reason or another (many of these are noted in the "Documents Index," which indexes the documents that have been printed; any reference librarian can show you how to use it); and there are pension records.

There is in Washington a great building devoted to the National Archives. Here, where they can be properly housed, listed, cared for, and made available to the public, the older records from the various departments, bureaus, and offices of the national government have been concentrated. The use of these records has been greatly facilitated by the introduction of modern methods of arranging them, and by the many lists, calendars, and catalogs compiled by the staff; and copying is made much easier by the use of photographic processes of one sort or another. You should write to the National Archives and Records Service, General Services Administration, Washington, D.C. 20408, for information regarding what records are available for use and whether or not your question can be answered by this office. Extensive research is generally turned over to a research worker whom you select and pay. *Genealogical Records in the National Archives* (General Information Leaflet, Number 5), obtainable free, is a twenty-page description of records of value to the ancestor hunter to be found in the archives. You also should request a copy of the free pamphlet, *Genealogical Sources Outside the National Archives* (General Information Leaflet, Number 6), which will be of assistance in your research. In fact the General Services Administration has a kit that it will send free of charge. It includes the leaflets, forms to be filled out, and prices for photocopies of certain records. There is also a more extensive (114 pages) *Guide to Genealogical Records in the National Archives*, by Meredith B. Colket, Jr., and Frank E. Bridgers. This is on sale by the Superintendent of Documents, U.S. Government Printing Office, Washington, D.C. 20402, for 65 cents. As you get into genealogical research you will probably want your own desk copy of this valuable guide to public records.

## Searching in Military Records

Nearly every generation of American families has been touched in a direct and personal manner by war: perhaps a husband, brother, or son has served in one of the armed forces and returned home safely or has been wounded or killed in the course of military action. The time line of our family's history has been punctuated in the twentieth century by the tragic rhythms of the wars in Viet Nam and Korea and by World Wars I and II. During the nineteenth century we recall the Spanish-American War, the Civil War, the Mexican-American War, and the War of 1812. The colonial period of America's past was marked by the various colonial wars of the seventeenth and eighteenth centuries and capped by the Revolutionary War. The records that were created as a result of military service throughout America's history are of genealogical and historical interest.

Military records are significant for this reason: it was necessary to verify and certify personal information to qualify for the benefits of service. A military file will give us information regarding the serviceman, his family, military experience, and places of residence. Also, when a widow makes application for benefits, she is required to prove her marriage to the serviceman with supporting documents from the clergyman who married them or from relatives or friends. The same procedure is followed, too, by the heirs of veterans seeking service-related benefits.

## How Do I Begin?

Begin your search for genealogical and historical information gathered from military records by gathering those military documents that you may have found in the bottom drawer of the family desk or chest: records such as registration for the draft, enlistment, promotion, transfer, discharge, and, of course, the military units in which the veteran served as well as the wartime career. We should remind you that for seventy-five years after a serviceman's discharge his records are generally restricted and not available for your use. Information from the files may be requested from the Military Personnel

Records Center (GSA), 9700 Page Boulevard, St. Louis, MO 63132. For information regarding Navy officers separated since 1902, and enlisted men separated since 1885, and Marine Corps officers and enlisted men separated after 1895, inquiries should be made to Military Personnel Records (GSA), 9700 Page Boulevard, St. Louis, MO 63132.

## Draft Records

Certain draft records are available through the National Archives, information that for World War I includes such data as the name, address, age, birthdate, race, citizenship, and nearest relative and address. For copies of World War I draft records, you need to know your relative's address and then send your query to the Federal Archives and Records Center, GSA, East Point, GA 30344.

Federal draft records for the Civil War are located at the National Archives in Washington, D.C. Arranged by state and Congressional district, these records note the name, residence, age as of 1 July 1863, occupation, marital status, and the state territory, or country of birth. However, it is essential for you to know the registeree's place of residence at the time of his enrollment to gain access to this information.

We should mention that the archives of the various states should also be consulted for data regarding draft registration. This is particularly so for the Confederate states, since their records were not deposited in the National Archives.

## The Records of Various Wars

For the several wars that were waged between the close of the Civil War and World War II, the various Indian Wars in the West, the Spanish-American War (1898–99), and the Philippine Insurrection (1899–1902), inquire at the National Archives since the records for veterans of these wars are deposited there.

When requesting a search of the military service records at the National Archives for the Civil War, use GSA Form 6751, "Order and Billing for Copies of Veterans Records," and do be certain to complete as much of the form as possible. Although the National Archives is the depository for Union Army personnel records, remember that it also has some Confederate military records, but that your search should be supplemented by investigating the State Archives of former Confederate States and the Confederate Memorial Building in Richmond, Virginia. Since there are several potentially rich sources for you to consider as you search for the Civil War military records of your ancestors, do read the booklets printed by the National Archives relating to military records for guidance. You will want to know how and when to use the "Confederate Citizens File," the "Union Provost Marshal Citizens File," or "Amnesty Oaths" records in the course of your careful research.

Your ancestors may have served in the Mexican War (1846–48), or one of the several Indian Wars before the Civil War, or the War of 1812 (1812–15) and if so you should check the records at the National Archives for assistance. There are three key collections to check for veterans of these wars: first, the service records of the particular war, second, the veterans' records for the appropriate war, and third, the bounty-land warrant application files based on service between 1775 and 3 March 1855.

Although the National Archives has some Revolutionary War records, the collections are incomplete because fires in Washington, D.C. on 8 November 1800 and 24 August 1814 destroyed many records. It is essential to check the National Archives and appropriate state archives since your ancestor may have served whether in the Continental Army (in which case the records that survive are at the National Archives), or in the state militia (records at the state archives), or both.

## Claims for Pensions and Bounty Land

Since the Revolutionary War period many laws have been adopted awarding money and land to Army, Navy, and Marine veterans and their widows and dependents. Each application for a pension or bounty land is filed under the name of the veteran on whose service the petitioner based his or her claim. Bounty land warrant application files for service in wartime between 1775 and 1855 and pension application files for service between 1775 and 1916 are deposited at the National Archives. Incidentally, for pensions based on military service for the Confederate States of America which were authorized by some southern states but not by the federal government until 1959, inquiries should be addressed to the appropriate state archives at the capital of the veteran's state of residence after the war.

The form and content of applications for claims have changed through the years and thus the kind of information recorded has varied. There are, however, certain important distinctions:

1. A veteran's claim will probably show his place and date of birth, place of residence after service, and a brief account of military service.

2. A dependent's claim generally includes the dependent's age and residence, relationship to the veteran, and date of the veteran's death.

3. A widow's application includes her maiden name, the date of her marriage to the veteran, and the names of their children.

You should submit your inquiries about pension and bounty land claims to the National Archives on GSA Form 6751, "Order and Billing for Copies of Veterans' Records." Instructions are printed on the form for its use. When a claim file is found, documents that usually contain information of a personal nature about the veteran and his family will be selected and photocopied and sent to you with a bill for the cost of service. A very helpful tool for access to certain pension records is the

*Index of Revolutionary War Pension Applications*, published by the National Genealogical Society (1976 edition) of Washington, D.C.

Perhaps your ancestor served in one of the colonial wars: French and Indian War (1754–63), King George's War (1740–48), War of Jenkin's Ear (1739–42), Queen Anne's War (1702–13), or King William's War (1689–97). These wars were fought to protect the colonies and colonists from the intrusions of the French and Spanish, and shaped in an important manner the path to independence from Great Britain. The records of colonial war service are generally deposited in the appropriate state archives, state library, or state historical society in which your ancestor resided and served. Many of the records have been published in records series sponsored, say, by the state, a historical society, or the Society of Colonial Wars. These materials are frequently found in libraries with substantial genealogical collections.

# CHAPTER 11

# How to Arrange a Genealogy

Now THAT you have gathered together a mass of notes on your ancestors, you will want to arrange them in some orderly fashion, especially if you propose to print or publish them in some way. You will probably plan to preserve what you have dug out of the various original records and hand it on to your children, your nephews, nieces, cousins, aunts, and uncles. In distributing copies of your genealogy, keep in mind the help you have had from the printed books and genealogies at your favorite library, and deposit a copy of it there and perhaps in one or two other genealogical collections, for others to use.

In using genealogies, especially those found in the *New England Historical and Genealogical Register*, you have undoubtedly noted the string of names, each with a superior number attached to it, printed in italic type and enclosed in parentheses, following the name of the head of the family. This is an abbreviated way of showing a descent in the successive generations from the emigrant ancestor or the progenitor of the family, the superior figure indicating the number of the generation, thus (*James*[4] *John*[3] *Henry*[2] *John*[1]). This, interpreted, means that James was of the fourth generation and a son of John the third generation, who was the son of John the emigrant, or the progenitor of the family.

Because of this custom of using superior figures to indicate the generations, which has developed through long usage, it is unwise and confusing to use the same device in a genealogy for reference to footnotes or authorities, in the way such numbers are used in histories and other works. For this purpose it is better to use letters of the alphabet, or figures enclosed in parentheses, thus (1), or the customary symbols (*, †, ‡, § ||, ¶, etc.).

You should write first the account of the progenitor (or emigrant ancestor) of the family whose genealogy you have been preparing. In the first paragraph should be given the dates of his birth and death, his parentage (if known), and the authorities for these statements. Incidentally, if only one fact is taken from some authority that source should be cited immediately following the information gained from it; if more than one fact comes from that authority, the reference may be cited at the end of your account of that generation and referred to by a superior letter or figure in parentheses.

The next paragraph should contain the record of the progenitor's marriage, giving the place and date if known (or, if not known, the approximate date and the reasons supporting it), the bride's full name and her parentage, as well as the dates of her birth and death. If she was a widow, the name of her first husband should be given; and if she married a second or a third time, the name or names of her successive husbands should be noted — this is all a part of her history. Interesting details of her life and accomplishments can be reserved for a later paragraph.

If this progenitor had two or more wives, we prefer to give a separate paragraph to each marriage and the vital details about each wife. It sets the successive marriages apart in the text and enables anyone using the genealogy to quickly find the data for which he or she is searching.

Following the marriage paragraph (or paragraphs) should come the account of the life, activities, and accomplishments of the head of the family — his military service, the offices which he held in civil life, the migra tions he made, and all details that will help you or your prospective reader paint a picture of him.

In a paragraph by itself should be given an abstract of his will and that of his wife (or widow) if she made one. In abstracting a will you should note the relationship of the heirs to the testator, as mentioned in it, and any other interesting details you think should be noticed. The date of the will and the date of probate should always be given. In the absence of a will, any details gleaned from the administration of the estate should be given, as well as abstracts of any deeds or conveyances that contain genealogical evidence.

Then, beginning a final paragraph with some such phrase as "The children of . . . and . . . (. . .) . . ." or simply the word "Children" or "Issue," you should list in columnar form all the children of this progenitor or head of a family. We like to follow the "Register form," as the style used in the *New England Historical and Genealogical Register* is called, using small Roman numerals to indicate the order of birth (even if, in the absence of specific evidence, you have had to arrange them hypothetically), and reserving the Arabic numerals for the child (or, in the case of a comprehensive genealogy of all the descendants of the progenitor, the children) whose line is carried on.

Following the account of the children, you can list the general references used in building up the history of this generation of the family. In giving references to books you should always use the author's name and the title of the book as given on its title page, rather than the "binder's title," or title from the back of the bound volume (binder's titles may vary in different libraries, but the title page is always the same wherever you use the book). If there is a date of publication on the title page, it should be cited in parentheses following the title of the book; if there is no date on the title page, use the copyright date given on the back of the title page, or the date at the end of the preface. Any of these dates not only serves to identify the edition of the book that you have used, but indicates the approximate time when the record you abstract from that book was obtained by its author.

Now let us see what this looks like in printed form. We are writing up, as an example, an imaginary family in which all names, places of residence, and other data are fictitious. We give the "records" of two generations and two families only, but my use of Arabic numerals indicates that this is a comprehensive genealogy of all John Jones's descendants.

### The Descendants of John Johns

#### GENERATION I

1. JOHN JONES was born, probably in England, about 1750–51; he died in Pollock, Blank County, N.Y., 23 April 1833, aged 83 years, according to his gravestone in the Pine Grove Cemetery there. His parentage is unknown, but it has been said that he was the younger son of a prominent English family and that he came to America as an officer in the British Army during the Revolution. Convinced of the righteousness of the American cause, he resigned his commission, assumed the name of Jones, and enlisted in the Continental Army. He never disclosed his real name, and no evidence of it has been found. There can be little doubt of his English origin, for he was referred to as "John the Englishman" in the Pollock Town Records, apparently to distinguish him from another John Jones living in Pollock at that time (Pollock Town Records, Book B, p. 26).

He married, 1 May 1783, at Allen, Mass., Mary Smith, daughter of James and Mary (Hancock) Smith. She was born in Allen, 3 August 1760; she died in Pollock, N.Y., 29 January 1851, and was buried beside her husband in the Pine Grove Cemetery.

John Jones served in the Massachusetts Line in the Revolutionary War from 1780 to 1783. He claimed a pension in 1820. His pension record in Washington shows his service, but gives no indication of his birth or parentage. His widow received a pension, and her papers give the place and date of their marriage and contain a transcript of the Bible records of their children. (The Bible appears to be lost.)

After his marriage, John Jones and his wife lived in Allen,

Mass., for two or three years. About 1786 they removed to New York state, and were living in Pollock by 1790 [U.S. census, 1790, New York, p. 221]. He was a miller and is said to have established the first mill in Pollock. He held several town offices, and was a member of the Congregational Church in Pollock.

His wife, Mary, is said to have been a woman of considerable ability as a nurse. The obituary notice of her in the Pollock *Messenger*, 31 January 1851, comments on her kindliness and notes the great esteem in which she was held by the community.

John Jones's will was dated 30 March 1833, and probated 6 July 1833. He mentioned his wife, Mary, eldest surviving son, Henry, sons Eugene, George W. (if he is found within two years), and Jonas; and his daughters Mary Martin and Almira Martin (deceased), and her son John Jones Martin. (Surrogate court records, Blank County, N.Y., Book D, pp. 195–201.)

Issue:

|   |        |                                                                              |
|---|--------|------------------------------------------------------------------------------|
|   | i.     | John, Jr., b. in Allen, Mass., 21 June 1784; d. 22 June 1784.                 |
|   | ii.    | Mary, b. in Allen, Mass., 15 June 1785; d. young.                            |
| 2.| iii.   | Henry, b. in New York, 5 July 1787.                                          |
| 3.| iv.    | James Smith, b. 28 June 1789; removed to Michigan.                           |
| 4.| v.     | Mary, b. in Pollock, N.Y., 1 July 1791; mar. Henry Martin.                   |
| 5.| vi.    | Almira, b. in Pollock, N.Y., 6 September 1793; mar. John Martin.             |
|   | vii.   | Eugene, b. 15 September 1795; d. unmar. 29 March 1850.                       |
|   | viii.  | George Washington, b. 1 September 1797; disappeared in the West before 1833. |
|   | ix.    | John (twin), b. 6 April 1800; d. 15 April 1800.                              |
| 6.| x.     | Jonas (twin), b. 6 April 1800.                                               |

*References:*

Biographical sketch of John Jones in William Johnson's *History of Blank County, N.Y.* (1879), pp. 345–46.

*Vital Records of Allen, Massachusetts to 1850* (1910), p. 37.

Pension records of John Jones, No. W. 56,666, Washington, D.C.

Surrogate Court Records, Blank County, N.Y., Book D
pp. 195–201.

Inscriptions, Pine Grove Cemetery, Pollock, N.Y.

2. HENRY JONES (*John*[1]), son of John and Mary (Smith)
Jones, was born, probably in Pollock, N.Y., 5 July 1787; he
died in Whosset, Iowa, 31 December 1869, and was buried
in the Center Cemetery, Buren, Ill., beside his wife.

He married, in Pollock, N.Y., 25 December 1810, Sarah
Allen, daughter of Joseph and Sarah (Smith) Allen, and sis-
ter of his brother James's wife. Her mother is supposed to
have been a sister of his mother. Sarah Allen was born in
Allen, Mass., 25 December 1790; she died in Buren, Ill., 2
June 1860, and was buried in the Center Cemetery there.

Henry Jones served in the War of 1812 and was present at
the Battle of Lake Erie. For this service he received a pension
in 1858, which was continued until his death. (Pension
records, Washington, D.C.)

As the western country was opened up in the years following the War of 1812, he became interested, and finally
moved to Buren, Black County, Ill., about 1840. He lived
there until the death of his wife, and then went to Iowa to
live with his son John.

In his will, dated 16 March 1867 and proved 5 January
1870, he mentioned his deceased wife, Sarah, and expressed
a desire to be buried beside her. He named also his sons
John, Henry, George, and Joseph; his daughter Sarah Martin; his grandchildren Henry and Sarah Griffith, children of
his deceased daughter Mary; and his grandson James, son of
his son John.

Issue (all born in Pollock, N.Y.):

7.   i. Mary, b. 10 October 1811, d. 16 June 1849; mar.
        Jonathan Griffith.
8.  ii. John, b. 29 March 1815.
   iii. Henry, b. 4 April 1817; living in 1867.
9.  iv. Sarah, b. 17 March 1819; mar. Joseph Martin.
     v. Hannah, b. 25 October 1821; d. 3 January 1822;
        bur. in Pine Grove Cemetery, Pollock, N.Y.
    vi. Jane, b. 13 October 1823; d. 6 July 1830; bur. in
        Pine Grove Cemetery, Pollock, N.Y.
10. vii. George Washington, b. 9 February 1826.
11. viii. Joseph, b. 29 February 1828.

*References:*

Bible record in possession of Mary Jones, eldest daughter of John Jones, Whosset, Iowa.

Smith, William E., *History of Blank County, Illinois* (1886), p. 801.

*Vital Records of Allen, Massachusetts to 1850* (1910), p. 10.

Will of Henry Jones, Blank County Probate Office, Ill., Book 9, pp. 222–23.

If you want to write up your direct line of descent from, let us say, John Jones, you should give Arabic numerals to that child in each successive generation from whom you descend.

Your pedigree blanks form only a skeleton of your pedigree. The complete details of each line of descent should be written up in the style just given. If you want to examine a fine example of this type of genealogy, one in which the ancestry of a man has been worked out in detail, look at Mary Walton Ferris's *The Dawes-Gates Ancestral Lines*, in which she worked out in elaborate detail the ancestry in all lines of Rufus Dawes and his brother, General Charles Dawes.

An excellent example of the comprehensive genealogy of the descendants of an immigrant, worked out in detail and noted for its accuracy is Donald Lines Jacobus's *Bulkeley Genealogy: Rev. Peter Bulkeley, Being an Account of His Career, His Ancestry, the Ancestry of His Two Wives, and His Relatives in England and New England, Together with a Genealogy of His Descendants through the Seventh American Generation.*

These books are models you should study and follow in writing up the account of your family, for each has been compiled and written by an accomplished genealogist, whose ability and reputation for accurate, painstaking, documented work is well known.

# DESCENDANTS OF JOHN JONES, OF POLLOCK, N.Y.

*1 May, 1783*

JOHN JONES = MARY SMITH
b. in England, ca. 1750/1
d. Pollock, N.Y. 23 Apr. 1833,
age 83; served in the
Revolution; miller

daughter of James and Mary
(Hancock) Smith
b. Allen, Mass., 3 Aug. 1760;
d. Pollock, N.Y., 29 Jan. 1851

JOHN b. 1784; died young
MARY b. 1785; died young

**HENRY** = **SARAH ALLEN**
b. in N.Y., 5 July 1787
d. Whosset, Ia., 31 Dec. 1869;
served in War of 1812;
farmer, Buren, Ill.

*25 Dec. 1810*

daughter of Joseph
and Sarah (Smith)
Allen: b. 25 Dec. 1790;
d. 3 June, 1860

**JAMES**
b. 1789, settled
in Michigan
married and
had issue

**MARY** = **HENRY MARTIN**
b. 1791
had
issue

ALMIRA = JOHN MARTIN
b. 1793;
had issue

EUGENE
b. 1795;
d. 1850
unmarried

GEORGE WASHINGTON
b. 1797;
went West

JOHN (twin)
b. 1800;
d. an infant

JONAS (twin)
b. 1800; married
and had issue

MARY = JONATHAN GRIFFITH
b. 1811
had issue

JOHN
b. 1815;
married and
had issue

HENRY
b. 1817;
living 1867

SARAH = JOSEPH MARTIN
b. 1819;
had issue

HANNAH
b. 1821;
died young

JANE
b. 1823;
died young

GEORGE W.
b. 1826
married and
had issue

JOSEPH
b. 1828
married and
had issue

FORM 4. The "English" Type of Pedigree

This is a type of graphic pedigree much used by English genealogists but somewhat less common in America. It presents in greatly condensed form the data given in my genealogy of the hypothetical Jones family as printed on pages 133–35.

# CHAPTER 12

# Odds and Ends to Help Your Search

### The Calendar

A STUMBLING block for many an ancestor hunter, when attempting to check the dates of forebears, is a mysterious discrepancy of either a few days or a year which throws out calculations. If this does not arise, then the "double" date in some old record may cause the searcher to wonder why those who made the contemporary record did not know whether the child was born in 1701 or 1702. If you have much experience with them, you will note that these double dates occur in the old records only in January, February, and March — never in any other months and never after 1752.

This system of double-dating arose as a result of a change made in the calendar in 1582. Before that date the so-called Julian calendar was used throughout the Christian world. It was established by Julius Caesar, hence its name. This system, which divided the year into 365 days, plus an extra day every fourth year, was officially adopted at the sitting of the Nicene Council in A.D. 325. As it became possible to measure more accurately the length of the solar year, it was found that the Julian system of measuring exceeded the solar year by eleven minutes, or twenty-four hours every 131 years, and three days every 400 years. This excess amounted to about ten days between A.D. 325 and A.D. 1582. Thus the date of the vernal equinox had been thrown back, by

that time, from 21 March to 11 March and the calcula
tions for Easter were thrown out.

In 1582 Pope Gregory XIII, then head of the Roma
Catholic Church, ordered that ten days be dropped ou
of the calendar, thus restoring the equinox to its accus
tomed date, 21 March. To prevent the recurrence of thi
error, he ordered further that, in every four hundre
years, leap year's extra day should be omitted thre
times. To accomplish this in an orderly fashion it was t
be omitted on centennial years of which the first tw
digits could not be divided by four without a remainder
Thus it was omitted in A.D. 1700, 1800, and 1900, bu
will not be omitted in A.D. 2000. Moreover, the decre
changed the beginning of the new year from 25 March t
1 January. This system, known as the Gregorian calen
dar, now prevails and we are right with the sun.

Following the edict of the Pope, all Catholic countrie
adopted the new system of reckoning. But England, i
difficulties with the Church of Rome and always reluc
tant to accept a new and untried idea, even though sci
entifically proved, refused to adopt the new calenda
officially and did not adopt it until 1752, or 170 year:
later, when the difference between the calendar and th
sun was a little more than eleven days. So in English
speaking countries (including the English colonies) an
in Russia, the Julian calendar continued to prevail as th
official system of counting time. Throughout that time
(that is, until 1752) the new year did not begin until 2!
March, and there was still a difference of eleven day:
between the English calendar and that used in the res
of Europe.

In spite of this difference in the official calendar, many
people began to use the Gregorian system. Hence, i
many of the early colonial records you will find "double
dates," generally written like this: "9 March 1656/57,"
indicating that, although it was officially still 1656, some
people considered it as 1657. Governor Winthrop dated
a letter to his wife 22 March 1629; six days later he wrote
another and dated it 28 March 1630.

Incidentally, in dates of the seventeenth century you will frequently find the month indicated by its number rather than its name. This was primarily because most of the months had "pagan" names and hence those names were disliked by the Puritans, and even more by the Quakers, who believe in simplicity carried to its extreme. Since, before 1752, March was considered the first month of the year, even though the twenty-fifth was the day on which the year changed, we must interpret the old records with that in mind. Thus "13th, 2nd month, 1644"; becomes "13 April 1644"; or "3:12 mo:1639" becomes "3 February 1639" (that is, 1640). Generally the day was given first and the month second, but you should always make sure by comparing the date with others in the same record, remembering that there were but twelve months and a possible thirty-one days. If you find that a date is given as 3:28:1644, you know that "3" represents the month — May; but if the record is 3:8:1644, you should try to find in the same record a date that definitely establishes the first figure as that of the month, as 4:15:1644.

In 1752, when the British government finally decided to recognize the fact that a mistake had been made in calculating the length of the solar year, and to shift into line with the other countries of Europe in the use of the calendar, Parliament passed an act by which the Gregorian system was officially adopted. It is said that there were riots in some of the rural sections of England because the act ordered that eleven days should be dropped out of the calendar following 2 September (making the next day 14 September). The people thought that the government was trying to cheat them out of eleven days of their lives! (Incidentally, the bill enacting the change was introduced in the House of Lords by the Earl of Chesterfield whose *Letters to His Son* is one of the classics of English literature.)

To cite an example of what this change meant, let us consider the birth date of George Washington. He was actually born, according to the official calendar in force at the time, 11 February 1732. But, with the change in the calendar in 1752, he changed his birthday to conform with the new calendar and thus made it 22 February in order to celebrate, we suppose, the exact anniversary of his birth. Therefore, to state his birth date accurately, we should write: "Born 11 February 1731, O.S. (that is, old style), or 22 February 1732, N.S. (new style)." When attempting to correlate birth records, the genealogist should always remember this difference of eleven days and the change in the beginning of the new year. If your ancestor's gravestone states that he died "August 31, 1810, aged 81 years, 6 months, 19 days" and you figure back from that record and determine that he was born 12 February 1729, and then you find the date of his birth in the vital records of his native town as 1 February 1728, you can account for the discrepancy by this change in the calendar, for 12 February 1729 would be the "new style" of reckoning, and 1 February 1728 the "old style."

Most people do not change into new style the dates of these old records, when both of the dates (that is, those of birth and death) occurred before the change in the calendar. Even if one date is old style and one new style, it is not necessary to make the change, for it can be designated by the initials "O.S." or "N.S." to indicate that you have noted any discrepancy that you have found. In the case of the "double dates" occurring between 1 January and 25 March, the year is generally designated "1640/41" or, as some of them have been printed, "16$^{40}$/$_{41}$."

Frequently this matter of the change in the calendar will explain the birth of two children apparently within too short a period. Thus, if you have collected the data on the births of the children of a family from different sources, you can reconcile them by studying the calendar. Suppose that you find, from one source, that John and Mary Jones had a son, named Henry, born 27 March 1640, and from another record a daughter, named Hannah, born 28 February 1640. This looks very strange until you remember that the 28 February 1640 was "old style" and actually, according to modern reckoning, 28 February 1641; therefore, you can figure that these two children were born eleven months apart, instead of twenty-seven days apart.

## Terms of Relationship Used in Early Records

One matter very confusing to those who begin to dig for ancestors in the early records is that of the terms used to designate relationships in ancient wills, deeds, diaries, and letters. Unless you are familiar with the variant meanings these words had in the seventeenth century, you are likely to make some serious errors.

One of the most tricky terms of this sort is "cousin." Today we think of a cousin as the son or daughter of one of our uncles or aunts, or someone more remotely related but descending from a common ancestor, and we speak of "first cousins," "cousins-german," or "own cousins" to indicate an exact degree of cousinship — that is, a son or daughter of a brother or sister of either of our parents. "Second cousin" means a grandchild of our great-uncle or great-aunt, and so forth. The child of a "first cousin" or "own cousin" is our first or own cousin once removed. But in seventeenth-century wills one frequently finds the term "cousin" applied to any relative who is not a brother or sister, son or daughter. Thus a man, making his will in 1650, might call his grandchild "cousin," or he might use the term to refer to a nephew, niece, uncle, aunt, or any other close relative except blood brother, sister, son, or daughter. Thus John Hubbard is called "cousin" in the wills of both Robert Merriam and Mary Merriam of Concord in the seventeenth century. Since no records of the exact relationship have been found, all we can assume is that John Hubbard was in some way connected with Robert Merriam or his wife Mary and may have been a nephew.

"Son-in-law" and "daughter-in-law" were terms which sometimes had a different meaning in seventeenth-century records. A man was quite likely to call a stepchild (that is, child of his wife by a former marriage) "son-in-law" or "daughter-in-law" in his will.

On the other hand, "son" and "daughter" were sometimes used in that period in the sense in which we use "son-in-law" and "daughter-in-law." You have to reason out just what was meant by the term and try to find evidence of the exact relationship.

"Brother" is another tricky term. Sometimes it meant blood brother, sometimes stepbrother, sometimes brother-in-law, and frequently "brother in the church," as it is still used in some evangelical sects. Wordy old Judge Samuel Sewall, he of the *Diary*, frequently called a man "brother" who had no degree of relationship with him. He appears to have attended the funerals of innumerable "brothers" or "sisters" who were in no way related to him or his several successive wives. In other records, even in such serious documents as wills, the term was used to designate even the husband of a sister-in-law. In a letter written by Thomas Hungerford of Connecticut in 1657 to Anne, wife of John Leigh, of Ipswich, Mass., he calls her "sister" and thanks her for her offer to take care of his motherless daughter, Sarah. On the basis of this letter it has been assumed that John Leigh's wife, Anne, was Thomas Hungerford's sister. There is no other evidence of the relationship, although John Leigh, in his will dated in 1671, made a bequest to this Sarah Hungerford. It seems more likely that Anne Leigh was a sister of Thomas Hungerford's first wife, whose maiden surname is unknown. Thomas Hungerford was about to marry a second wife in 1657, when this letter was written, so it is quite possible that he should send his young daughter (Sarah was born about 1654) to her mother's sister and keep with him his son, Thomas Jr. (born about 1648). Neither John Leigh, nor his widow, Anne, mentioned Thomas Hungerford's son or his daughter Hannah (by his second wife) in their wills.

"Mother" and "father" are likewise terms that did not

always imply the relationship with which they are associated today. They might mean "mother-in-law" or "father-in-law" or even a stepparent acquired through the remarriage of a parent.

Frequently old records will refer to "Mrs." or "Mistriss" Sarah Jones, let us say. If you find such a title before a girl's name in a colonial marriage record, it does not mean necessarily that she was a widow or had been married before. In the seventeenth and even in the eighteenth century the title "Mistriss" (often abbreviated to "Mrs." in records) was one of social distinction as a general rule. Its use did not necessarily mean that the woman to whom it was applied was, or had been, married, as it does now. Records of the 1690s exist in which the title was given to an unmarried girl of seventeen who belonged to a family of considerable standing in the community. Sometimes the recorder used the term "widow" if the bride had been married before and had lost her husband, although in some records you will find "Mrs." meaning widowhood. As you work with the records, you will learn to distinguish the meaning and use the title correctly.

In early colonial days, "Mister" (or Mr.) was a title of respect given only to those who held important civil office or were of gentle blood before coming to America. If a man did not act in accordance with the dignity of the title "Mr.," it was taken away from him, as some of the old records show. About the only title that outranked it was "deacon." For instance, in the early records of Plymouth Colony, Dr. Doane's ancestor was called "Mr. John Done," but after he was made a deacon he was always referred to as "Deacon John Done," thus indicating the attitude of the times toward titles.

"Goodman" and "goodwife" were titles applied to those who had the respect of their fellow colonists but who did not quite merit the titles "Mr." and "Mrs." A man who had the right to vote or conduct business in the community was entitled to be called "freeman." When a man was "admitted freeman" in a community, it indicated that he was not an indentured servant any longer (if he had been one) and was free to commit himself in trade and to vote.

The inexperienced genealogist will do well to study carefully all the available records of a family before he or she accepts too literally in the modern sense any of the terms expressing relationship, particularly when he finds them in old documents originally written in the seventeenth century. Inaccurately interpreted or unthinkingly accepted, they may lead you into difficulty and cause you to claim as ancestors people whose blood does not flow in your veins.

## The Family Coat of Arms

The use of a coat of arms in the United States is a matter of personal taste. Unless you have a coat of arms that is registered as a trademark in the Patent Office, there is no government authority that can prevent any other individual from using it. Moreover, there is no law by which you can obtain a coat of arms. Since our government does not recognize coat armor, it has become a matter of custom that we use a heraldic insignia only from personal choice. In using it, we should abide by the laws governing its use in the country in which our family originated. Moreover, laws or customs regarding the right to use arms vary from country to country, so the native land of the progenitor has a bearing on our "right" to arms.

Heraldry is of truly ancient origin. There is evidence that in ancient Greece and Rome family insignia were used. By the time of the Norman conquest of England, many individuals throughout Europe used such devices. As the use of armor developed and it became impossible to distinguish one man from another when the visor of his helmet was closed, it came to be the custom to wear a surcoat over the metal armor, on which were embroidered the "arms," or insignia, which the individual used to distinguish himself. Usually this was identical with the insignia on the banner that his men carried, and it came to be known as the "coat of arms" of his family, as it was handed on from generation to generation. Gradually laws were made governing the use of coats of arms, and by the fifteenth century a definite code had been established. In the sixteenth century, in England, the College of Heralds, under whose jurisdiction the use of coat armor was placed, began a series of "visitations" of the several counties of England to determine what arms were being borne and who was entitled to them. These visitations, containing as they do thousands of pedigrees, are a source of knowledge for the genealogist as well as a record of arms. Since that time, arms have been granted by the Crown on the authority of the College of Heralds, and today you must either prove your right to bear a coat that has been confirmed by the College or pay a fee for a grant of arms.

In various western European nations there is today a strong interest in heraldry, and many articles and books are published on a variety of aspects of the subject. The key organization promoting professional attention in this field is the International Confederation of Genealogy and Heraldry, directed by Monsieur Roger Harmignies and located at B 1150 Brussels, Rue Martin Lindekins 57, Brussels, Belgium. It is composed of the key institutions in western Europe that pursue these interests as well as by the New England Historic Genealogical Society, in Boston. Should you want to pursue your heraldic research further, we would suggest you do so by contacting the center for heraldic study in the particular country from which your ancestors migrated.

(1) England, Wales, and Northern Ireland. The Royal College of Arms, Queen Victoria Street, London, E.C.4V 4BT grants arms for these areas.

(2) Scotland. The Lord Lyon, Lyon Office, New Register House, Edinburgh EH1 3YT controls grants of all coats of arms in Scotland. You need to make application to the Lord Lyon for a grant of your Scottish ancestor's coat of arms, or if your ancestor did not have a coat of

arms, you make application to receive a grant of arms for that ancestor. After that procedure has been completed, you may request that the arms be reassigned to you.

(3) Republic of Ireland. To check for your ancestral coat of arms, write to the Chief Herald of Ireland, Dublin Castle, Dublin 2.

— (4) Austria. The official use of coats of arms has been forbidden in this country since 1919. Before that, after 1760, arms were restricted to use only by the nobility. For assistance, however, write to: Heraldisch-genealogische Gesellschaft "Adler," Haarhof 4a, A 1010 Wien, Austriche.

(5) Belgium. Your inquiries should be directed to Le Conseil Héraldique, 85 Rue du Prince Royal, Brussels.

(6) France. The Société Française d'Héraldique, 113 Rue de Courcelles, Paris, is the center for study in France. The country enjoys a splendid heraldic heritage, particularly during the fifteenth, sixteenth, and seventeenth centuries: the French Revolution and later political developments arrested modern interest in heraldry and abolished the college of arms which had been established in 1406.

(7) Germany. For assistance with questions regarding the coat of arms of your German ancestor write to: Verein "Der Herold" zu Berlin, D 1000 Berlin 33 (Dahlem), Archivstrasse 12–14, Allemagne, and Deutsche Arbeitsgemeinschaft genealogischer Verbände, D 7000 Stuttgart 1, Fichtestrasse 18, Allemagne.

(8) Italy. Write to Araldica, Instituto Genealogico Italiano, Largo Chigi 19, 00187, Roma, for help in gathering details about your Italian ancestors who may have obtained a coat of arms.

(9) Spain. The Instituto Internaciónal de Genealogia y Heraldica, Apartado de correos 12-079, Madrid, Espagne, is the agency in Spain to which you should send your questions about your Spanish ancestor's right to arms.

For any other country, such as the Netherlands, Sweden, or Switzerland, we suggest you contact the particular nation's embassy in Washington, D.C. for advice and assistance on how to go about obtaining heraldic information about your ancestor. You will find that the staffs of the embassies are helpful in responding to your important questions.

In using a coat granted or confirmed several centuries ago, you must prove your descent from the family that originally used that coat and establish your right to the same arms. The right to bear arms descends in the male line only. Even if you assume a coat of arms without the authority of a heraldic institution in Europe, England, Scotland, or Ireland, you should use only the arms that have been borne by your paternal line. A woman did not go to war in the Middle Ages and hence did not bear arms and wear coat armor. Therefore, although it is perfectly proper for you to blazon your mother's family arms in your account of her descent, you should not assume those arms as your device. According to the English law, you can quarter your father's arms with your mother's, provided she was an "heiress" and had no brothers. But we do not propose to go into the matter of quartering arms here, for it is too extensive a subject; in some of the books to which we shall refer you, it is treated fully.

Looking up your surname in some armory (such as Burke's *General Armory*) and assuming that you have a right to the coat of arms described therein is not enough. You must prove your descent from the family to whom those arms were granted or confirmed by the appropriate heraldic institution. If you are willing to go to the expense of having those arms confirmed to you, or if you wish a new coat granted to you, you must apply to an agency such as the College of Heralds in London, England, or the Lord Lyon's Court in Edinburgh, Scotland, and go through the same procedure that any English person would go through in a similar case.

For example, although your name may be an unusual one, such as Hungerford, you should find proof of the connection of your immigrant ancestor with the family who bore the arms in England. In the case of the Hungerford family, we lack any evidence whatsoever of the English connection of Thomas Hungerford in Connecticut (1639), Thomas in Maryland (1641), or William in Maryland (1642). All were undoubtedly of the same blood as the English family of that name, but until their places in the English pedigrees are established, their descendants have no right (according to English law) to use the Hungerford arms as given in Burke's *General Armory*.

Because of the interest in coat armor in America, the New England Historic Genealogical Society of Boston, Mass. has a Committee on Heraldry. Since 1864 this committee has investigated the claims of over seven hundred American families to bear coat armor and has published a roll of authentic coats of arms. This is as near as we come on this side of the ocean to anything like the distinguished English College of Heralds.

We should note a book or two that may be useful to you in your preliminary efforts to identify your ancestor's coat of arms.

An excellent book on the use of coats of arms is *The Right to Bear Arms*, which was published anonymously in England several years ago. The standard book on heraldry is Boutell's *Manual of Heraldry* — there is a revised edition by J. P. Brooke-Little (1973). Another good one is Francis J. Grant's *The Manual of Heraldry* (1924). Of the older armories, the best known is Sir John Bernard Burke's *The General Armory of England, Scotland, Ireland, and Wales* (1878), generally referred to as *Burke's Armory*. The 1884 edition was reprinted in 1969. It is useful because it attempts to list all known coats of arms ever used in England.

A brief, interesting, and informative little book is that by Sir Anthony R. Wagner, K.C.V.O., D. Litt., Clarencieux King-of-Arms, the College of Arms Heralds, London, *Heraldry in England* (King Penguin Books, 1946). Here is one sentence from it: "An honest pedigree, however unambitious, and a new shield [that is, grant of arms] though without pretence to nobility, may warm its owner's heart, make him hold his head higher and feel himself the heir of a great tradition" (page 24).

For other countries we would suggest the following: Scotland, Sir Thomas Innes's book, *Scots Heraldry*; France, the *Grand Armorial de France*; Germany, Forest E. Barber's work, *Genealogisches Handbuch des Adels*; Italy, Giustino Colaneri's useful book, *Bibliografia Araldica e genealogica d'Italia*; and for Spain the reference work, *Heraldic and Genealogical Encyclopedia: Spanish American* is helpful for arms of families not only in Spain but also in the various Latin American countries.

## Bound Boys and Orphans

Several have asked what it means when one discovers a tradition, or the fact, that great-grandfather, let us say, was a "bound boy" or an "indentured servant," or was taken from an orphanage. The old, reliable *Century Dictionary* (10 vols., 1896), a useful tool for quick reference because it includes phrases and illustrative quotations as well as words, defines "bind" (in this sense) as "to indenture as an apprentice: often [used] with out." A son was "bound out" by his father, his widowed mother, or his guardian to give him training in some craft or trade, or, perchance, to relieve the parent from the expense of feeding and clothing him during his minority. Orphanages regularly bound out boys and girls in the same way that they might be trained to support themselves. This system of indentured apprenticeship undoubtedly had its origin in the trade guilds of the Middle Ages. During the course of the centuries, various laws governing and controlling it have been enacted, but we need not go into its history here — if you are interested, read the short but excellent article in the 11th edition of the *Encyclopaedia Britannica* as an introduction and then Abbot Emerson Smith's *Colonists in Bondage: White Servitude and Convict Labor in America, 1607–1776* (1947), noting especially the bibliographical appendix, pages 397–417.

For our purpose, it is sufficient to say that, from early colonial days, a boy might be "bound out" to a master, who, under the terms of the indenture (or legal agreement), had to provide him training in his craft or trade and give him board, lodging, and clothes, and perhaps pay him a stipulated sum at the end of his term. This was usually seven years or, in some instances, until the boy came of age. A farmer, lacking sufficient help, would take a boy in this way to help him with the farm work, or a girl to help his wife spin and weave and cook; a goldsmith, or printer, or paper-maker would do the same to get assistants and to train them. The boy so indentured would, in seven years, learn the craft and be able to take care of himself at the end of the contract. A widow, bereaved of her husband and left with little support, might bind out one or more of the elder children in order to provide them with a trade and at the same time relieve herself of their support.

An indentured servant was generally one who, wanting to migrate to America, the land of golden opportunities, where he thought he would have a better chance of improving his condition than he would in his native country, would sell his services (the only asset he might have) to someone by indenturing himself as a servant in return for the passage money he needed to get to the New World. By this indenture he contracted to work for the man who advanced the money for a specified number of years. Some of the passengers on the famous *Mayflower* were such servants, Dr. Doane's ancestor, George Soule, among them.

Some masters were exacting, severe, even cruel and inhuman in their treatment of their apprentices and "indentured servants," in fact used them like slaves; others were fair and kindly, even though they may have been strict and insistent upon full service and good workmanship; and some went further and treated their "bound boy" or girl as a member of the family.

Although it may be difficult, it is not always impossible to find the parentage of a bound boy, or an orphan.

Indentures of apprenticeship were generally matters of public record, so the records of them may be found in county courthouses or other repositories such as the state archives — the custodianship of such records varies in different periods and in the several states. In some, for instance, there is an orphans' court in the county organization; in others the records may be kept in some division of the municipal government. See, for example, pages 55–58 in Rosalie Fellows Bailey's *Guide to Genealogical and Biographical Sources for New York City (Manhattan) 1783–1898* (1954) for her account of the records of orphans and apprentices in that city. Perhaps the best way to locate records of indenture or orphanage is to write to the county clerk and ask for information — failing that, try the secretary of state at the state capitol. Again, let us warn you, in writing to an official for the records of a specific individual, give in concise form all the data you have and especially the approximate date, if you do not have a specific date.

To descend from a bound boy, an orphan, or an indentured servant is nothing to be ashamed of or be sensitive about. Poverty is not a disgrace nor is orphanage, whatever the circumstances that brought it about. Not all children in orphanages were illegitimate or of unknown parentage, but all were wards of the state through no fault or act of their own and should be respected as human beings and treated with sympathy and understanding, if for no other reason than that they were deprived of parental affection and normal family life.

### Illegitimate and Adopted Children

Speaking of illegitimate and adopted children: we have been asked how such cases should be dealt with in a genealogy or family history. This may well become a moot point when the genealogies of many twentieth-century families are compiled, considering some attitudes now prevalent. Many illegitimate children are acknowledged by their fathers, or their fathers are identified in records. In some instances they even bear the father's name. In fact, in the New England colonies, an illegitimate birth was frequently recorded under the mother's name and the child given its father's surname; in some instances the birth may be recorded under both names, paternal and maternal. We have found such cases in Rhode Island records. An illegitimate child is in no way to blame for the accident of his or her birth, though in times past many were stigmatized by a cruel, inhuman society. In our time, we trust, we are less censorious and more willing to accept men and women on their merits.

Certainly in the compilation of a genealogy, illegitimate or adopted children bearing the surname of the family should be given full treatment if they live to adulthood and have progeny and hence are carried forward as heads of family groups. Although adopted children usually do not have the "blood," they too bear the name and hand it down to their descendants. When the actual parentage of an adopted child is known, it should be recorded in the genealogy. That is what we have advised when we have been consulted. The fact of illegitimacy or adoption can be given in a footnote, with as much detail as the compiler decides to use. When such a person is carried forward as the head of a family group, such information need not be repeated or amplified if the compiler has any qualms about it.

During the past few years there have appeared on the pages of newspapers and magazines happy and sad accounts of adopted children seeking reunion with their biological parents and birth mothers searching for a long-relinquished child. It is usually a story of anxiousness and frustration; of restrictions established by law in the various states; of bureaucratic procedures rigidly fixed by social agencies; of the adoptee's innate desire to know "Who am I?" and the natural parent's right to privacy. A strong advocate of the adopted person's right to know is Betty Jean Lifton, an "adoptee" herself.

She has written two important books on the subject: the first, *Twice Born: Memoirs of an Adopted Daughter*

(New York, 1975), recounts her own painful but persistent search to know and find her biological parents. The
second, *Lost and Found* (New York, 1979), focuses on the
experiences of other adoptees in their search for blood
relatives. It is an eloquent and thoughtful book which
speaks at once about the genealogical questions which
confront an adoptee and the urgent need to compas-
sionately revise the present rules governing adoption.

## Where to Go to School

Opportunities for instruction in family history research
have increased considerably in recent years. Today,
across the United States and Canada public libraries,
state and local historical and genealogical societies,
adult education centers, and colleges and universities
offer courses for those searching for their ancestors.
Probably your nearby library or historical society can
help you locate a course being offered in your area. Before taking such a course, it is well, however, to have
gathered at least a few records of your progenitors,
gained a little experience, and know what your problems are. In many of these, in addition to lectures, there
is some type of laboratory work, and you are graded, in
part at least, on the way you handle a problem. The
instructor may assign to you a case that will involve
using the kinds of records which he or she has been
discussing, or may have you take one of your own problems and apply to it the principles you have been taught
and expect you to use the appropriate sources in your
efforts to find the solution. This is good practice, for you
have expert guidance in your searching.

During the summer months the New England Historic Genealogical Society in Boston, Mass., usually offers a two-week seminar at Harvard University on either
introductory or more advanced topics of interest to a
researcher on family history. The participants live in
Harvard dormitories and eat in the college dining hall.
The resources of the New England Historic Genealogical
Society Library, the Harvard University Library, Mas-

sachusetts State Archives, as well as the many other important research libraries located in the greater Boston area, are available for research purposes. For information and registration materials, write to the New England Historic Genealogical Society, 101 Newbury Street, Boston, MA 02116. Incidentally, the Society also offers annually one-day lecture programs in many cities across the United States and Canada on such key research topics as how to use census, church, and military records in your research work, as well as discussions on problems encountered in genealogical research and methods of organizing and writing your family story.

In Washington, D.C., the National Archives and Records Service holds a seminar on genealogy each summer. Drawing on the important resources available for research use in the Washington neighborhood, the course usually covers the techniques of genealogical research, research in various geographical areas and in special fields, with visits to special libraries such as the Daughters of the American Revolution Library in Memorial Continental Hall in Washington, the Library of Congress on Capitol Hill, the Maryland Hall of Records in Annapolis, and the Virginia State Archives in Richmond. For information about the program and registration forms write to the National Archives and Records Service, General Services Administration, Washington, D.C. 20408.

At least one large university, the Brigham Young University, in Provo, Utah, offers a special course of studies in genealogy and research techniques as part of a four-year course leading to a degree. Write to the Supervisor, Genealogy Technical Research Program, Brigham Young University, Provo, Utah 84601 for detailed information.

One of the valuable results of such courses is fellowship with other hunters and the opportunity to talk over some of your problems with them. Clarifying a problem in your own mind in order to state it clearly to someone else helps you see it more objectively. And sometimes having a day or week or two in which to do nothing but pursue an elusive ancestor is fun and refreshing.

## The Spacing of Generations

Questions are sometimes asked about the number of generations that are likely to occur in a given span of years, say a century. We generally figure three or four generations to a hundred years — in rare instances only two, in others five. The average span between one generation and the next is about twenty-five to thirty years, so, in the space of 350 years, you can estimate that there will be about twelve generations. At the tercentenary of the landing of the Pilgrims at Plymouth, most of the applicants for membership in the Society of Mayflower Descendants were of the 10th generation in descent, few were of the 9th, few of the 12th.

There are, of course, exceptions to any rule of thumb. Only a short time ago we read in the newspaper about a boy of twelve who was willing to help support his new-born child whose mother was thirteen. Occasionally one hears of other instances of extraordinarily youthful parentage. Maurice Berkeley, who later became Lord Berkeley, was born in 1281 and married in 1289 at the age of eight to the heiress of considerable property who was also eight. Their first child, Thomas, was born about 1291: he was thirty-five when he succeeded his father in the peerage. His son, another Maurice, also married at the age of eight another heiress, but this young couple was not permitted to live together for several years.

In the days of increasing longevity and youthful marriages, one quite frequently sees in the newspapers pictures of "five generations" — say a great-great-grandmother seated in the center of a group, holding an infant in her arms. She is usually in her eighties, if not her nineties, and the infant is a few months old. Five generations in less than a century! True, but the span between each generation is still twenty to thirty years. Say the great-great-grandmother was born in 1890; her son, the great-grandfather, in 1915; his daughter, the grandmother, in 1937; her daughter, the mother, in 1958; and the infant in 1980.

At the other extreme, it is not unusual for a man to be forty, fifty, or even sixty before he marries or his first child is born; and in rare, but nonetheless authentic, cases an octogenarian may father children. The late Richard T. Ely, a noted economist, was born in 1854. He married his second wife in 1931 when he was seventy-seven. Before he died in 1943 he had fathered a son and a daughter by that wife, the youngest born when he was about eighty-four years old — two generations in eighty-four years.

## Names

Because we are occasionally asked about surnames, their meaning or origin, we shall take a little space (beyond the mention in Chapter 1) to briefly introduce the subject, knowing full well that what we write is but a mere shadow of what you should know if you become really interested in the subject.

Surnames did not come into general use until about the thirteenth and fourteenth centuries, although there are traces of them long before that. The earlier names were usually locative, referring to a place. Such names as De Courtenay (later just Courtenay) indicated that the men so called were of the noble family ruling a region and having a chateau of that name in France. Descendants, who came to England in the days of the early Norman kings, kept the designation of their "hometown" as their name. This type of name belongs to one of the four main classes of surnames as the specialists in the study of names arrange them. It is called *topponym* and has two subclasses, the locative, derived from the name of a place, as Courtenay is, and the topographical, derived from the designation of a physical or geographical feature, such as Hill or Wood. Another class consists of patronymics, rarely metronymics, names inherited from the father like Johnson, Adams (that is, Adam's son, the suffix having been dropped sometime over the centuries). Another class is the occupational surname, derived from the occupation of the bearer, such as Chandler (candlemaker), Sherman (shear man, one who sheared cloth: note that shearer was one who sheared sheep). The fourth class is made up of nicknames, pet names, diminutives. Many names that seem strange to us today fall in this class, such as Calef (a calf), White or Blount (a blond), Tubbe (a fish found off the coast of Cornwall, where there was a family of this name). Some names may be classified in two categories, such as Robinson (Robin, a nickname or diminutive for Robert, to which the patronymic suffix has been added).

Changes in spelling through the years have so altered the original form of some names that it is difficult to discover the earliest form and hence the meaning, unless one is a scholar versed in onomatology (the history of names). Therefore, it is best to consult a good book on the subject. The best, a combination of an excellent and readable essay on surnames and a lengthy list, is the late P. H. Reaney's *A Dictionary of British Surnames* (1961). Dr. Reaney's "dictionary" is not as extensive as we might wish, although it runs to several hundred pages. It does not include many Irish or Scottish names. For the Scottish, see George Black's *The Surnames of Scotland*, published as a bulletin of the New York Public Library in 1966; and for the Irish, Edward MacLysaght's *The Surnames of Ireland*, published in Shannon, Ireland, by the Irish University Press, in 1969. The latter is not as comprehensive as Dr. Black's.

There is always a tendency among us amateurs to make assumptions. However, assumptions in genealogy, especially in claiming relationship because of identity of family names, are treacherous. As Dr. Black observes in his discussion of the name Stewart (Stuart and any other spelling), many noblemen, as well as successive sovereigns, had stewards. Steward (Stewart) is an occupational surname. Stewards were not uncommon in noble households in both England and Scotland.

Hence the word may have become a surname almost simultaneously in different areas. Therefore, not all Stewarts (Stuarts, etc.) are Scots, nor do they all descend from a common progenitor, or even a family of stewards, although the office of steward was sometimes hereditary. So it is with many other surnames. In Dr. Doane's case (the name means a dune, or hill), he has found Doanes whose name was originally Dohn, the progenitor having come from Germany, and others who came from various parts of England and Scotland, some spelling the name Don, some Doun, some Doone, any of which may be transformed into Doan or Doane as some have. So do not rely upon the name alone.

# PART II
## Special Searches

CHAPTER 13

# Searching for Ethnic Origins

### Native Americans

DURING THE past decade persons of Native American ancestry have become interested in searching for their ancestors. Their interest is reflected in the broader interest by members of many ethnic groups to define and recover their family heritage. The plight of the American Indian through the past three and a half centuries parallels the rhythms of mistreatment that punctuate and measure the harsh treatment of Black Americans. Many Indian groups today, the Penobscots in Maine and the Mashpees on Cape Cod in Massachusetts, are seeking legal action in the courts in hopes of reclaiming a portion of their ancestral lands and a share, if any, of a financial settlement. Accordingly there is a need to define a person's Indian ancestry and also to determine what is a tribe and who comprises it. Incidentally, should one wish to establish tribal membership, it is necessary to file papers with the Secretary of the Interior and in particular the Tribal Enrollment Section of the Bureau of Indian Affairs in Washington, D.C.

The constant conflict that shaded relations between the Native Americans and the whites from the earliest settlement at Jamestown, Virginia in 1607 to the massacre at Wounded Knee, South Dakota in 1890 made the accumulation and care of records difficult indeed. You may find some information on Indian ancestry in the records that have survived for the Indians in the eastern United States, particularly eighteenth- and nineteenth-century records. However, should your ancestors have been converted to Christianity at one of the Franciscan missions in the Southwest, or at one of the missions in New England sponsored by the Society for the Propagation of the Gospel among the Indians, or at a Jesuit mission in the Great Lakes region there may be church records to assist you in your search.

During the years between 1830 and 1850 the United States government pursued an active policy of removing Indians on lands east of the Mississippi River and settling them on lands west of the river. At the National Archives in Washington, D.C., there are two helpful sets of records for this period: an 1832 Census of the Creek Nation and an 1835 Census of the Cherokee Nation, and the muster lists. These censuses were taken before the Indians of these two tribes were uprooted from their ancestral lands and sent west. The removal muster rolls are arranged chronologically, list individuals, and are indexed. Names are given of the individuals who migrated westward and occasionally the number of persons in each family is noted by age and sex.

We should indicate that because the policy of the United States government was to isolate Indians on tribal reservations, especially west of the Mississippi River, and to exclude them from the privileges of the 14th Amendment to the Constitution, no reference was made to Indians until the Federal Census of 1860. It was not until 1890 that there was an effort to include all Indians in the Census.

America has not proved to be a melting pot for American Indians because tribal Indians have continued to live apart from American life. Nonetheless, there are government records to aid you in pursuing your ancestors. For the Indians who became a part of the non-Indian community, information may be sought in the usual public and private records sources.

Our cardinal principle, to learn as much about our

families as possible from our relatives, is important for Indians. Moreover, since Indians frequently used several Indian names during their lifetime and may also have used an English name in their contact with federal officials, you must try to learn all the names, Indian and English, of your various ancestors as you chat with your older relatives.

The Indian tribal records at the National Archives in Washington, D.C. are significant because they contain such materials as lists of Indians removed from the eastern sections of the United States, especially for the Cherokees of the southeast, and several Indian censuses. These records are open for research on your ancestry, and if you provide certain basic information, such as your ancestor's name, the name of his tribe, and the approximate date of this tribal association, a staff member at the National Archives will undertake a search for you.

At Regional Federal Records Centers you will find the records of the Bureau of Indian Affairs for the area in which your ancestor lived. Covering the years between 1850 and 1952, the records include birth, marriage, and death data as well as educational records and censuses of tribes.

Should you be unsuccessful in locating information on your ancestors at either the National Archives or at a Federal Records Center, you should check the office of the federal agency in charge of your tribe's records. Write to the Bureau of Indian Affairs, 1951 Constitution Avenue N.W., Washington, D.C. 20245, and ask for the name and location of the agency responsible for your tribe.

There are two sorts of census records that you must consult at the National Archives. First, the United States Censuses beginning in 1860 for those persons in the category of "Indians taxed, that is living off the reservation and among the white population," should be searched. Second, beginning in 1885, the federal government took an annual census of Indians living on reservations, and since most Indians did live in those communities, the returns are helpful. These records continue for most reservations until 1940.

Also at the National Archives is a four-volume "Special Census of Indians Not Taxed" undertaken in 1880 for particular tribes in the territories of North and South Dakota and Washington and the state of California. There are scattered earlier censuses too which should be studied at the National Archives if your ancestors were of the Creek or Cherokee nations.

Do not overlook the valuable records called annuity rolls which the government maintained for the period between 1850 and 1887. These records, which relate to several tribes, note the annual payment of money or goods to heads of Indian families. Occasionally the sex and age of each member of the family is recorded. Beginning in the 1870s, several school censuses of Indian children were taken from time to time by the Bureau of Indian Affairs. These should be checked since they do list the students, their ages, where they were born, and frequently the names of their parents.

Another significant source for genealogical data is the Allotment Registers. The federal government, by the terms of the General Allotment Act, began in 1887 to convey to Indians, who proved they were able to supervise their own affairs, tracts of land. When an Indian died, all of his or her heirs had to be identified and their relationship to the deceased described. The registers were used during the period between 1905 and 1930 although some of the family information is carried back to the early decades of the nineteenth century. Here you will find the Indian and English names of the allotted person as well as age, birth date, and the names, ages, and relationships of several members of the family.

You should inspect, too, at the National Archives the *Sanitary Record of Sick, Injured, Births, Deaths, etc.* maintained by the Bureau of Indian Affairs. Beginning late in the nineteenth century the Bureau's medical service listed those persons who had been treated for physical or mental illnesses. For births, you will find the date noted and the names of the parents; for deaths usually the date is indicated.

After 1910, with approval of the commissioner of Indian Affairs, an Indian could prepare and file a will. These too will be found at the National Archives, along with other supporting papers, and they do detail such information as name, tribe, residence, date of death, age at death, name of spouse, date of marriage, names and dates of marriage of parents, and the names of brothers, sisters, and children.

## Canada

The first permanent settlement in Canada was established in 1608 at Quebec City by the Frenchman Samuel Champlain. For the next one hundred and fifty-five years the French strengthened and advanced their claims in Canada, although it is a story punctuated by the various colonial wars against the British. European imperial politics, commercial rivalries, and maritime power were mirrored in North America in the geographical areas of present-day Canada and the United States. Following the French and Indian War, France's stake in the New World ended under the terms of the Treaty of Paris of 1763. Now under British control, Quebec province was divided into Upper and Lower Canada by the Constitutional Act of 1791. Fifty years later, in 1841, following the Rebellion in 1837–38, the two Canadas were reunited as the Province of Canada. In 1867 the English Parliament approved the British North America Act which created the Dominion of Canada, a confederation of provinces consisting of Nova Scotia, New Brunswick, and Lower and Upper Canada. The remaining provinces, which comprise present-day Canada, joined the confederation on various later dates.

For an understanding of the history of Canada and its people, look at the following books: John B. Brebner, *Canada: A Modern History* (Ann Arbor, 1960) and Edgar McInnis's work, *Canada* (Toronto, 1969). Both books, through text and bibliographical suggestions, will lead you to books related to your special areas of interest in Canada's past.

Genealogical research in Canada has been significantly aided by the publication of Eric Jonasson's book *The Canadian Genealogical Handbook* (second edition, Winnipeg, 1978). It is an informative and instructive guide to the materials that are available at the local, provincial, and national levels to assist the researcher who is studying his or her family's history.

The maintenance of civil registration for births, marriages, and deaths did not begin until 1869 in the province of Ontario. Unlike European countries, Canada has no central national registry office for civil registration; such records are kept at the Vital Statistics offices in each of the ten provinces and two territories. The correct addresses are listed in *The Canadian Genealogical Handbook*.

Church records throughout Canada generally remain in the hands of ministers or clerks of local congregations. Again, we must emphasize that should you wish to use this sort of record to identify a particular event in an ancestor's life, it is essential to determine the religious affiliation of the ancestor and then locate the records of the particular church of which he or she was a member. The Roman Catholic church, the first religious group to come to what is today Canada, was established in Quebec City as early as 1614. Today nearly half the population of twenty-three million people is attached to the Roman Catholic church. The second largest denomination in the country is the United Church of Canada, composed by union during the past fifty years of the Congregational, Presbyterian, and Evangelical United Brethren churches. For aid in finding church records helpful to you in your research, address your inquiry to: The United Church of Canada, Committee on Archives, Victoria University, Queen's Park Crescent East, Toronto, Ontario, M5S 1K7. The Anglican Church of Canada is the oldest Protestant church and the third largest religious group in the nation. Records remain in the hands of the local parish or diocesan offices. For information about the addresses of local diocesan offices, write to: The Anglican Church of Canada, 600 Jarvis Street, Toronto, Ontario, M4Y 2J6.

In this brief overview of Canadian resources for the study of family history, we can direct you only to the several provincial archives and libraries throughout the country that hold materials relating to the development of the various regions and their peoples. We do wish, however, to bring to your attention the excellent resources of the Public Archives of Canada since it is the largest repository of historical, governmental, and genealogical records in Canada. Here you will find census records and military records helpful to you as well as emigration materials and records relating to the many ethnic groups that have settled in Canada. An excellent feature of the Public Archives system for researchers who live at a distance from the headquarters in Ottawa is the inter-library loan of microfilm. Generally, any material that has been microfilmed at the Public Archives is available for use at your local library, so do ask your librarian about the procedures to be followed to use this service. Make your inquiries to: Public Archives of Canada, 395 Wellington Street, Ottawa, Ontario, K1A 0N3.

The publications program of the Public Archives has provided several helpful guides to its collections: Maureen Hoogenrood's pamphlet *Genealogical Sources at the Public Archives of Canada*, and the booklet *Tracing Your Ancestors in Canada*. For information regarding the purchase of these and other publications, write: Publications Division, Public Archives of Canada, Postal Station B, 59 Sparks and Elgin, 6th Floor, Ottawa, Ontario K1A 0N3.

## Mexico, Puerto Rico, and Cuba

The opportunities are rich for pursuing the study of family history in Central and South America and the Caribbean islands. In particular, after family records, the researcher will find the civil, church, and notorial records of most assistance. Since the greatest number of United States residents with Latin American backgrounds have come from Mexico, Puerto Rico, and Cuba, we will focus our attention on the records in these three countries. An indispensable guide for use in our survey, as well as for all of the other Latin American states, is Lyman De Platt's comprehensive *Genealogical and Historical Guide to Latin America* (Detroit, Michigan, 1978). You will want to be familiar with the valuable and instructive contents of this work before you launch your search further afield.

## MEXICO

The world of the Aztecs was conquered by the Spaniard Hernando Cortez in 1517, and the viceroyalty of New Spain was established in 1535. The territory of New Spain included Florida, Texas, New Mexico, Arizona, California, Mexico, and most of Central America. Although settlements in all of these areas were established, in the sixteenth century, it was not until the late eighteenth century, particularly in California, that these areas were significantly settled. Mexico's political history has at times been turbulent, not only before gaining independence in 1821 but since then as well. Nonetheless, Mexico is a country with rich collections of genealogical and historical materials.

Civil registration of births, marriages, deaths, divorces, annulments, fetal deaths, adoptions, and acknowledgment by fathers of illegitimate children is maintained at the municipal level of government in Mexico. The procedure began in 1859, although in some places it started earlier and in other communities it was initiated later, and is the key source for doing genealogical research for the past one hundred years.

These materials compiled by the state should be used to supplement and complement church records. Since between ninety and one hundred percent of the population of Mexico, or any other country in Latin America, before 1900 was Roman Catholic, it is to the registers of Catholic parishes we must look for assistance. Many parish registers have been lost or destroyed through the decades, but those that do survive give you information regarding the baptisms, confirmations, marriages, and dates of burial of your family members.

We should call to your attention that the Genealogical Society of Utah, an organization of the Church of Jesus Christ of Latter-Day Saints, in Salt Lake City, Utah, has microfilmed many of the civil records and church registers in Mexico and throughout Latin America. These microfilms are available for public use at any of the Mormon branch libraries throughout the United States, Canada, indeed the world.

In the Latin world, both in Europe and in Central and South America, another important source for genealogical information, especially before the keeping of civil records, are the notorial records. This sort of record is based on Roman law and was translated to Latin America from Spain. The registers kept by the notaries public contain several sorts of legal transactions: wills, buying and selling of land, letters of indebtedness, etc. These records are deposited in nearly eight hundred notorial archives located throughout Mexico, although many states have brought the materials within their jurisdiction under the supervision of the state archives or special notorial archives. Although each state in Mexico has its own major archives, the most important archives in the country for genealogical research is the Archivo General De La Nacion (National Archives), Palacio Nacional, Mexico 1, D.F.

PUERTO RICO

Attached to the viceroyalty of New Spain between 1534 and 1821, it became a dependency of Spain from 1821 until the Spanish American War in 1898. After that war, Puerto Rico became a protectorate of the United States which in 1952 declared it a free territory under its jurisdiction. During the years since the end of World

War II there has been a substantial emigration of Puerto Ricans to the United States.

Vital statistics since July 22, 1931 are filed at the Division of Demographic Registry and Vital Statistics, Department of Health, San Juan, Puerto Rico 00908. Earlier records, dating from about 1880, are kept at the office of vital statistics in the particular municipality.

Parish registers in Puerto Rico, should they survive, will be either in the hands of the local parish priest or at the Ecclesiastical Archive of San Juan (the Archbishop's Archive). A complete guide to the available parish registers has been compiled by the Genealogical Society of Utah and is of interest to those persons searching for ancestors in Puerto Rico.

A major center for genealogical and historical resources is the Archivo General de Puerto Rico (National Archives), Av. Ponce de Leon 500, Puerta de Tierra, San Juan, Puerto Rico 00905. The notorial records are of special interest as is the alphabetical card index to the names of Puerto Ricans which are found in the records deposited in institutions in Spain. The index notes the name, document, and source of the information, and new information is constantly added to it.

CUBA

The viceroyalty of New Spain supervised Cuba from 1535 until 1821, save for an interlude in 1762 and 1763 when the British controlled the island. Under Spanish rule until the Spanish American War, it became an economic and political protectorate of the United States in 1899. Since 1934 dictatorial rule of one fashion or another has governed the fortunes of the country. Particularly, before and immediately after the revolution led by Fidel Castro in 1959, many Cubans emigrated to the United States, especially to Florida. During the past twenty years, with an interruption of cultural and diplomatic relations between the United States and Cuba, our knowledge of Cuban affairs has been restricted, too. This is certainly true regarding our understanding today of genealogical and historical materials available in Cuba for the researcher's use. We can note only that civil registration began 31 July 1889, and that these records, should they have survived the various military uprisings, are in the hands of the Civil Registry of the town in which the birth, marriage, or death occurred. Parish registers, where they exist, are in the hands of the local parish priest. The notorial records are preserved in the archives of the notorial districts and generally note materials dating from the early eighteenth century. The Archivo Nacional (National Archives), Copostela y San Isidro, Havana 1, Cuba, has such genealogical and historical materials of interest as census returns, military records, and land petitions.

# CHAPTER 14

# Bridging the Seas

"How DO I go about finding my ancestors in the old country?" This question is asked frequently by those who have traced their American ancestors back several generations and who meet the immigrant ancestor.

All we can do to help you with this problem is to suggest what you can do before you initiate any research overseas, and call your attention to several sources of more specific direction which will tell you better than we can what to do when you are ready to start searching overseas. In other words, there is a certain amount of hunting that you must do right here in the United States, and there are places to which you can write for records once you have gathered as many facts as you can.

Your very first step, regardless of the nationality of your immigrant progenitor, is to marshal all the facts and traditions you can collect from your relatives, whether by personal interview or by correspondence. You may find that you should do a little traveling in the United States before you plan to cross the seas; and, if you are able to get to Salt Lake City, you may be able to do a considerable amount of digging right there, where the Genealogical Society has microfilm copies of many overseas records and genealogists who are trained to read them. It also has publications on genealogical research in several countries, giving the location of the archives office and other repositories, if any.

From your own family records, you need to assemble all the facts you can and arrange them in clear and logical order. From your own knowledge, or perhaps from your grandfather or great-aunt, you know or learn that your progenitor was English, Swedish, or Italian. Perhaps there is a vague recollection that your grandfather, before he died, said that he came from northern England, but beyond that, when you commence your search, about all you know is that his name was Thomas Ackroyd. That much as been handed down!

Interview as many of the older relatives as you can, and quiz them about any old letters or papers they may have. If they won't let you take that bundle of old letters home to read or copy at your leisure, go through them then and there and note carefully the names of all persons and places mentioned in each letter, the date of the letter itself, and the names of the writer and recipient. One of your older cousins, perhaps, adds a piece to the puzzle when she tells you that her mother said the family came from Yorkshire; but another cousin tells you that his father said they came from Liverpool. As you poke around you find that many of the nineteenth-century emigrants from England sailed from Liverpool, so both of these cousins may have been right, and Thomas Ackroyd was a Yorkshireman who sailed from that port. Then you pick up the story that he landed in New York on the Fourth of July and was "rather" surprised at the celebration he found in progress. But as yet you know nothing about his age when he came, or even the year in which he arrived.

But you do know that the family has lived in Wisconsin for four or five generations, so you begin to search for records of them. You find in the State Historical Society the 1850 census and a card index to it which tells you that in the township of Vienna, Dane County, there was, in 1850, a Thomas Ackroyd who was the head of a family, and another Thomas Ackroyd who was younger and single and working as a laborer on a farm. One of your problems now is to distinquish between these two.

As a hypothesis you settle on the head of the family and begin to analyze the record. You note that Thomas and his wife Mary and the two eldest children in their family were born in England before 1840, and that the next five children were born in Wisconsin between 1840 and 1850. The significant fact is that sometime between 1838, when the younger of the two older children was born, and 1840, when the first child born in Wisconsin arrived, the family must have come to the state. As you look at the records of other families in the township, you find that there are several of English origin, and the same pattern prevails in some of them — sometime between 1838 or 1839 and 1840 or 1841 each came to Wisconsin. So it appears that there was a group of English immigrants that probably came together. Note the names (at least the surnames) of these, for they may be useful to you in identifying the ship on which they came and even the community in England from which they came.

Then some fine day you drive out from Milwaukee, where your family has lived for two generations, and see what you can find in Norway Grove, the most central village in the township of Vienna. At least you will visit the cemeteries and perhaps you can find the gravestone of Thomas Ackroyd. At the grocery store in the small village you find a man who tells you that there are still descendants of some of the English families left there and that old Miss Green up the road a half mile knows more about them than anyone else, because she was related to some of them. You go and talk with her and she gives you an earful indeed! The main facts you glean from her are that there was a "shipload" of Englishmen and their families who came to Vienna in the summer of 1840, for they landed in New York on the Fourth of July and came straight out to Wisconsin. She recollects that her grandmother told her the ship was called the *Aniseed*, which always struck her as odd, naming a ship after a plant seed. She, too, thought that the ship sailed from Liverpool, but her own people were from Yorkshire. You ask her about cemeteries, and she tells you where most of the English families were buried and that you will find some of the Ackroyds there, although most of the family left Vienna before she was born.

In the cemetery you are somewhat disappointed. But you do find the gravestones of Thomas Ackroyd and his wife Mary and two or three other Ackroyds whose names you recognize from the census records, and you carefully copy the inscriptions. You look at the other stones of the same general period, and you find more names which you have seen in the census records. One of them, quite near the Ackroyd stones, is that of John Darcy, who was born in York, England, 16 February 1818 and died 6 August 1885. Some of the others have the words "born in England" on them, but Thomas Ackroyd's gives merely the date of his death and his age at that time, so you can figure about when he was born, say 1810.

Your next step, now that you have some definite dates, is to search the newspapers of that area — the county weeklies are more likely to carry obituary notices of the inhabitants of the countryside and the small villages and towns than the city dailies are. In one of these you find an obituary notice of Thomas Ackroyd which states that he came to the county in 1840, bringing with him his wife and two children, his nephew Thomas, and his wife's brother, John Darcy. His age checks pretty closely with that given in the 1850 census. So you have him pretty well pinpointed.

You may summarize the facts you have gathered: You have your ancestor's name and age, his wife's name, the names of the children who were born in England, and you may assume that his wife was a Darcy, since her brother, John Darcy, came with them. You may assume also that the ship on which they came was named something that sounds like *Aniseed*, and that it sailed from Liverpool and arrived in New York about the Fourth of July, 1840.

The last you should verify by writing to the National Archives and Record Service, General Services Administration, Washington, D.C. 20408, and asking if such a ship arrived at that time and if so, was Thomas Ackroyd a passenger. If your date is correct and there was such a ship, an assistant in the National Archives will check the record for you. But suppose that he writes back that they were unable to find such a ship listed, or it didn't arrive that week. You can employ a professional searcher to check the lists of passengers on ships that did arrive about that time and he may find the ship's name was the *Anglesea* — the old lady probably never knew how its name was spelled and remembered only that it sounded like anise seed. Moreover, the *Anglesea* docked on 2 July 1840, having sailed from Liverpool with Captain So-and-So as the master.

Even with as much information as this, and it is more than some have been able to gather, you should continue your search on this side of the water. Look for old family letters, the family Bible — it may be in some cousin's hands in California or Texas! Look at any other old books that may have names written on the flyleaves or letters or clippings tucked between their pages. Sometimes a battered old prayer book will turn up and indicate that even though the groups of English families that settled in Vienna in 1840 were Methodists (or Wesleyans), the Ackroyds may originally have been members of the Church of England, as this old prayer book indicates. Say it has the name Roger Ackroyd, 1776, written on one of its leaves. Could he have been the father of Thomas? Or the grandfather? You recall that one of Thomas's sons, as given in the census, was R. Ackroyd. His name could have been Roger, rather than Richard, as you guessed it was. This Roger may be an important clue when you get your English genealogist to work for you.

There is another important source we have overlooked. Just as you think you have gotten about everything you can find and have wearied all your relatives in pumping them for details, you suddenly think of naturalization. Was Thomas Ackroyd ever naturalized? A news item in the evening paper telling about the swearing in of some new citizens at the county courthouse suggests that you find out where the old records of naturalization are. So you get on the trail. You have four names: Thomas Ackroyd and his nephew Thomas, Roger Ackroyd, relationship unknown, but a possible clue, and John Darcy. Perhaps one of these will produce information that will lead you to a specific spot in England somewhere in Yorkshire, possibly the city of York. Even if the clerk of the court is discouraging, try to find someone who can tell you where the old records are. One of our friends had to use a little "influence" and asked a lawyer friend of her husband's to prod one of the officials; she then learned that what she wanted was in Chicago. More influence was needed to get at it, but she finally found the record and it gave her some valuable information about date and place of birth, etc.

Once you have pinned an ancestor down to a specific parish in England, you can write to the vicar and make arrangements to have the parish register searched for baptisms, marriages, and burials — Crockford's *Clerical Directory* will give you the vicar's name. Remember, by English law, he is entitled to a fee for searching his register, which forms part of his income.

Let us summarize what you should do before you think of writing overseas for information. The principles are the same for all countries. You must have names and dates, even though the latter are only approximate. You must try to associate the name with some particular locality, or it will be like finding a needle in a haystack. You should have some idea of when your ancestor migrated. If you can find the names of contemporary relatives, it will aid greatly in the search. Put all your facts into a logical order (see pages 140–44 for an example of how to arrange your data about your immigrant ancestor).

## Tools for Your Search

Before you go any further, we suggest that you get a copy of Timothy Field Beard's very helpful book, *How to Find Your Family Roots* (1977). In particular, become familiar with his valuable suggestions regarding genealogical sources in each state of the United States and for each country in the world. Note carefully his suggestions about books and articles that may be of assistance to you for the region in which you are searching for your ancestors. Another helpful feature of this book is that the author has carefully noted the names and addresses of the key archives, libraries, and historical and genealogical societies here and overseas. This book will give you some idea how to proceed in hunting for the records you want in a particular country, or how to get in touch with the proper authorities or a genealogist there. Some knowledge of the language of the country is a great asset, but it is not impossible to accomplish a great deal without it. Another useful book along this line is *Genealogical Research: Methods and Sources*, by the American Society of Genealogists (vol. I, 1960, vol. II, 1971), which has several important chapters on resources available for pursuing your research in England, Scotland, Wales, Ireland, and European countries.

Some overseas countries have published leaflets that give considerable information about research in these particular countries: The British Tourist Authority, 680 Fifth Avenue, New York, N.Y. 10019, has published "Tracing Your Ancestors in Britain." The Royal Norwegian Ministry of Foreign Affairs, Office of Cultural Relations, Oslo, Norway, has a booklet called "How to Trace Your Ancestors in Norway" (written in English). The Royal Ministry for Foreign Affairs, Press and Information Service, Stockholm, Sweden, has a brochure entitled "Finding Your Forefathers: Some Hints for Americans of Swedish Origin." Recently one was issued for the Netherlands. It is possible that other countries have issued similar booklets. There may be a small charge for some of these. You might try writing to the embassy of the country in which you are interested and asking for information — they all have offices in Washington, D.C., which will at least refer your request to the proper official.

## Black Americans

Alex Haley has charted the course for black persons searching for their ancestors. He systematically read the census records of Almance County, North Carolina, available to him at the National Archives in Washington, D.C., and reconstructed the family's oral history which he had heard and learned from his grandmother as a boy, supplementing and complementing the story whenever possible with evidence from printed or authentic sources. Finally he traveled to Africa, visited the village of his ancestors, and confirmed the lesson he had learned as a child from a family member who had kept alive the ancient custom of committing to memory the history of the family.

Our knowledge of American history recalls that wave after wave of immigrants stepped on the shores of the New World from 1607 to 1920. We should recall too that the black people had been captured in Africa, transported in bondage across the Atlantic, and sold into slavery in America. Families had been broken forever, husbands and wives, parents and children, children and children, never to see each other again. For blacks the New World meant not only slavery but also a new climate and scenery, new customs and language, and a land filled with people of a different color.

The stirring interest since the late 1950s in the Civil Rights Movement led by the eloquent Martin Luther King has encouraged the development of a black consciousness. Now the African languages are offered in black studies departments on college and university campuses throughout the United States.

## WHERE DO I BEGIN?

Fortunately there are now two very instructive books for the study of black genealogy: Alex Haley's inspirational account of his search for his ancestors, *Roots*, and a guide to printed and manuscript sources and government records that are helpful in the study of black family history entitled *Black Genesis* (1978). We are in debt to the authors, James Rose and Alice Eichholz of Queens College, Flushing, New York, for providing us with a map to do black family history. The book notes that the records available for research are massive, and the account state by state of the materials of interest to us is probably only the tip of the iceberg. *Black Genesis* calls our attention to the genealogical collections at the Schomburg Center for Research in Black Culture at 135th Street and Lenox in New York City and The Southern Historical Collection at the University of North Carolina in Chapel Hill. The Schomburg Center has material on black life not only in the United States but also in Africa; the resources in The Southern Historical Collection are particularly strong for those southern states in which slavery was practiced.

For the past one hundred or so years, back to 1870, you can use such sources as vital records, church records, cemetery inscriptions, and census records to solve genealogical questions. You should also check the city directories for the towns in which your families lived for the surname you are tracing. Your nearby public library may have copies or be able to direct you to a collection. The city directories published before the Civil War may tell you if a person was black or may have a special code to denote a black person.

During the nineteenth century, in northern cities such as Philadelphia, New York, and Boston, beneficial societies were established for blacks. The purpose of the societies was to provide such benefits as assistance to the poor, sick, and aged as well as burial insurance. Regretfully many of the records of these societies have been lost; however, it would be useful to check the central public library in each major city for such material and the key local historical societies: in Philadelphia, The Historical Society of Pennsylvania, in New York, the New York Historical Society, and in Boston, the Massachusetts Historical Society. Furthermore, black newspapers, usually published in the larger cities and towns, should be searched for family names and information — perhaps of a birth, a wedding, or a death.

*Census Records* • Census records, available at the National Archives in Washington, D.C., or at one of the Federal Records Centers across the country, should be searched too. The first federal census was undertaken in 1790 and there is available for use at the National Archives a useful *List of Free Black Heads of Families in the First Census of the United States, 1790*. There was no special procedure for noting free blacks in the first census, so they were frequently recorded in the "other category" which also included American Indians. Furthermore, the census enumerators freely noted that a family was Negro, mulatto, or free, but some received no racial designation at all. Until 1850 only the heads of households were identified by name. For every state, until 1860, slave schedules were prepared on a county basis, with slaves recorded under the owner's name.

Incidentally, for the 1830 census you may find it helpful to consult two books prepared by the distinguished black historian Carter G. Woodson: *Free Negro Heads of Families in the United States in 1830* and *Free Negro Owners of Slaves in the United States in 1830*.

*Military Records* • The National Archives, or its branch federal records centers, should be consulted for black military records. Since the Revolutionary War, black soldiers have distinguished themselves in battle. There are several key reference tools you should look at in this regard: *List of Black Servicemen Compiled from the War Department Collection of Revolutionary War Records; The Negro in the Military Service of the United States, 1639–1886;* and an *Index to Compiled Service Records of Volunteer Union Soldiers Who Served with United States Colored Troops.* The payroll records of the Continental Army, also at the National Archives, should be checked too for military service during the Revolutionary War. You should not overlook the records of the hereditary society, Negro Descendants of the American Revolutionary War, which may be useful in your search for an ancestor.

Black persons participated in a full way in the War of 1812 (1812–15), although by the time of the Mexican American War (1846–48) army regulations had been revised to exclude blacks except as stewards, cooks, or servants. During the Civil War, more than 186,000 black soldiers served in either the Union or Confederate forces. For records of such service you should check not only the materials at the National Archives in Washington, D.C., but also at the state archives, or state library, or state historical society of the state in which the black soldier was a resident.

In the Spanish American War blacks served in the armed forces, and in World War I more than 350,000 blacks served. More than one million blacks were in the various branches of the armed forces during World War II, and thousands served in both the Korean and Vietnam wars. Again, your first step in searching for the military records of your ancestors should be the National Archives.

*The Business of Slavery* ● Slavery in the New World altered the family life the blacks had known in Africa. On the wretched sea journey in prison ships, death separated many black families. Ashore in America, in Charleston, Mobile, or New Orleans, the auction block dramatically separated spouses and children from one another. Black men and women, boys and girls, were bought and sold as a business transaction. For a black slave at work on a plantation, family life was maintained with great difficulty. Blacks were not equal, which the

Constitution assured from 1789 until Articles XIII, XIV, and XV were adopted between 1865 and 1870. Marriage was not legally binding for blacks, and family records of, for example, births, marriages, and deaths, were of little interest to the slave owner.

We talk about the need to provide proof of our family's past. This is very difficult to do for the families of slaves. Many of the detailed records of the southern plantations were lost or destroyed in the course of the Civil War. Some may remain in private hands, the descendants of slave owners. You will find some records in the state libraries, archives, and historical societies of each of the former Confederate States. However, it requires much time, patience, and not a little serendipity to find a clue or two, or more important, some evidence. In any event, before you begin your search, you must know the name of the slave owner and the location of the plantation. Should you know the names of the slaves, you will be greatly aided when consulting the plantation record books. Also, since slaves were considered property and passed from one generation to another through wills, do look at the wills, estate inventories, and tax records of the slave owners and their children; you may find important information.

There are a variety of other sources for you to pursue when attempting to establish proof of your ancestry. First, is the manumission record, a formal statement that the slave master gave to the slave declaring his freedom. Such documents may be part of a will or other legal document. These papers, although occasionally in the hands of families, are frequently found in the collections of research libraries. Second, newspapers of the day published advertisements of runaway slaves, vital information for you since each ad gave such important information as the name of the slave owner and details of the physical features and vocational skills of the slave. However, because newspapers are seldom indexed, you will need to carefully review each issue in your search for clues. Generally, back-runs of newspapers can be found at university libraries or at historical societies. Third, the station keepers of the Underground Railroad network occasionally left records of the names of those persons whom they helped to freedom. Although certain northern cities, such as New York, Philadelphia, and Pittsburgh had anti-black riots during the 1840s and 1850s, many slaves traveled on the Underground Railroad network to towns in Canada, particularly in southern Ontario. Blacks settled in towns such as Wilberforce, St. Catherines, and London. If you know the town in which your relative settled, you should write to the local historical society for information.

Mixed marriages, blacks and whites, present special problems. Such liaisons were a feature of plantation life until the end of the Civil War and in the South during the years afterward. In nearly all black families in America, there are white members. Therefore, the genealogies of the white families may be helpful to you in turning up information about your ancestors.

*Bridging the Atlantic* • Bridging the Atlantic, from the United States to Africa, is the last, and difficult, step. You need to know three important facts: First, you must identify the precise point-of-entry of the slave ship to the United States. Was it Savannah, Georgia; Charleston, South Carolina; Roanoke, Virginia; Baltimore, Maryland; Philadelphia, Pennsylvania; New York; Newport, Rhode Island; or Boston, Massachusetts? Second, you must identify the slave ship and the ports it called at on its voyage from Africa to the United States. Most of the ships stopped at ports in the West Indies, Cuba, Jamaica, Brazil, and other Latin American countries. Third, locate the port from which the ship sailed in Africa.

We recognize at the outset that connecting the family from America to Africa will be difficult. A leading scholar of the Atlantic slave trade, Professor Philip D. Curtin, has observed that possibly less than ten percent of the slaves from Africa arrived in the United States.

Many died at sea and many were sold at ports in the Caribbean and in South America. Accordingly, black families were separated from one another at every stage of their captive journey.

The African slave trade was substantially aided by the bitter conflicts between the various tribes. To make your family's connection to the other side of the Atlantic, you will need to know the general area from which your ancestor came. Since most slaves came to the Americas from West Africa, your search should focus on the nations and tribes of that region. Several of the key peoples of that area are the Guros, who live in the backcountry of the Ivory Coast; the Hausos, who populate the northwestern region of Nigeria and the eastern section of Niger; the Ibos, in the eastern region of Nigeria; the Senufo tribe, which inhabits the West Coast of Africa; and the Yorubas, who live in southwestern Nigeria and in southeastern and central Dahomey.

A trip to Africa may be necessary. Do consult the appropriate African embassies in Washington, D.C., and at United Nations headquarters in New York for help in directing you to archives and records centers in Africa.

The family tree is central to African cultural and religious life. The family, or clan, is bound entirely on kinship, from descent from a common ancestor. The small village was the stage for clan life while the tribe, which claimed for themselves descent from the same ancestor, was spread over a broader geographical area. Within the tribe, members learn the same customs and language, and learn of the several groups that compose the tribe. Tribes may be organized in two ways: ancestry may be traced through the father's line or the mother's. These ancestral systems have been significant in African cultural life since they influence education, profession, and class.

Alex Haley had the good fortune during his trip to Africa to meet a person in his ancestral village whose vocation is to commit to memory and recount orally the history of a clan or village. Although today these persons, called *griots*, work at other jobs too, they are really walking and talking libraries.

## Jewish Family History

Interest in Jewish ancestry has enjoyed the same kind of dynamic development in recent years as has that for all other national and ethnic groups. One person whose knowledge, energy, and enthusiasm has shaped in a large way the present-day curiosity about Jewish family history is Rabbi Malcolm H. Stern. By lecturing to audiences from Boston to Los Angeles and taking pen to paper to inform readers through the printed pages of various genealogical journals, he has shared with many people, both Jew and non-Jew, the fruits of his persistent and broad research efforts. His most recent contribution to our understanding of Jewish ancestry is the recently published compendium, *First American Jewish Families. 600 Genealogies, 1654–1977.* (Cincinnati, Ohio: American Jewish Archives; Waltham, Mass.: American Jewish Historical Society, 1978). A massive project, Rabbi Stern's book treats in alphabetical order by surname nearly forty thousand individuals, generally Sephardic Jews, whose ancestors settled in what is today the United States between 1654 and 1840. He notes such details as dates and places of births, marriages and deaths, and military service. It is an important work not only for Jews but also for non-Jews, since during the past three hundred and twenty-five years there have been many marriages between the groups.

Persons of Jewish ancestry must accomplish the basic research tasks facing all family historians before they can direct their attention to special problems: talking with a family member who has kept alive the family's history; gathering copies of birth, marriage, and death records in the United States; searching synagogue and cemetery records, as well as checking for information regarding the immigration and naturalization of family

members. You should not overlook federal census and
military records for details, as well as ships' passenger
lists, city directories, and obituaries.

Another important book on Jewish genealogy which
has appeared in recent years is *The Unbroken Chain: Biographical Sketches and the Genealogy of Illustrious Jewish
Families from the 15th–20th Century*, by Dr. Neil Rosenstein (New York, 1976). Beginning with Rabbi Meir, the
talmudic scholar of fifteenth-century Padua, Italy, the
author, records the many lines of the Katzenellenbogen
family descendants to the present day. The account
bridges not only the centuries but also national boundaries and the seas as the author examines four hundred
years of genealogical history.

Jewish emigration from Europe to the western hemi-
sphere began in the sixteenth century in the Spanish
and Portuguese territories of Latin America. By 1641 a
Jewish congregation was organized in the Dutch city of
Recife in Brazil. The Portuguese forced the Dutch out of
their South American colony in 1654, prompting many
Jews to return to Holland while others settled in the
West Indies and one small group moved to New
Amsterdam. Four years later a Jewish community was
established in Newport, Rhode Island, and in the 1730s,
40s, 50s, and 60s Jewish settlements were founded in
Savannah, Philadelphia, Charleston, and Montreal. Although the earliest of the Jewish colonists were
Spanish or Portuguese origin, Jews of German origin
were represented, too. There were major waves of
Jewish immigration to America during the 1840s and 50s
from German states and Austria in the wake of revolution in those countries and from eastern Europe, particularly Poland and Russia between 1880 and 1920. The
movement of America's frontier westward also found
Jewish families moving to and settling in inland cities
during the nineteenth century, cities such as Cincinnati,
Chicago, St. Paul, St. Louis, and San Francisco. Emigration was nearly brought to a halt after 1924, as the

United States Immigration Law set quotas on the number of immigrants from each country who could enter the United States.

Special exceptions have been made during the last half century to the number of Jews allowed to enter and settle in America: during the 1930s and Hitler's policy of suppressing Jews in Germany; following the Hungarian revolt of 1956; and during the 1960s and 70s in response to Russia's harassment and persecution of Jews.

Before striking out on your own, read the very valuable book, *Finding Our Fathers: A Guidebook to Jewish Genealogy* (New York, 1977) by Dan Rottenberg. Prompted by the study of his own family's history, this manual is indispensable for the study of your Jewish ancestors. He identifies the libraries and archives throughout the United States and in key countries overseas that have materials in their collections relating to Jewish families.

Rottenberg calls attention to the microfilm collections of the Genealogical Society of Utah in Salt Lake City which are of help, not only to Mormons, but to many people seeking to compile their family's story. He notes the strengths of the American Jewish Archives, 3101 Clifton Avenue, Cincinnati, Ohio 45220, the American Jewish Historical Society, 2 Thornton Road, Waltham, Mass. 02154, and the YIVO Institute for Jewish Research, 1048 Fifth Avenue, New York, New York 10028, whose collections are strongest for families with origins in East European Jewish communities. The resources of the Leo Baeck Institute, 129 East 73rd Street, New York, New York 10021, which focus on German-speaking Jews and their European cultural ties, is recognized too.

Overseas, the Central Archives for the History of the Jewish People, Sprinzak Building, Hebrew University (Givat Ram Campus), P.O. Box 1149, Jerusalem, Israel, has gathered from around the world registers and records relating to Jewish history in the Diaspora from the twelfth century to the present. It is a very important collection of family histories, town-by-town registration of Jewish births, marriages, and deaths in Germany between 1800 and 1876. The bulk of the materials in the Central Archives comes from Germany, Austria, France, and Italy. The Yad Vashem Archives Har Hazikaron, P.O. Box 84, Jerusalem, gathers materials on Jewish persons and communities that were destroyed during the Nazi Holocaust. It is especially rich with materials on Eastern European Jews, in particular the *yizkor* (memory books), books for some six hundred East European towns.

Jewish naming practices do present some difficulties in compiling your family story. It was uncommon for Jews in Germany and Europe to have a surname until early in the nineteenth century, although some Jews in Spain, Portugal, and Italy had family names since the tenth and eleventh centuries. Also after family names were introduced, persons frequently modified or changed their names when they moved from one country to another. Some Jews, having fled Europe, anglicized their name upon arrival in America, making it very difficult now to trace their origins. Do look at the section of Dan Rottenberg's book entitled "Alphabetical List of Family Names" for a more comprehensive discussion of this matter, as well as the fascinating and valuable book by Rabbi Benzion C. Kaganoff, *A Dictionary of Jewish Names and Their History* (New York, 1977).

Before we leave this part of our discussion about researching our family's story, we should urge you to look at two periodicals that publish articles of interest to persons with Jewish ancestry. The first publication, the *American Jewish Historical Quarterly*, has appeared since 1892 and has printed on its pages many genealogies, biographies, and vital records. Since 1977 a bimonthly publication *Toledot: The Journal of Jewish Genealogy* has appeared; it has become a vital reference work in the field.

## England

The era of Henry VIII in England (1509–47) witnessed the introduction of a systematic effort to maintain public

records. Beginning in 1538 Thomas Cromwell, Vicar
General to Henry VIII, ordered that parish records
should be kept in the churches of England and Wales.
The local clergy were to keep records of births, marriages, and burials within their parishes. Before 1837
when civil registration was introduced in England, it is
essential for you to search parish registers for information about your ancestors. The records of baptisms,
marriages, and deaths remain in the hands today of the
clergyman of the particular Church of England parish.
Should you know the name of the particular parish in
which your ancestor lived, write to the priest in charge
of the church. Incidentally, sometimes the early parish
registers have been deposited in the diocesan headquarters or the local or county record offices. However, the
parish priest is responsible for the materials and should
be able to answer your questions.

We have mentioned here only the records kept by the
priests of the established church, but, we ask ourselves,
"Where will I find the records of Baptist, Presbyterian,
and Methodist churches?" The records may be found in
two places. First, beginning in 1695 it was required by all
persons in England under the terms of the Registration
Act, except for Quakers, Jews, and many Roman
Catholics, to register their family's births, marriages, and
deaths with the Anglican minister in charge of the local
parish. Thus you should also check this source for family information. Second, many of the records of non-
Church of England churches can be found at the Public
Record Office in Chancery Lane in London. For Baptist
records you should also check the famous Dr. Williams
Library, Gordon Square, London. The Society of
Friends maintains records in the library at its headquarters, Friends House, Euston Road, London, N.W.1. A
number of Catholic records have been published by the
Catholic Record Society through the years: inquiries
should be sent to the Secretary, Catholic Record Society,
Archbishop's House, Westminster, London, S.W.1.

Since there are no Jewish registers deposited in the Public Record Office, you may find it helpful to seek assistance from the Board of Deputies of British Jews, Woburn House, Upper Woburn Place, London, W.C.1.

For information about your ancestor who was born, married, or died since 1 July 1837, you should pursue your research at St. Catherine's House, London. The required records for civil registrations of England and Wales are kept there. The address to which you write is: Register General, General Register Office, St. Catherine's House, 10 Kingsway, London WC2 1LR.

When requesting information from this office, or from any civil registration office in any country for that matter, supply as many of the basic details as you can about your ancestor. For example, when seeking a copy of a birth certificate, you should give the first and middle names, the family (surname) *at* birth (since it may have been changed for one reason or another later), day, month, year, and place of birth, full name and family name of father, father's occupation, and mother's maiden name. You may not have in hand all of this information, but provide as much as possible. We hasten to add that in England it is possible to obtain two kinds of birth certificates: a complete one, which states all the data we have just noted and a short certificate, which is nearly useless to a genealogist because of its key purpose of protecting the illegitimate from knowledge of their parents.

When seeking copies of marriage certificates, do try to give the first name and family name of the groom as well as the bride's first name and family name, and, of course, the date and place of the wedding. The certificates include additional helpful information such as noting whether it was a second marriage for either party, and the current addresses, occupations, names and family names of the fathers of the bride and groom.

For copies of death certificates, it is most helpful if you can supply the first name, family name at death, date and place of death (which, incidentally, need not be the deceased's residence), age, occupation, and marital status.

The first census in England and Wales that is useful for genealogical purposes was taken in 1841. The 1851 census records the full names, exact names, and relationship of each member of the household to the head. Also recorded was the sex, occupation, and birthplace of each person recorded in the return. Microfilm copies of the census returns for 1861 and 1871 are also available for research, and they may be consulted at the Public Record Office in London. Although there is no charge for examining the microfilm records in person, a fee is required if searches are requested by correspondence.

We all know of the assistance that wills provide us in researching our family history. Since 1 January 1858 a copy of every will proved in England and Wales has been deposited at the Principal Probate Registry, Somerset House, London WC2 1LR. A photocopy of a will can be requested at a modest cost. Before 1858 our problems in locating wills are somewhat more complicated, since wills were generally proved in church and manor courts. These records are now deposited either in county or local records offices, or in the Lambeth Palace Library in London, or in the Public Record Office. Before undertaking your search for an ancestor's English will, read Anthony J. Camp's important book *Wills and Their Whereabouts*.

Several reference books that no doubt would be of help to you as you plan and pursue your investigation of ancestors in England are Anthony Camp's *The Genealogists' Handbook* (London, 1969) and his *Tracing Your Ancestors* (London, 1972), or his *Everyone Has Roots* (London, 1978), as well as David E. Gardner and Frank Smith's instructive work, *Genealogical Research in England and Wales*. For students who have advanced experience with materials in libraries and county records offices, I suggest Sir Anthony R. Wagner's *English Genealogy* (second edition, Oxford, 1972).

As in the United States and Canada, numerous genealogical and family history societies have been established throughout England during the past ten or fifteen years. The flagship of these organizations is the Society of Genealogists which maintains its headquarters and library at 37 Harrington Gardens, London, SW7 4JX, England, and publishes the excellent periodical *The Genealogists' Magazine*, which is devoted to special problems of genealogy, genealogical methods, as well as extracts from various kinds of source material. The Society of Genealogists has focused its work on developing a collection of typescript and manuscript copies of parish registers and indexes of these for its readers' use.

## Wales

A comment or two about Wales and Welsh records is in order. Since 1535 England and Wales have been administratively united, and, accordingly, Welsh records and family papers have found their way into libraries and records offices in both Wales and England. An excellent guide to introduce you to Welsh genealogical research is David E. Gardner and Frank Smith's book, *Genealogical Research in England and Wales*. The National Library of Wales at Aberystwyth has received through the years many important genealogical collections, including court records and parish registers. The British Library at Kew in London and the Public Record Office also in London should be consulted, too, for resources. Do keep in mind that you must cover the same sort of ground and sources pursuing your Welsh ancestors as you do for your English family members: search parish registers, check for civil registrations, censuses, wills, and land records, naval and military records.

## Scotland

The history of a country, region, or town complements and supplements our genealogical research. It is always essential for us to acquaint ourselves with the history of the area and times in which our ancestors lived in hopes of understanding the rhythms and events that shaped or bruised their lives. The history of Scotland is at once complex, dramatic, and colorful: a nation formed politically and culturally by its many clans at home and by early Norse invasions and English wars triggered from abroad. A useful introduction to the social history of this great country and its people is T. Christopher Smout's book, *A History of the Scottish People, 1560–1830* (London, 1969). A more detailed account is the multi-volume work, *The Edinburgh History of Scotland*, sponsored by Edinburgh University and under the general editorship of the distinguished historian Professor Gordon Donaldson.

There are several tools to use in finding one's way to and through the various records in Scotland as one compiles information about the family's past. Before you launch your research efforts, be sure to consult Margaret Stuart's book *Scottish Family History*. It is a very helpful guide to many reference works on the history and genealogy of Scottish families. Do not overlook Joan P. S. Ferguson's volume, *Scottish Family Histories held in Scottish libraries*; she lists existing books and in the libraries in Scotland where they may be found. Another particularly useful introduction to research in Scotland is Gerald Hamilton Edward's, *Tracing Your British Ancestors: A Guide to Genealogical Sources*, second edition. His account on resources in Scotland for the study of family history is at once comprehensive and suggestive. Another valuable guidebook in your search for Scottish ancestors is Donald J. Steel's *Sources for Scottish Genealogy and Family History* (London, 1970).

Generally, parish registers in Scotland do not record baptisms, marriages, or burials earlier than 1700. The registers are of the parishes of the Kirk of Scotland, the Established Presbyterian church. We should call to your attention the fact that unlike Great Britain, Scotland has no county record offices and only a handful of the large cities maintain archivists to look after their records: consequently, there has been a considerable centralization of local records in the Scottish Record Office. At the New Register House in Edinburgh, the registers from the more than nine hundred parishes in Scotland have been gathered for safe-keeping and research use. Another possibly important source of information about your family may be the Kirk Session Papers. Maintained by the local church minister, these records list the names and dates persons received letters of permission to leave the parish to move to another village or town or perhaps to the United States or Nova Scotia.

Since 1855 Scotland has required the civil registration of births, marriages, and deaths, and you may request copies of these records from the Register General, New Register House, Edinburgh EH1 3YT, Scotland. Census records are available for use in Scotland after seventy years, which means you can use the materials on your ancestors in the 1901, 1891, and earlier decennial censuses. These also may be consulted at the New Register House.

Scottish law and legal terms are somewhat different from the procedures and language used in, say, England or the United States. You will want to be aware of such differences when you consult land records or wills and estate papers. Before 1836 Scottish wills were proved before the Commissary Courts, an old ecclesiastical court that operated in a similar fashion to those in England until 1858. After 1830 jurisdiction in matters relating to marriage, divorce, and legitimacy was transferred to the Court of Sessions from the Commissary Court. Should you wish to check on a will relating to one of your ancestors, again, make inquiry at the New Register House. Registers of land sales and transfers since the early seventeenth century exist and are available at the Scottish Record Office, P.O. Box 36, H.M. General Register House, Edinburgh EH1 3YT, Scotland.

The role of Scottish emigration to the New World — to Nova Scotia and Prince Edward Island in Canada, and to Virginia, the Carolinas, New York, and elsewhere in what is today the United States — is a story of hope and tragedy, of achievement and disillusionment in new places overseas and in familiar neighborhoods in Scotland. Our understanding of this migration is greatly aided by Professor Gordon Donaldson's book *The Scots Overseas* (London, 1966) and the excellent volume by Professor Charles W. Dunn of Harvard University *Highland Settler: A Portrait of the Scottish Gael in Nova Scotia* (Toronto, 1953).

## Republic of Ireland

Immediately we must acknowledge that the turbulent course of Irish history, crowned by the burning of the Public Record Office in Dublin on 13 April 1922, has created irreparable gaps in our knowledge of Irish genealogy. Not all of Ireland's records were burned in the wake of the civil war, since many records had not been sent to Dublin but remained in the hands of local authorities. The fire in 1922 destroyed about one thousand Protestant parish registers, bishops' transcripts, civil registrations, census returns, wills, and estate papers — records that were not available in any other depository either in Ireland or in London. Consequently, searching for your Irish ancestors is a difficult task. It is important for you to have a basic understanding of the civil and ecclesiastical organization of Ireland before and after the division of the country in 1922. You may find on the United States immigration records that your ancestor noted his birthplace in Ireland, or stated the province, county, parish, or diocese in which he was born or lived before coming to the United States. At the Registrar General's Office, Old Customs House, Dublin, you will find arranged on a county basis births, marriages, and death records since 1864 because such information had to be registered. Protestant marriages were registered from 1 April 1845.

Because England governed Ireland until 1922, the favored religious denomination was the Church of England, which practiced the liturgy and doctrine of the Anglican tradition; parish registers for Roman Catholic churches are sparse. Records for Catholic and Church of

Ireland parishes are generally in the hands of the particular parish priest, and you should make inquiries to the priest in charge of the congregation of which your ancestor was a member.

The Public Record Office of Ireland (Oifig Iris Puibli), Four Courts, Dublin 7, has microfilm copies of church registers, both Catholic and Protestant, and some manuscript collections of genealogical interest such as the abstracts compiled from wills by Sr. William Betham, Ulster, extracts from parish registers, and many collections of family papers. Also the National Library of Ireland, Kildare Street, Dublin, has a substantial collection of printed and manuscript materials relating to Irish family history.

An excellent reference guide to assist you in your research work in the Republic of Ireland and Northern Ireland is Margaret Dickson Falley's two-volume *Irish and Scotch-Irish Ancestral Research: A Guide to the Genealogical Records, Methods and Sources in Ireland*. It is an indispensable survey of the public records, church records, printed books, and manuscript collections available throughout Ireland and Northern Ireland. In particular, we urge you to read Mrs. Falley's instructive chapter "Preliminary Research in the United States" before attempting research efforts anywhere in Ireland; her suggestions will provide you with the necessary framework to build your story. Another readable and suggestive handbook is the volume prepared by Heraldic Artists Ltd. of Dublin, *Handbook on Irish Genealogy: How to Trace Your Ancestors and Relatives in Ireland*.

### NORTHERN IRELAND

Until 6 December 1921 the six northern counties that are a part of the United Kingdom were a part of Ireland, and the public records were at the office of the Registrar General in Dublin. Since 1922 such records for Northern Ireland are kept at the Central Registry Office, Fermanagh House, Ormean Avenue, Belfast BT2 8HX.

The registration of marriages, except Roman Catholic

marriages, began on 1 April 1845, and of births, deaths, and Roman Catholic marriages on 1 January 1864. These records are in the hands of local registrars and clergymen. The Public Record Office in Belfast has some materials before 1922 of genealogical interest: wills and probate records, Tithe Apportionment Books, Poll Tax Records, Militia Yeomanry and Muster Rolls, parish registers for the Church of Ireland, Roman Catholic, and Methodist, etc. churches, Voters Poll, and some census records.

## Scandinavia: Sweden, Norway, Denmark, Iceland, and Finland

Many Americans, particularly in the farming and urban communities of the middle-west and far-west, have ancestral roots in one or more of the Scandinavian countries. Indeed, during the nineteenth century 1,228,000 Swedes migrated to the New World, as did 814,000 Norwegians, 340,000 Danes, and 22,000 Finns. The figure for Finland is somewhat misleading since immigrants from that country were included with the statistics for Sweden before 1918. Because Iceland was a dependency of Denmark until 1944, the figures for immigrants from that country are included in the category for Danes.

Research in the Scandinavian countries is a pleasure because the public records have been so efficiently maintained through the centuries. If you know the name of your Swedish ancestor and the place in Sweden where he or she lived before traveling to America, you will find numerous sources to assist you in your hunt.

Since 1686 ministers have been required by law to maintain parish records. Occasionally you will find useful church records before 1686. The pages of the church registers, when they were earnestly kept, include much information of a genealogical interest. You will find not only records of births, marriages, and deaths, but also communion records and notes regarding the movements of persons in and out of the parish. Since about

1750 the household examination rolls contain records of the households in the parish, including all their members. After World War II, in 1946, certain revisions were introduced into the system of keeping parish records: a record of each individual is completed in the parish, and when he or she moves, it is sent to the parish where he or she now lives. If he or she dies or emigrates, the record is deposited in the Central Bureau of Statistics in Stockholm. When the parish records do not contain the information you need to locate, pursue your research at the regional district and city archives. The national archive, Riksarkivet, located in Stockholm may be useful, although it is primarily a depository for papers of the central government and its various agencies, the parliament, courts, and certain notable families. Census materials and real estate books are also included in the collections of the Riksarkivet.

In Norway church records should be consulted as noted. They hold the usual information about baptisms, marriages, and deaths as well as the confirmation dates of persons and the movements of people in and out of the parish. The parishes were ordered to keep registers beginning in 1687 and are now under the supervision of the Central Bureau of Statistics in Oslo.

The census records at the national archives, Riksarkivet, are particularly useful after 1865 because the place of birth of the individual was first recorded by the census-taker for the census of that year. Norway has undertaken a census of its population nearly every tenth year since 1801 and without interruption since 1890.

Regional state archives are located in seven cities of Norway and preserve wills that have been proved in the courts of the district as well as the records of the Probate Court. The oldest registers of the Probate Court date from 1660.

### DENMARK

Like Sweden and Norway, parish registers are the most important tool for research in Denmark. The clergy were required by law in 1645 to keep records of the vital statistics of the parish, although frequently you will find that parish registers were kept as early as 1600. After 1814 the state ordered that two copies of parish registers should be kept, one by the clergyman of the parish and the second by the local teacher. Parish registers before 1891 are collected in four regional register offices. Copenhagen, Aabenraa, Viborg, and Odense. Since 1831 the procedure has been to deposit one copy of the registers for the past thirty years in the archives after being completed.

The Danish State Archives Department in Copenhagen is the key national archives. Founded in 1889, the Riksarkivet maintains the records of the various departments and agencies of the government.

## ICELAND

From 1380 to 1944, Iceland was a possession of Denmark. Now an independent nation, its records are marked by the style and procedures practiced in Denmark. The records of births, confirmations, marriages, and deaths were kept by the clergy by royal decree since 1746. The clergy are required to file an annual report to the Statistical Bureau of Iceland, and all parish records are deposited with the national archives, Thjodskjalosfr Islands, in Reykjavik. Copies of wills are also deposited in the archives. In 1703 a census of Iceland was undertaken to record the name, occupation, residence, and age of every person in Iceland. The 1816 census return was the first to note place of birth. Besides the census records, and Iceland undertook a census nearly every ten years between 1703 and 1960, you should also check church records for information.

A useful book for families in the United States and Canada of Icelandic descent is Olafur S. Thorgeisson's *Almanach Fyrir*. Published in 1895, it notes genealogical and historical information for many of the nineteenth-century Icelandic settlers.

## FINLAND

Finland has historical ties to both eastern Europe and Sweden. Finland was conquered by Sweden in 1157, and the Swedish language, religion, and civilization have markedly influenced cultural development in Finland. Until 1809 Finland was under Swedish control; then control passed to Russia. After World War I and a brief military regency, Finland received its independence.

Church registers are important tools for undertaking Finnish genealogical research. Following the pattern of record-keeping throughout Scandinavia, the parish registers record in chronological order the births, marriages, deaths, and moves in and out of the parish. Dating from about 1650, the National Archives, Valtionarkisto/Riksarkivet PL274, SF-00171, Helsinki 17, Finland, has in its collections copies of all pre-1850 church registers.

Civil records date back only to 1918 and they are not compulsory. Citizens can choose either civil or church registrations for births, marriages, and deaths, but not both procedures.

An interesting tool for Finnish genealogical research is Alf Brenner's book *Slaktforskning: Praktisk Handbok for Finland*.

## The Netherlands

Since the settlement of New Netherlands (New York) in 1624, there has been a close relationship between the Dutch and Americans. As elsewhere on the European continent, the Dutch churches, Protestant and Catholic, maintained registers, and these have been placed in the various national archives located in each of the provincial capitals. After the conquest of the Netherlands by Napoleon in 1811, civil registration was introduced. These records are preserved in several locations: the Central Archives of the State, Algemeen Rijksarchief, Bleijenburg 7's Gravenhage, Netherlands, and at eleven excellent and helpful provincial archives. With the aid of excellent register indexes you are able to put your hand on much genealogical information, at least to 1811, in a speedy manner. Another key aid is the Bevolking register (population register), which notes the ancestry in all directions of the entire population of Holland as far back as 1811. Write to the Central Archives for information and you will be directed, when necessary, to the appropriate provincial or town archive. Beginning in 1850 each town kept a register noting details about the persons who lived in the community. It is a very useful resource for information on family members, since the period of heavy Dutch immigration occurred after that date.

A word of caution: one of the difficulties in Dutch genealogy is that before 1811 there were few real surnames. Patronymics were in use but not surnames. Napoleon's decree that all should take names and register them has produced to the present nearly 87,000 family names in Holland. By careful analysis of the names you can determine the region of origin, which may give you a clue to the area of your family's residence.

## Belgium

During the period between 1500 and 1830 Belgium was at one time or another under Spanish, Austrian, French, and Dutch rule and, accordingly, Belgian records were removed to other lands. Before 1795 the local parish priests maintained registers of baptisms, marriages, and burials, and these are now deposited either in the state archives or in town or commune halls. More recent parish registers remain in the hands of the local priest. The French introduced civil registration in 1795, and these records are kept at the town and commune halls throughout the country. The Archives Générales du Royaume, rue de Ruysbroeck 2–6 1000 — Brussels, Belgium has many materials of genealogical interest. Included in its collections are some parish registers, many family archives, and a variety of state judicial and administrative papers of assistance in family research.

## France

One of the benefits of the French Revolution for genealogists was the introduction in France in 1789 of civil registration for births, marriages, deaths, and divorces. The records have been preserved in the communes, and you may write to the Office of the Mayor of the appropriate town for copies of your ancestor's birth and marriage records.

The Catholic Church maintained parish registers for baptisms, marriages, and burials before the French Revolution. The local parish priest was required to keep such a record of his parishioners since the sixteenth century. Pre-1789 parish registers have been deposited in the archives of each municipality. Since 1789 the parish priests have continued their practice of maintaining records, but they now keep one record in the parish and forward another to the headquarters of the bishop of the diocese. In searching for your French ancestors, as in any other country, it is important to know the department (département) of origin to aid the archivist in informing you of your relative's commune of origin.

The Archives Nationales de France, 60 rue des Frances-Bourgeois, 75141 Paris CEDEX 03, should be consulted for such information as immigration records (including ships' passenger lists), military records, and some property and probate records.

There are many publications available to assist you in your French genealogical research. The following are of particular interest: *Bibliographie Généalogique Heraldique et Nobiliaire de la France* by Gaston Saffroy (3 vols., 1970, 1974) and Pierre Durge's *Genealogy: An Introduction to Continental Concepts*, translated into English by Wilson O. Clough.

## Switzerland

Before 1848 civil registration in Switzerland was in the hands of each of the three political units, the cantons — Uri, Schwyz, and Nidevalden. The churches actually carried out the responsibility until 1876 when the duty was taken over by the civil authorities. Birth, marriage, and death records for the period between 1834 and 1875 were deposited in the registry office of each canton.

Censuses of families living in particular parish areas have been listed in Haushaltungsregisters which provide such data as the names, dates, and places of birth of family members: parents, grandparents, brothers, and sisters. This source of information should be supplemented by checking for related family certificates (Familienschein) at the Zivilstandesamt. At the place of citizenship in Switzerland, family details are recorded and maintained for several generations.

## Spain

The genealogical resources in Spain are indeed rich. The Catholic parish registers are acknowledged to be the oldest in Europe. Beginning in 1570 the parish priests were charged to note the baptisms, marriages, and burials in their parishes. In fact, more than 1,600 of the 19,000 Spanish parishes have registers that record information before 1570. A useful handbook about the Spanish Catholic church, *The Guidebook of the Spanish Church*, published by the General Office of Information and Statistics of the Church, lists all the parishes in Spain, noting their dioceses and the date of the earliest register for baptisms, marriages, and burials. You may inquire at the public library or Spanish Consul's headquarters to learn if they have a copy of the book.

In 1870 civil registrations began in Spain under the supervision of the justices of municipalities, of districts, and of the peace. The municipalities maintain the records today, and you will want to make your inquiries to the town office in the particular town in which your ancestor resided.

For assistance on Spanish family research, there is a very useful institution in Madrid which you should consult either by correspondence or during a visit to Spain. It is the Instituto Internacional de Genealogiá y Heraldica, y Federación de Corporaciones Afines (the International Institute of Genealogy and Heraldry and Federation of Similar Corporations). You should address your correspondence to Apartado de Correos 12, 079, Madrid, Spain.

For Spanish American families, that is Latin American families, you should consult the *Enciclopedia Heraldica y Genealogica: Hispano-Americana* by Alberto and Arturo Garciá Caraffa. It is a significant compilation of the histories of many families in Spain and Latin America.

## Portugal

Like Spain, Portugal has much material that is helpful in the preparation of a family history. Parish registers in many instances date back to at least 1570. During the past century, the registers were to be kept in the civil registry office, or the central archives in Lisbon, or in the district archives. However, not all the parish registers have been so neatly deposited, and the best course to follow would be to send an inquiry to the central archives. The address is Arquiro dos Registos Paroquiais, Rua dos Prazeres 41 — r/c, Lisbon, 2, Portugal.

Civil registration began in 1878 and the registers are under the supervision of local officials. Since there was a form of civil registration in Portugal between 1832 and 1878, you should send inquiries to the Inspector Superior of Libraries and Archives; there is one in every county for information regarding records for this forty-five-year period. For details regarding birth, filial descent, marriage, pre-nuptial contracts, deaths, emancipation, care or guardianship of minors, write to the Direccâo-Geral do Registo e Notariodo do Ministerio da Justiçia, Lisbon, Portugal. Incidentally, records are available for Portuguese citizens and for foreigners residing in Portuguese territory.

The Arquiro Nacional da Torre do Tombo (National Archives) has in its collections materials of genealogical interest. You will find not only early Portuguese parish registers but also wills. We hasten to add that many old registers were lost in the Lisbon earthquake of 1755, but some survived and others have been deposited since that disaster.

## Italy

More than 4,775,000 Italians migrated to the United States between 1820 and 1920. Italian Americans who seek to locate information about their family in Italy will find that genealogical research is, at best, difficult. Until 1870 when it was united under King Victor Emmanuel II, Italy was composed of many separate states. Consequently, for our purposes, the keeping of records was fragmented. The first national census was undertaken in 1861 and has been repeated at ten-year intervals. Since 1851 there has been civil registration of births, marriages, and deaths, but the records are best kept for the period since 1870. For information on a civil registration, write to the Vital Statistics Office of the particular town where your ancestor's birth, marriage, or death took place. For census information you should write to the Istituto Centrale di Statistica, Via Balbo 16 00100, Rome, Italy.

Before 1870 and civil registration, church registers are our best source. Many of the parish record books remain to this day in the hands of the local parish priest. Some registers have been transferred to the custody of the local bishop and the diocesan archives.

Incidentally, do not overlook the collections at the town libraries or offices of the State Archives located in many towns throughout the nation, since both institutions may have information relating to the history of local families.

## Germany

More than 6,250,000 Germans have migrated to America since the mid-eighteenth century. However, the peak period for immigration was the eighty-year period between 1820 and 1900, when more than 5,000,000 Germans made their way to the United States to establish new homes. The difficult path to follow to do research in Germany has been made considerably easier recently with the publication of Professor Clifford Neal Smith and Anna Piszczan-Czaja Smith's *Encyclopedia of German-American Research* and *American Genealogical Resources in German Archives* (1976, 1977). Begin by reading the final section in the *Encyclopedia of German-American Research* entitled ''German-American Genealogy.'' These two books should be consulted before pursuing serious research in Germany either in person or by correspondence.

Divided for more than four centuries by religion, Catholic and Protestant, and until 1871 by numerous political states, today Germany is divided as it has been since the close of World War II into two geographical and political areas: the Federal Republic of Germany (Bonn) and the Democratic Republic of Germany (East Berlin). A successful research should be acquainted with the contours of the country's history.

It is best to know if your ancestor was a Protestant or a Catholic. Parish records begin to be numerous about 1550 and remain in the hands of either the local parish or the bishop of the diocese. Civil registration was begun on 1 January 1876 and each community in Germany had to have its own registry office (Standesamt). Births, marriages, and deaths are recorded at these offices. Each town has its own archives as does every German province, and you will want to search both repositories to find information useful to you in your quest for genealogical records.

### Austria

Until 1938 the parishes in Austria registered births, marriages, and deaths. Record-keeping dates from about 1550, although occasionally you will find earlier baptismal registers. To locate the numerous parishes in the country, consult the *Austrian Official Calendar*, a printed book that is available in key libraries and at the Austrian consulates. For Protestant church records, and some do exist, send a letter of inquiry to the High Church Council, Vienna I, Schellinggasse 12, Austria. It is the administrative agency for several Protestant denominations.

For civil registrations since 1938, write to the appropriate town registry office for your information.

### Poland

During the period between 1572 and 1795, Poland fell prey to the political designs of her powerful neighbors — Russia, Prussia, and Austria. In fact, after 1795 and until 1918 Poland disappeared from the map of Europe. After World War I and the establishment of the Treaty of Versailles, Poland became an independent state. For our purposes it is important to acknowledge that Polish record-keeping varied according to the interests of the occupying nation. In brief, before 1918 the clergy maintained the vital records in the area ruled by Russia; in the Austrian-dominated territory, the parish clergy were treated as state officials; in the Prussian section, the records were kept by public officials. To find our way through the maze of political interests to the necessary records, it is essential to know the voivodship (wojewodzkie), meaning roughly county, in which your ancestor resided. Looking at a map of Poland, we can recognize that the Prussian-governed area included the western and northern voivodships and the northern section of the Katowice voivodship; the Russian territory covered the eastern voivodships and the eastern area of Bialystok voivodship; and the Austrians dominated the central and Silesian voivodships. Parish records may exist for a period before 1795, but little is known about that material.

It was not until after World War II, in 1946, that civil registration was introduced for the entire nation. However, should your ancestors have lived in Warsaw, where civil records were introduced about 1870, you may request a copy of the records of births or marriages from either the Vital Statistics Office for Central Warsaw (Urzad Stanu Cyivilnego, Warszawa-Strodmiescie) or from the Vital Statistics Office for Praga (Urzad Stanu Cyivilnego, Warszawa-Praga), depending on the exact area in which the birth or marriage occurred. If your ancestor was born or married in a city outside of Warsaw, you should request a copy of the appropriate record from the local Vital Statistics Office. For other communities in Poland a copy of the records can be obtained from the Communal Vital Statistics Office (Urzad Stanu Cyivilnego, Gminnej Rady Narodowej) established for the town or village.

### Albania, Bulgaria, Greece, and Rumania

The shadow of Turkish domination of the Balkan peninsula between 1460 and 1912 resulted in an unevenness in the public records of use for genealogical information. Before declaring its independence from the Turks in 1912, Albania's vital records were maintained by the clergy of the parishes of the Roman Catholic and orthodox churches. The Muslims are a sizable minority of the population, but their records were not as carefully maintained as those of the Christian churches. This procedure was followed until 1929 when civil registration was set up in each municipality. Unfortunately, many church records have been destroyed by the Communists, making it exceedingly difficult to search for one's ancestors.

Bulgaria reached partial independence in 1878 at the close of the Russo-Turkish Wars and full independence in 1908 under the rule of Prince Ferdinand of Saxe-Coburg-Gotha. In 1860 the Bulgarian Church became independent of the Greek Church and parish registers were introduced. Certificates of baptisms and marriages can be obtained from the church where the ceremony occurred. The maintenance of civil vital records did not begin until 1893, and these records, of births and marriages, are filed in the office of the appropriate district People's Council where the event took place.

Parish registers of the Greek Orthodox Church provide the genealogical researcher in Greece with helpful information. Only since 1912 has it been required by law for registers to be maintained in all of the parishes: records of baptisms, marriages, and deaths. Earlier church records, should there be any, will probably, at best, be incomplete. Civil registration began in 1925, and births are recorded in special registration offices in each city and town. Marriage certificates are issued by the metropolitan, a church official, in the area in which the wedding took place. For assistance regarding civil registrations of your family members, write to: Recording Office, Ministry of the Interior, 57 Punepistimiou Avenue, Athens, Greece, and for inquiries relating to church records, write to: Greek Orthodox Archdiocese, 21 Aghias Filotheis Street, Athens, Greece.

In 1831 civil registration was established in Rumania and the registers were kept by the clergy of the parishes of the Orthodox Church. Until 1865 the clergy recorded the births, marriages, and deaths in their neighborhood when the duty was passed on to offices in the city or town government. However, the clergy were required to continue to maintain registers in their churches of baptisms, marriages, and burials. Before it became compulsory to keep these registers, the churches had maintained their own records of births, marriages, and deaths. In Transylvania, civil registration was introduced in 1895. Before that date civil records were listed in the parish registers. You may obtain request copies of civil records from the Office of Vital Statistics (Oficiul Staru Civile) of the People's Council (Sfatul Popular) of the particular community in which your ancestor was born, married, or died.

## Yugoslavia

As elsewhere on the European continent, parish registers were kept in Catholic and Protestant churches. Beginning in 1895 civil registration was established in the territory of Voivodina, and since 1946 it has been the law throughout Yugoslavia. The State Secretariat for Internal Affairs compiles the information provided by persons concerning births, marriages, deaths, adoptions, etc. Birth certificates are issued by the Registrar of the People's Committee in the appropriate village, town, or city.

## Czechoslovakia

Composed of the former countries of Bohemia, Moravia, Slovakia, Ruthenia, and Silesia, the Czechoslovakia we know today was formed by the Treaty of Versailles following World War I. Again, as for every other European nation, parish registers, both Catholic and Protestant, are important resources in Czechoslovakia. It was not until after World War I, in 1918, that civil registration was introduced in a limited way, limited because it was not required of church members. The state in 1950 took over the duty of recording vital statistics, and copies of records of births and marriages may be obtained from the office of the Local National Committee in the community in which the event occurred. Incidentally, when the state took over the parish registers in 1950, they were deposited in the various district archives. Should you seek information from a parish register make a request to Central State Archives (Státní Ústřední Archiv, Karmelitská 2 Prague I, Czechoslovakia). The embassy of the Czechoslovak Socialist Republic, 3900 Linnean Avenue, N.W., Washington, D.C. undertakes to issue documents regarding the birth, marriage, or death of a Czech ancestor. Write to the embassy about this service and the fees charged and any other genealogical research with which they may be able to assist you.

An exceedingly helpful tool for genealogical research in Czechoslovakia is Olga K. Miller's book *Genealogical Research for Czech and Slovak Americans*. The author identifies a variety of sources for research in Czechoslovakia, such as land records, census materials, and military records, as well as directing the reader to the location of the many county and state archives.

## Union of Soviet Socialist Republics

Since the ninth century Russia has played a key military and political role in eastern Europe and in the Balkan countries. Millions of persons have come under Russian jurisdiction in their daily lives, and that influence has been stamped both within and outside Russia's boundaries.

Peter the Great, Czar of Russia between 1689 and 1725, introduced many "westernizing" features during his reign. One of the innovations was the keeping of civil records by the ministers of religion. Begun in 1722, the system required that the established Orthodox clergy keep records relating to the baptisms, marriages, and burials within their parishes. Outside the Orthodox Church, clergymen of other denominations, such as Roman Catholic, Lutheran, as well as Muslim and Jewish, were also required to keep such records for their congregations.

Civil registration of births, marriages, and deaths was introduced by the new Soviet government in 1918. It was at this time, during the formative months of the Russian Revolution and the creation of a new national government, that the Orthodox Church was disestablished. Consequently, civil records were kept at town and city offices under the supervision of the Ministry of Internal Affairs of the national government. The birth records note the first name and family name of the child, and the names, ages, address, and occupations of the parents.

Obtaining copies of Russian public records is at best difficult. American citizens seeking such data should write to the Consular Section, American Embassy — Moscow, c/o Dept. of State, Washington, DC 20521 and request the information sheet and order form used to submit requests for copies of public records in the Soviet Union. The completed form is returned to the American Embassy with a charge of $2.25 for each requested document. The fee is not refunded even if your request is not fulfilled. Generally, it takes from six months to one year before the American Embassy receives a response to a request to Soviet officials for a copy of a public document. Frequently the record is reported to be unavailable because of the damage and destruction of public records in World War II.

## China

After the Civil War many Chinese laborers were brought to California and dispatched to remote posts in various western states to assist in the building of railroad lines. However, anti-Chinese sentiment on the Pacific coast led to violence and the first Chinese Exclusion Act which Congress passed in 1882. The Act prohibited the entry into the United States of Chinese workers for a period of ten years, and it was extended for a similar period in 1892 and in 1902 was indefinitely extended. Consequently, the Chinese population of the country declined from 107,000 in 1890 to 75,000 in 1930, which virtually ended anti-Chinese outbursts. The laws were repealed in 1943, and Chinese immigrants were admitted into the United States under the Quota Law of 1921.

Today the cultural contributions of the Chinese community are felt not only in California and Hawaii but also in cities like San Francisco, New York, and Boston. The population of Chinese-Americans now stands at 435,062.

You should, of course, first follow the fundamental steps necessary for all persons who research their family history. Talk with older relatives about the family's past, and consult the vital records and census records whenever possible to establish supporting evidence.

Because ancestor worship was an important aspect of Chinese cultural and religious life through the centuries, the preservation of a family's lineage was common. Before 1949 the Census Section of the Civil Affairs Department of each precinct had charge of registering all births, marriages, and deaths within its jurisdiction. The records were held by the precinct, and when a family moved to another precinct, it was necessary to inform

the Census Section so that its records could be passed to
the next precinct.

## Japan

Their early story in America is similar to that of the
Chinese. Japanese laborers were not allowed to go
abroad to work until 1886, and after five years only one
thousand Japanese were in the United States. During
the period between 1906 and 1924 the Japanese were
excluded primarily by the discriminatory laws of the
state of California, although it was, in fact, a national
policy under the 1907 "Gentlemen's Agreement" of
President Theodore Roosevelt. With the passage of the
Immigration Act of 1924, such exclusion was enforced
by a statute that remained in effect until the
McCarran-Walter Act of 1952. One of the blights on the
record of America's treatment of minority groups was
the confinement during World War II of citizens of
Japanese ancestry.

Registration of vital statistics in Japan is regulated by
the comprehensive Family Registration Law. Under the
terms of the law, family registration is to be handled by
the head of the local government. Information to be included in the registration is: birth, adoption, dissolution
of adoptive relations, recognition (generally of a chld to
be legitimated), marriage, divorce, parental power and
guardianship, death and disappearance, resumption of
surname by surviving spouse and dissolution of mat-
rimonial relations, disinheritance of a presumptive successor, entry into or separation from a family, acquisi-
tion of a name or surname, and transfer of registered
locality of family and establishment of a family register.
Write to the Civil Affairs Bureau, Minister of Justice,
Tokyo, for information on these details.

The family register establishes that all matters relating
to a Japanese citizen are recorded from cradle to grave. It
is not only the record of the individual's status but also
the collective record of all those who are related to that
person.

# APPENDIXES

# APPENDIX A

# *Bibliography*

The following lists of books are not to be regarded as exhaustive. They are intended to serve as a guide to the most used books in each indicated field. The individual starting out to search for ancestors must remember that no one book can tell him or her how to work out his or her lines, for each line presents its own problems. Therefore, these lists suggest the starting points for further research in books, once the hunter has reached the point where he or she can begin to work with printed material. You will note that no histories of individual families are suggested. For references to printed genealogies of specific families, consult especially the bibliographies listed in Sections C and D. Section E lists the better-known general magazines of genealogical interest. Section F contains atlases and gazetteers, which are indispensable tools for understanding the history of the western world. Maps were guides to the explorers and to our ancestors as they traveled from the old world to the new, and from the Atlantic coast, across the Great Plains and Rocky Mountains to the Pacific coast. Section G notes key reference works for the study of heraldry.

## A. Handbooks and Guides

American Society of Genealogists. *Genealogical Research: Methods and Sources*. 2 vols. Washington, 1960, 1971. (A collection of essays by Fellows of the Society. Vol. I: Part I, General considerations; Part 2, Materials for research; Part 3, Regional genealogy; Part 4, Pre-American ancestry; Part 5, Special fields of investigations. Vol. II: Part 1, Regional genealogy, with essays on eleven midwestern states; Part 2, Special studies — Ontario, Huguenot migrations, Jewish migrations.)

Beard, Timothy Field, with Denise Demong. *How to Find Your Family Roots*. New York, New York, 1977.

Bell, James B. *Family History Record Book*. Minneapolis, 1980.

225

Blockson, Charles L. and Fry, Ron. *Black Genealogy*. Englewood Cliff, New Jersey, 1977.

Camp, Anthony J. *Everyone Has Roots: An Introduction to English Genealogy*. Baltimore, Maryland, 1978.

Camp, Anthony J. *Wills and Their Whereabouts*. London, 1974.

Colket, Meredith B., Jr., and Bridges, Frank E. *Guide to Genealogic Records in the National Archives*. Washington, D.C., 1964.

De Platt, Lyman. *Genealogical Historical Guide to Latin America*. Detroit, Michigan, 1978.

Everton, George B., Sr. *A Handy Book for Genealogists*. Sixth edition, Salt Lake City, Utah, 1971.

Falley, Margaret Dickson. *Irish and Scotch-Irish Ancestral Research. Guide to the Genealogical Records, Methods and Sources in Ireland*. Evanston, Ill., 1962. Vol. 1, Repositories and Records, Vol. II, Bibliography and Family Index.

Gardner, David E. and Smith, Frank. *Genealogical Research in England and Wales*. Salt Lake City, Utah, 1956. 1959.

Greenwood, Val D. *The Researcher's Guide to American Genealogy*. Baltimore, Maryland, 1973.

Hamilton-Edwards, Gerald. *In Search of Scottish Ancestry*. Second edition. Baltimore, Maryland, 1972.

Helmbold, F. Wilbur. *Tracing Your Ancestry: A Step by Step Guide Researching Your Family History*. Birmingham, Alabama, 1976.

Heraldic Artists Ltd., *Handbook on Irish Genealogy: How to Trace Your Ancestors and Relatives in Ireland*. Dublin, 1970.

Jonasson, Eric. *The Canadian Genealogical Handbook*. Second edition, Winnipeg, Manitoba, 1978.

Kirkham, E. Kay. *Simplified Genealogy for Americans*. Salt Lake City, Utah, 1977.

Lichtman, Allan J. *Your Family History: How to Use Oral History, Personal Family Archives, and Public Documents to Discover Your Heritage*. New York, New York, 1978.

Linder, Bill R. *How to Trace Your Family Tree*. New York, New York, 1978.

Mitler, Olga. *Genealogical Research for Czech and Slovak Americans*. Detroit, Michigan, 1978.

Rose, James and Eicholz, Alice. *Black Genesis*. Detroit, Michigan, 1978.

Rottenberg, Dan. *Finding Our Fathers: A Guidebook to Jewish Genealogy*. New York, New York, 1977.

Steel, D. J. assisted by the late Mrs. A. E. F. Steel. *Sources for Scottish Genealogy and Family History*, in *National Index of Parish Registers*, Vol. XII. London, 1970.

Stevenson, Noel C. *Search and Research*. Salt Lake City, Utah, 1977.

Stryker-Rodda, Harriet. *How to Climb Your Family Tree: Genealogy for Beginners*. New York, New York, 1977.

Williams, Ethel W. *Know Your Ancestors: A Guide to Genealogical Research*. Rutland, Vermont, 1960.

Wright, Norman E. *Building an American Pedigree: A Study in Genealogy*. Provo, Utah, 1974.

Zabriskie, George O. *Climbing Your Family Tree Systematically*. Salt Lake City, Utah, 1969.

## B. Reference Books

Barton, H. Arnold. *The Search for Ancestors: A Swedish-American Family Saga*. Carbondale and Edwardsville, Ill., 1979.

Black, George F. *The Surnames of Scotland: Their Origin, Meaning, and History*. New York, New York, 1946.

Colket, Meredith B. *Founders of Early American Families: Emigrants from Europe, 1607–1657*. Cleveland, Ohio, 1975.

Dubester, Henry J. *State Censuses. An Annotated Bibliography of Censuses of Population Taken after the Year 1790, by States and Territories of the United States*. Washington, D.C., 1948.

Franklin, W. Neil, compiler. *Federal Population and Mortality Census Schedule, 1790–1890, in the National Archives and the States: Outline of a Lecture on Their Availability, Content, and Use*. Washington, D.C., 1971.

Fucilla, Joseph G. *Our Italian Surnames*. Evanston, Ill., 1949.

Haley, Alex. *Roots*. New York, New York, 1976.

Hassall, W. O. *History through Surnames*. Oxford, England, 1967.

Jacobus, Donald Lines. *Genealogy as Pastime and Profession*. Second edition. Baltimore, Maryland, 1968.

Kazanoff, Benzion C. *A Dictionary of Jewish Names and Their History*. New York, New York, 1977.

Kirkham, E. Kay. *Some of the Military Records of America Before 1900: Their Use and Value in Genealogical and Historical Research*. Salt Lake City, Utah, 1964.

Kirkham, E. Kay. *The Land Records of America and Their Genealogical Value*. Provo, Utah, 1972.

Kirkham, E. Kay. *A Survey of American Church Records*. Fourth edition. Logan, Utah, 1978.

Lifton, Betty Jean. *Twice Born: Memoirs of an Adopted Daughter*. New York, New York, 1975.

Lifton, Betty Jean. *Lost and Found: The Adoption Experience*. New York, New York, 1979.

MacLysaght, Edward. *The Surnames of Ireland*. Shannon, Ireland, 1969.

Matthews, Constance M. *English Surnames*. New York, New York, 1967.

Maudell, Charles R. *The Romance of Spanish Surnames*. New Orleans, Louisiana, 1967.

Parker, J. Carlyle. *City, County, Town and Township Index to the 1850 Federal Census Schedules*. Detroit, Michigan, 1979.

Reaney, Percy H. *A Dictionary of British Surnames*. London, 1966.

Rosenstein, Neil. *The Unbroken Chain: Biographical Sketches and the*

*Genealogy of Illustrious Jewish Families from the 15th–20th Century*. New York, New York, 1976.

Round, J. Horace. *Family Origins and Other Studies*. 1930, reprint. Baltimore, Maryland, 1970.

Smith, Clifford Neal. *A Calendar of Archival Materials on the Land Patents Issued by the United States Government, with Subject, Tract, and Name Indexes, 1788–1810*. Federal land series. Vol. 1, Chicago, Ill., 1973.

Smith, Clifford Neal. *Federal Bounty-Land Warrants of the American Revolution, 1799–1835*. Federal land series. Vol. 2. Chicago, Ill., 1973.

Smith, Clifford Neal and Piszczan-Czaja Smith, Anna. *Encyclopedia of German American Genealogical Research*. New York, New York, 1976.

Smith, Clifford Neal and Piszczan-Czaja Smith, Anna. *American Genealogical Resources in German Archives: A Handbook*. New York, New York, 1977.

Stern, Malcolm H. *Americans of Jewish Descent: A Compendium of Genealogy*. New York, New York, 1971.

Stern, Malcolm H. *First American Jewish Families: 600 Genealogies, 1654–1977*. New York, New York, 1979.

Stevenson, Noel C. *The Genealogical Reader*. Salt Lake City, Utah, 1958.

Stevenson, Noel C., J.D., F.A.S.G. *Genealogical Evidence: A Guide to the Standard of Proof Relating to Pedigrees, Ancestry, Heirship and Family History*. Laguna Hills, California, 1979.

Stewart, George R. *American Given Names: Their Origin and History in the Context of the English Language*. New York, New York, 1979.

Wagner, Sir Anthony. *English Genealogy*. Second edition. Oxford, England, 1972.

## C. Indexes to "Buried" Genealogies

*A Survey of American Genealogical Periodicals and Periodical Indexes*. By Kip Sperry. Detroit, Michigan, 1978.

*Almanach de Gotha: annuaire genealogique diplomatique et statistique* 1763–1944. Published at various locations.

*The American Genealogical Index*. Edited by Fremont J. Rider. 48 vols. Middletown, Conn., 1942–52. (Indexes the individual names in a selected list of several hundred family histories and the federal census of 1790.)

*The American Genealogical-Biographical Index*. Edited by Fremont J. Rider. Middletown, Conn., 1952—. (Continuation of preceding, now being published. In addition to providing the histories of more families, it includes all the names in the *Boston Evening Transcript*, 1906–41, and 63 volumes of lists of Revolutionary War soldiers and a few other military rosters. This useful tool will probably extend to at least 300 volumes.)

*Bibliographia genealogica americana: An Alphabetical Index to American Genealogies and Pedigrees Contained in State, County, and Town Histories, Printed Genealogies, and Kindred Works*. By Daniel S. Durrie.

Albany, 1868. Second Edition, revised and enlarged. Albany, 1878. Third Edition, revised and enlarged. Albany, 1886 (Supplement, 1888).

*Genealogical Periodical Annual Index*. 1962–65, compiled by Ellen Stanley Rogers; 1966–73, compiled by George E. Russell; 1974—, compiled by Laird C. Towle. Bowie, Maryland, 1962.

*The Grafton Index of Books and Magazine Articles on History, Genealogy, and Biography Printed in the United States on American Subjects during the Year 1909*. New York, New York, ca. 1910.

*Index to American Genealogies and to Genealogical Material Contained in All Works Such as Town Histories, County Histories, Local Histories, Historical Society Publications, Biographies, Historical Periodicals, and Kindred Works*. Fourth Edition, revised, improved, and enlarged, containing nearly 40,000 references. Albany, 1900 (Supplement, 1900–8, Albany, 1908). (Munsell's, Joel, Sons).

*Index to Genealogical Periodical Literature, 1960–1977*. By Kip Sperry. Detroit, Michigan, 1979.

*Index to Genealogical Periodicals*. By Donald Lines Jacobus. 3 vols. New Haven, 1932–53. (The third volume contains the late Mr. Jacobus's "Own Index," a key to many excellent studies of ancestral lines buried in the lineages of individuals, such as Ferris's *The Dawes-Gates Ancestral Lines*.) Baltimore, Maryland, 1973.

*The Library of Congress Index to Biographies in Local Histories*. Microfilm. 40 rolls. Baltimore, Maryland. References extracted from state and regional histories and biographical collections from every part of the United States.

*Munsell's Genealogical Index*. South Norwalk, Conn., 1933.

## D. Bibliographies

*Bibliography of Lists of New England Soldiers*, compiled by Mary Ellen Baker. Addenda by Robert MacKay. Boston, Mass., 1977.

Brigham, Clarence S. *History and Bibliography of American Newspapers, 1620–1820*. Two volumes. Worcester, Mass., 1947.

Brigham, Clarence S. *Additions and Corrections*. Worcester, Mass., 1961.

Filby, P. William. *American and British Genealogy and Heraldry: A Selected List of Books*. Second edition. Chicago, Ill., 1975.

Freidel, Frank, ed. *Harvard Guide to American History*. Revised edition. Two volumes. Cambridge, Mass., 1974.

Kaminkow, Marion J. *United States Local Histories in the Library of Congress: A Bibliography*. Four volumes. Baltimore, Maryland, 1975.

Kaminkow, Marion J. *Genealogies in the Library of Congress: A Bibliography of Family Histories of America and Great Britain*. Baltimore, Maryland, 1974.

Long Island Historical Society. *Catalogue of the American Genealogies in the Library*. Prepared under the direction of Emma Toedteberg. Reprint. Baltimore, Maryland, 1969.

New York Public Library. *Dictionary Catalog of the Local History and Genealogy Division, the Research Libraries of the New York Public Libraries*. Eighteen volumes. Boston, Mass., 1974.

New York Public Library. *United States Local History Catalog*. Two volumes. Boston, Mass., 1974.

Newberry Library, Chicago. *The Genealogical Index*. Four volumes. Boston, Mass., 1960.

Schreiner-Yantis, Netti, ed. *Genealogical Books in Print*. Springfield, Virginia, 1975.

## E. Current Magazines and Serials of General Interest

*American Genealogical Periodicals: A Bibliography with a Chronological Finding List*. By Lester J. Cappon. The New York Public Library. New York, 1964.

*American Genealogist* (formerly *New Haven Genealogical Magazine*). New Haven (Now Des Moines, Iowa), 1923—. (TAG.)

*Genealogical Journal*. Utah Genealogical Association. Salt Lake City, Utah. Vol. 1, 1972.

*Journal of Genealogy*. Robert D. Anderson, Publisher and Editor-in-Chief. Omaha, Neb. Vol. 1, Sept. 1976.

*National Genealogical Society Quarterly*. 1912—. (N.G.S.)

*New England Historical and Genealogical Register*. 1847—. (The *Register*.)

*New York Genealogical and Biographical Record*. 1870—. (The *Record*.)

*Toledot: The Journal of Jewish Genealogy*. New York, New York, Vol. 1, 1977.

## F. Atlases and Gazetteers

Adams, James T. *Atlas of American History*. New York, 1943.

*The American Heritage Pictorial Atlas of United States History*. New York, 1966.

Cappon, Lester J. *Atlas of Early American History: The Revolutionary Era, 1760–90*. Princeton, New Jersey, 1976.

*The Columbia Lippincott Gazetteer of the World*. New York, New York, 1962.

Gaustad, Edwin Scott. *Historical Atlas of Religion in America*. Revised edition. New York, New York, 1976.

Paullin, Charles O. *Atlas of the Historical Geography of the United States*. John K. Wright, editor. Washington, D.C. and New York, 1932.

Shepherd, William R. *Historical Atlas*. Ninth edition. New York, New York, 1964.

U. S. Geological Survey. *National Atlas of the United States of America*. Washington, D.C., 1970.

*Webster's Geographical Dictionary*. Springfield, Mass., 1962.

## G. Heraldry

Boutell, Charles. *Boutell's Heraldry*. Revised by J. P. Brooke-Little. New York, New York, 1973.

Brooke-Little, John P. *An Heraldic Alphabet*. Revised edition. London, 1975.

Burke, Sir John Bernard. *Burke's Genealogical and Heraldic History of the Landed Gentry, Including American Families with British Ancestry*. London, 1939.

Burke, Sir John Bernard. *The General Armory of England, Scotland, Ireland and Wales: Comprising a Registry of Armorial Bearings from the Earliest to the Present Time*. London, 1884. Reprinted, 1969.

*The Complete Peerage*. Vicary Gibbs, Editor. Thirteen volumes in fourteen. London, 1910–59.

Fox-Davies, Arthur C. *A Complete Guide to Heraldry*, 1909. Reprinted, revised, and annotated by J. P. Brooke-Little. New York, New York, 1969.

Grant, Francis J. *The Manual of Heraldry*. Edinburgh, Scotland, 1962.

Innes, Sr Thomas. *Scots Heraldry: A Practical Handbook on the Historical Principles and Modern Application of the Art and Science*. Second edition. Baltimore, Maryland, 1971.

London, H. S. *The Right Road for the Study of Heraldry*. Second edition. London, 1960.

Rietstap, Johannes B. *Armorial général; précedé d'un dictionnaire des termes du blason*. 1861. Reprint. Two volumes. Baltimore, Maryland, 1972.

Rolland, Victor and H. V. *General Illustrated Armorial*. 1903–26. Reprint. Six volumes in three. Baltimore, Maryland, 1967.

Rolland, Victor and H. V. *Supplément to the Armorial Général*. 1904–54. Reprint. Nine volumes in three. Baltimore, Maryland, 1969–71.

*A Roll of Arms: Registered by the Committee on Heraldry of the New England Historic Genealogical Society*. Parts 1–9. Boston, Mass., 1928–79.

Volborth, Carl A. von. *Heraldry of the World*. London, 1973.

# State Offices of Vital Statistics

Local records of births, marriages, and deaths are key sources of information for you in your search for your ancestors. During the twentieth century, particularly since the establishment of the social security system, record-keeping by each state has been considerably expanded and improved. The following list of state offices of vital statistics is presented for your convenience and should be consulted first in your quest for personal data. Do remember, however, that the records of the offices of vital statistics of the various states should be supplemented or complemented by the use of town or county records. For example, many county clerks' offices, to this day, are the repositories of marriage records.

When you write to a state, county, or town record office, be as precise as possible about the kind of information you are seeking: names, dates, and addresses. Ask for a "full copy" of the birth, marriage, or death certificate, since you want a complete copy of the information that is on file regarding your ancestor.

Because the procedures and fees charged for obtaining copies of records from the various offices of vital statistics vary, it is best to write in advance requesting information about such details.

### Alabama

Bureau of Vital Statistics
State Dept. of Public Health
Montgomery, AL 36104

(Births and deaths, 1908—
Marriages, Aug. 1936—; earlier, Probate Judge, County Court House)

### Alaska

Bureau of Vital Statistics
Dept. of Health and Welfare
Pouch "H"

Juneau, AK 99801

(Births, marriages, deaths: 1913—)

## Arizona

Division of Vital Records
State Dept. of Health
P.O. Box 3887
Phoenix, AZ 85030

(Births and deaths: July, 1909—; before 1909 abstracts from county clerk
Marriages: clerk of superior court of county where license was issued)

## Arkansas

Bureau of Vital Records
State Dept. of Health
4815 West Markham Street
Little Rock, AR 72201

(Births and deaths: Feb. 1914—
Marriages: 1917—)

## California

Bureau of Vital Statistics Registration
State Dept. of Health
410 N Street
Sacramento, CA 95814

(Births, marriages, and deaths: July 1905—; earlier at county recorder's office)

## Colorado

Records and Statistics Section
Colorado Dept. of Health
4210 East 11th Ave.
Denver, CO 80220

(Births and deaths: 1910—
Marriages: a statewide index of records for all years except 1940–67. Write to county clerk for copies)

## Connecticut

Public Health Statistics Section
State Dept. of Health
79 Elm Street
Hartford, CT 06115

(Birth, marriages, deaths: 1 July 1897—; prior records with town and city clerks and in the Barbour Collection at the State Library in Hartford)

Delaware

Bureau of Vital Statistics
Division of Public Health
Dept. of Health and Social Services
Jesse S. Cooper Memorial Bldg.
Dover, DE 19901

(Births, marriages, deaths: 1861–63; 1881—)

District of Columbia

District of Columbia Dept. of Human Resources
Vital Records Section
615 Pennsylvania Ave. N.W., Room 100
Washington, D.C. 20004

(Births: 1871—
Deaths: 1855—, except none during Civil War
Marriages: Clerk, District of Columbia
                    Court of General Sessions
                    Washington, D.C. 20001)

Florida

Dept. of Health and Rehabilitative Services
Division of Health
Bureau of Vital Statistics
P.O. Box 210
Jacksonville, FL 32201

(Births: 1865—
Deaths: 1877—
Marriages: 6 June 1927—; earlier, write to county judge's office)

Georgia

Vital Records Service
State Dept. of Public Health, Room 217H
47 Trinity Ave. S.W.
Atlanta, GA 30334

(Births and deaths: 1919—
Marriages: 9 June 1952—; earlier, county clerks or Clerk of the
Ordinary Court at county courthouse)

Hawaii

Research and Statistics Office
State Dept. of Health
P.O. Box 3378
Honolulu, HI 96801

(Births, marriages, deaths: 1853—)

Idaho

Bureau of Vital Statistics
820 Washington Street (building address)

State House (mailing address)
Boise, ID 83720

(Births, deaths: 1911—
Births, deaths: 1907–11, county recorder
Marriages: 1947—; prior, at county recorder's office)

Illinois

Office of Vital Records
State Dept. of Public Health
535 W. Jefferson St.
Springfield, IL 67261

(Births, deaths: 1916—
Marriages: 1962—
Earlier births, marriages, deaths at county clerk's office)

Indiana

Division of Vital Records
State Board of Health
1330 W. Michigan Street
Indianapolis, IN 46206

(Births: Oct. 1907—
Deaths: 1900—
Births and deaths prior, health officer of county or city
Marriages: 1958—; prior, clerk of circuit court or clerk of superior court)

Iowa

Division of Records and Statistics
State Dept. of Health
Des Moines, IA 50319

(Births: 1880—
Deaths: 1896—
Marriage records: 1916—; earlier, at clerk of district courts)

Kansas

Bureau of Vital Statistics
State Dept. of Health
6700 S. Topeka Ave.
Topeka, KS 66620

(Births, deaths: July 1911—; prior, at county clerk's office
Marriages: May 1913—; prior, probate judge of county)

Kentucky

Office of Vital Statistics
State Dept. of Health
275 East Main Street
Frankfort, KY 40601

(Births, deaths: 1911—
Marriages: July 1958—; prior, clerk of county court)

Louisiana

> Vital Records Registry
> State Dept. of Health
> P.O. Box 60630
> New Orleans, LA 70160
>
> (Births, deaths: July 1914—
> Marriages: 1946—; prior, clerk's office of parishes [counties])
>
> New Orleans: births, 1790—; deaths, 1803—; marriages, at
>
> Bureau of Vital Statistics
> City Health Dept.
> 1Wo3
> City Hall
> Civic Center
> New Orleans, LA 70112

Maine

> Office of Vital Records
> State Dept. of Health and Welfare
> State House
> Augusta, ME 04333
>
> (Births, marriages and deaths, 1892—; earlier, town clerk's office)

Maryland

> Division of Vital Records
> State Dept. of Health
> State Office Building
> 201 West Preston Street
> Baltimore, MD 21203
>
> (Births and deaths, 1898—
> Marriages, June 1951—; earlier, clerk of circuit court in county
> where license was issued
>
> Baltimore City Health Dept.
> Bureau of Vital Records
> Municipal Office Bldg.
> Baltimore, MD 21202
>
> Births, deaths, 1875—)

Massachusetts

> Registrar of Vital Statistics
> Room 103, McCormack Building
> 1 Ashburton Place
> Boston, MA 02108
>
> (Births, marriages, deaths, 1841—; earlier, city or town clerk's
> office)
>
> For Boston:
> City Registrar

Registry Division
Health Dept.
Room 705, City Hall Annex
Boston, MA 02133

(Births, deaths, 1639—)

## Michigan

Vital Records Section
Michigan Dept. of Public Health
3500 North Logan Street
Lansing, MI 48914

(Births, marriages, deaths, 1867—; earlier, county clerk's office)

## Minnesota

Minnesota Dept. of Health
Section of Vital Statistics
717 Delaware Street S.E.
Minneapolis, MN 55440

(Births, deaths, 1900—; earlier, clerk of district court of county;
City Health Dept. for Minneapolis or St. Paul
Marriages, 1958—; earlier, clerk of district court)

## Mississippi

Vital Records
P.O. Box 1700
Jackson, MS 39205

(Births, deaths: 1 Nov. 1912—; earlier, circuit clerk of county
Marriages: 1926—; earlier, circuit clerk of county where license
was issued)

## Missouri

Bureau of Vital Records
Division of Health
State Dept. of Public Health and Welfare
Jefferson City, MO 65101

(Births, deaths: 1910—; earlier, county clerk's office
Marriages: July 1948—; earlier, recorder of deeds of county where
license was issued)

## Montana

Records and Statistics Bureau
State Dept. of Health and Environmental Sciences
Helena, MT 59601

(Births, deaths: 1907—; earlier, county clerk's office
Marriages: July 1943—; earlier, clerk of district court where license
was issued)

## Nebraska

Bureau of Vital Statistics

State Dept. of Health
Lincoln Building
1003 "O" Street
Lincoln, NE 68508

(Births, deaths: 1904—
Marriages: 1909—: Bureau of Vital Statistics
                    State Dept. of Health
                    State Capital
                    Lincoln, NE 68509
earlier, clerk of county court)

Nevada

Dept. of Health, Welfare and Rehabilitation
Division of Health
Section of Vital Statistics
Capitol Complex
Carson City, NV 89701

(Births, deaths: 1911—; earlier, office of county recorder of each county
Marriages: office of county recorder of each county)

New Hampshire

Dept. of Health and Welfare
Division of Public Health
Bureau of Vital Statistics
61 South Spring Street
Concord, NH 03301

(Births, marriages, deaths: 1640—)

New Jersey

State Dept. of Health
Bureau of Vital Statistics
Box 1540
Trenton, NJ 08625

(Births, deaths: June 1878—
Marriages, state office or county clerk's office
For births, marriages, deaths: May 1848–May 1878, Archives and History Bureau, State Library Division, State Dept of Education, Trenton, NJ 08625

New Mexico

Vital Records
New Mexico Health and Social Services Dept.
PERA Building, Room 118
Santa Fe, NM 87501

(Births, deaths: 1880—; earlier, county clerk's office
Marriages, county clerk's office in county where license was issued)

New York

*except* for New York City

Bureau of Vital Records
State Dept. of Health
Empire State Plaza
Tower Building
Albany, NY 12237

(Births, deaths: 1880—; earlier, City Registrar of Vital Statistics
Births, deaths before 1914 for Albany, Buffalo, Yonkers, City Registrar of Vital Statistics
Marriages, 1880–1907; May 1915—; for 1908–April 1915, county clerk's office where license was issued
Marriages, from 1880 through 1907 for Albany, Buffalo, Yonkers, city clerk's office)

New York City, Borough of Bronx

Bronx Bureau of Vital Records
1826 Arthur Avenue
Bronx, NY 10457

(Births, deaths: 1898—; 1865–97 in Municipal Archives
Office of City Clerk
1780 Grand Concourse
Bronx, NY 10457
Marriages, 1914—)

New York City, Borough of Brooklyn

Brooklyn Bureau of Vital Records
295 Flatbush Avenue Extension
Brooklyn, NY 11201

(Births, deaths: 1898—; 1866–97 in Municipal Archives
Office of City Clerk
208 Joraleman Street
Brooklyn, NY 11201
Marriages, 1866—)

New York City, Borough of Manhattan

Dept. of Health of New York City
Bureau of Vital Statistics
125 Worth Street
New York, NY 10013

(Births, deaths: 1898—; births, 1866–97; deaths: 1798–1897
in Municipal Archives
Marriage License Bureau
Room 265, Municipal Building
New York, NY 10007
Marriages, 1866—; 1847–65 in Municipal Archives)

New York City, Borough of Queens

Queens Bureau of Vital Records
90-37 Parsons Blvd.
Jamaica, NY 11432

(Births, deaths: 1898—
Office of City Clerk
120-55 Queens Blvd.
Borough Hall Station
Jamaica, NY 11424
Marriages: 1898—)

New York City, Borough of Staten Island

Richmond Bureau of Vital Records
51 Stuyvesant Place
St. George, Staten Island, NY 10301

(Births, deaths: 1898—
Borough Hall
St. George
Staten Island, NY 10301
Marriages: 1898—)

North Carolina

Vital Records Branch
Division of Health Services
P.O. Box 2091
Raleigh, NC 27602

(Births, deaths: Oct. 1913—
Marriages: 1962—; earlier, register of deeds in county where marriage was performed)

North Dakota

Division of Vital Records
State Dept. of Health
Bismarck, ND 58505

(Births, deaths: July 1893—; earlier, clerk of district court
Marriages: July 1925—; earlier, county judge of county)

Ohio

Division of Vital Statistics
State Dept. of Health
G-20 State Department Bldg.
65 S. Front Street
Columbus, OH 43215

(Births, deaths: 20 Dec., 1908—; earlier, county probate court where event occurred
Marriages: Sept. 1949—; earlier, county probate court)

Oklahoma

> Division of Statistics
> State Dept. of Health
> Northeast 10th St. & Stonewall
> P.O. Box 53551
> Oklahoma City, OK 73152
>
> (Births, deaths: Oct. 1908—
> Marriages: county clerk of court where license was issued)

Oregon

> Vital Statistics Section
> State Board of Health
> P.O. Box 231
> Portland, OR 97207
>
> (Births, deaths: July 1903—
> Marriages: 1907—; earlier, county clerk's office where license was issued)

Pennsylvania

> Division of Vital Statistics
> State Dept. of Health
> 101 S. Mercer St.
> P.O. Box 1528
> Newcastle, PA 16103
>
> (Births, deaths: 1906—; earlier, register of wills, orphan's court, in county where birth or death occurred
> Marriages: 1941—; earlier, marriage license clerk, county court house)
>
> Births, deaths, Pittsburgh, 1870–1905:
> Office of Biostatistics
> Pittsburgh Health Dept.
> City-County Bldg.
> Pittsburgh, PA 15219
>
> Births, deaths, Philadelphia, 1860–1915:
> Vital Statistics
> Philadelphia Dept. of Public Health
> City Hall Annex
> Philadelphia, PA 19107

Rhode Island

> Division of Vital Statistics
> State Dept. of Health
> Health Bldg., Room 101
> Davis Street
> Providence, RI 02908
>
> (Births, marriages, deaths: 1853—; earlier, town clerk's office where birth, marriage, or death occurred)

### South Carolina

Division of Vital Records
Bureau of Health Measurement
South Carolina Dept. of Health and Analysis Environmental Control
2600 Bull Street
Columbia, SC 29201

(Births, deaths: 1915—; earlier, County Health Dept.

City of Charleston
Births: 1877—
Deaths: 1821—
Marriages: 1 July 1950—; earlier, county probate judge where license was issued; July 1911—)

### South Dakota

Division of Public Health Statistics
State Dept. of Health
Pierre, SD 57501

(Births, deaths: July 1905—
Marriages: July 1905—; earlier, county clerk of court where license was issued)

### Tennessee

Division of Vital Statistics
State Dept. of Public Health
Cordell Hull Bldg.
Nashville, TN 37219

(Births, deaths: 1914—; earlier, county clerk's office

For Nashville, June 1881—;
For Knoxville, July 1881—;
For Chattanooga, 1882—

Deaths, 1914—:

For Nashville, July 1874;
For Knoxville, July 1887—;
For Chattanooga, 6 Mar. 1872

Marriages, July 1945—; earlier, county court clerk's office, where license was issued.

Memphis: Shelby County Health Dept.
Division of Vital Statistics
814 Jefferson
Memphis, TN 38105

Births, April 1874–1887;
Nov. 1898–Jan. 1914

Deaths, May 1848–Jan. 1914)

Texas

  Bureau of Vital Statistics
  State Dept. of Health
  410 East 5th Street
  Austin, TX 78701

  (Births, deaths: 1903—; earlier, county clerk's office
  Marriages: county clerk's office where license was issued)

Utah

  Division of Vital Statistics
  Utah State Dept. of Health
  150 W. N. Temple
  Salt Lake City, UT 84110

  (Births, deaths: 1905—; earlier, county clerk's office
  Births, deaths, Salt Lake City, Ogden, 1890–1904, write to the City
  Board of Health
  Marriages, county clerk's office where license was issued)

Vermont

  Secretary of State
  Vital Records Dept.
  State House
  Montpelier, VT 05602

  (Births, deaths: 1760—
  Marriages: 1857—; earlier, contact town clerk's office in town
  where license was issued)

Virginia

  Bureau of Vital Records and Statistics
  State Dept. of Health
  James Madison Bldg.
  P.O. Box 1000
  Richmond, VA 23208

  (Births, deaths: 1853–Dec. 1896; 4 June 1912—; contact city or
  town health department for period between Dec. 1896 and 4 June
  1912
  Marriages: 1853—; earlier, clerk of county circuit court where
  license was issued)

Washington

  Vital Records
  Dept. of Health
  P.O. Box 9709
  Olympia, WA 98504

  (Births, deaths: July 1907—; earlier, office of county auditor where
  event occurred
  Marriages: 1968—; earlier, office of county auditor where license
  was issued)

West Virginia

   Division of Vital Statistics
   State Dept. of Health
   State Office Bldg., No. 3
   Charleston, WV 25305

   (Births, deaths: 1917—; earlier, clerk of county court where even
   occurred
   Marriages: 1921—; earlier, clerk of county court where license wa
   issued)

Wisconsin

   Bureau of Health Statistics
   Wisconsin Division of Health
   P.O. Box 309
   Madison, WI 53701

   (Births, deaths: 1852—
   Marriages: April 1835—)

Wyoming

   Vital Records Services
   Hathaway Bldg.
   Cheyenne, WY 82002

   (Births, deaths: July 1909—
   Marriages: May 1941—; earlier, county clerk's office in county
   where license was issued)

# APPENDIX C

## Location and Areas Served by the National Archives and Records Service Centers

Several kinds of federal records are a vital source of genealogical information: Census records, military records, pension records, bounty land records, passenger arrival lists, and passport applications, etc. Many of these materials have been microfilmed and may be consulted at the National Archives in Washington, D.C. or at one of its Regional Records Service Centers throughout the United States. The following list notes the location and geographical areas served by the Records Service Center. We suggest that you write to the Chief, Archives Branch, at the Federal Archives and Records Center nearest you and request a list of the materials in their collections which are available for your use. The materials may be used in the search room of the Records Service Center or borrowed by your local public library on the Interlibrary Loan Order service for your use in your hometown. There is no charge for these services. An indispensable aid to the riches of the National Archives and Records Service Centers is Meredith B. Colket, Jr. and F. E. Bridgers's *Guide to Genealogical Records in the National Archives*. Your local library may have a copy of this book, or it can be purchased for a small charge from the U.S. Government Printing Office in Washington, D.C.

Washington, D.C.
   National Archives and Records Service
   NNC
   Washington, D.C. 20408

Boston
   380 Trapelo Road
   Waltham, MA 02154
   (Serves Connecticut, Maine, Massachusetts, New Hampshire, Rhode Island, and Vermont)

New York

Building 22-MOT Bayonne
Bayonne, NJ 07002
(Serves New Jersey, New York, Puerto Rico, and the Virgin Islands)

Philadelphia

5000 Wissahickon Avenue
Philadelphia, PA 19144
(Serves Delaware and Pennsylvania; for microfilm loans also serves District of Columbia, Maryland, Virginia, and West Virginia)

Atlanta

1557 St. Joseph Avenue
East Point, GA 30344
(Serves Alabama, Georgia, Florida, Kentucky, Mississippi, North Carolina, South Carolina, and Tennessee)

Chicago

7358 South Pulaski Road
Chicago, IL 60629
(Serves Illinois, Indiana, Michigan, Minnesota, Ohio, and Wisconsin)

Kansas City

2306 East Bannister Road
Kansas City, MO 64131
(Serves Iowa, Kansas, Missouri, and Nebraska)

Fort Worth

4900 Hemphill Street (building address)
P.O. Box 6216 (mailing address)
Fort Worth, TX 76115
(Serves Arkansas, Louisiana, New Mexico, Oklahoma, and Texas)

Denver

Building 48, Denver Federal Center
Denver, CO 80225
(Serves Colorado, Montana, North Dakota, South Dakota, Utah, and Wyoming)

San Francisco

1000 Commodore Drive
San Bruno, CA 94066
(Serves California except southern California, Hawaii, Nevada except Clark County, and the Pacific Ocean area)

Los Angeles

24000 Avila Road
Laguna Niguel, CA 92677
(Serves Arizona; the southern California counties of Imperial,
Inyo, Kern, Los Angeles, Orange, Riverside, San Bernardino, San
Diego, San Luis Obispo, Santa Barbara, and Ventura; and Clark
County, Nevada)

Seattle

6125 Sand Point Way NE
Seattle, WA 98115
(Serves Alaska, Idaho, Oregon, and Washington)

APPENDIX **D**

# *Census Records*

Since 1790 the federal government has undertaken a census of the population every ten years. The schedules for censuses between 1790 and 1870, a microfilm copy of the 1880 schedules, the existing fragments of the 1890 schedules (the 1890 census was nearly completely destroyed by fire), and a microfilm copy of the 1900 schedules are at the National Archives.

For the period between 1790 and 1840 the census schedules give only the name of the head of household. Other family members are recorded by age and sex but are not named. The 1850 and 1860 schedules list slave owners and the age, sex, and color of each slave but not the name. The 1850 census is important because it was the first census to record the names of all persons in the household, and to ask for state, country, or territory of birth for all free members of the household. Additional information is included with each succeeding census after 1850.

Mortality schedules were compiled for the censuses of 1850, 1860, 1870, 1880, and 1885, which show the name, the month and cause of death, and the state, territory, or country of birth of each person who died during the year that preceded the taking of each of the censuses. The National Archives has microfilm copies of the mortality schedules for many of the states; for those states not represented, inquire for the materials at the appropriate state archives or state historical society.

The Works Project Administration during the 1930s produced an index system for the 1880 and 1900 censuses called Soundex. It is a helpful aid to readers searching for their ancestors because it gathers surnames that sound the same but that may be spelled differently. The surnames are arranged by the Soundex code and then alphabetically by the first names. You should consult the leaflet at the National Archives or at one of the branches of the archives regarding the procedures to follow when using the Soundex system.

In recent years many indexes to census records have been edited by Ronald V. Jackson and Garry R. Teeples and published by Accelerated ndexing Systems, Inc., Salt Lake City, Utah, and you should check those references before searching the records themselves. You may use microfilm copies of the various federal census records at the National Archives or its several branch centers, or the film may be borrowed and used at your local public library or at the genealogical branch libraries of the Church of Jesus Christ of Latter-Day Saints. It is also possible to purchase from the National Archives microfilm rolls of the federal census schedules at a modest charge.

In many states a census has been taken halfway between the federal censuses. For example, in New York there was a census in 1855, another in 1865, and so forth. The ancestor researcher should hunt around and try to find out what censuses have been taken in the locality in which he or she is interested. A helpful book in this regard and one that you should look at before undertaking work with this kind of material is *The United States Census Compendium* compiled by John "D" Stemmons and published in 1973 by The Everton Publishers, Inc., P.O. Box 368, Logan, Utah 84321. It is a directory of census records, tax lists, petitions, oaths of allegiance, church members, directories, poll lists, etc., which can be used as a census. The book notes the various material available for each state and for each county within the state, and identifies the name and location of the agency where the material may be consulted by a researcher.

## Population Schedules Missing, 1790 to 1820

This list of missing schedules is presented to save the ancestor hunter time and postage in writing to Washington, and in the hope that by lucky chance some reader of this book may find one or more of these schedules and notify the Bureau of the Census of the find so that copies may be made.

Census Records of 1800, 1810, and 1820 at the National Archives, Washington, D.C.

(Figures Indicate Number of Volumes)

| State Schedules | 1800 | 1810 | 1820 |
|---|---|---|---|
| Connecticut | 2 | 3 | 3 |
| Delaware | 1 | 1 | 1 |
| District of Columbia (in Maryland) | 1 | — | 1 |
| Georgia | — | — | 5 |
| Illinois | — | — | 2 |
| Indiana | — | — | 3 |
| Kentucky | — | 4 | 8 |
| Louisiana | — | 1 | 2 |
| Maine | 3 | 2 | 4 |
| Maryland | 3 | 4 | 7 |
| Massachusetts | 4 | 5 | 8 |
| Michigan | — | — | 1 |

(Figures Indicate Number of Volumes)

| State Schedules | 1800 | 1810 | 1820 |
|---|---|---|---|
| Mississippi | — | — | 1 |
| New Hampshire | 1 | 2 | 2 |
| New Jersey | — | — | — |
| New York | 8 | 9 | 18 |
| North Carolina | 5 | 6 | 6 |
| Ohio | — | — | 11 |
| Pennsylvania | 7 | 11 | 18 |
| Rhode Island | 1 | 1 | 1 |
| South Carolina | 2 | 2 | 3 |
| Tennessee | — | (1 county) | 3 |
| Vermont | 2 | 2 | 3 |
| Virginia | — | 6 | 11 |

## 1790 Schedules Missing

Delaware (all).

Georgia (all).

Kentucky (all).

Maryland (Alleghany, Calvert, and Somerset counties).

New Jersey (all).

North Carolina (Caswell, Granville, and Orange counties).

Tennessee (all).

Virginia (all — the printed volume of schedules is made up of state tax lists, not census).

## 1800 Schedules Missing

Georgia (all).

Indiana Territory (all).

Kentucky (all).

Maine (part of York County).

Maryland (Baltimore County outside of the city of Baltimore).

Massachusetts (part of Suffolk County).

Mississippi Territory (all).

New Hampshire (parts of Rockingham and Strafford counties).

New Jersey (all).

Northwest Territory Ohio River (all).

Pennsylvania (parts of Westmoreland County).

South Carolina (Richland County).

Tennessee (all).

Virginia (all).

## 1810 Schedules Missing

District of Columbia (all).

Georgia (all).

Illinois Territory (all except Randolph County).

diana Territory (all).

uisiana (all).

aine (part of Oxford County).

chigan (all).

ississippi (all).

ew Jersey (all).

ew York (Cortland and part of Broome counties).

orth Carolina (Craven, Green, New Hanover, and Wake counties).

hio (all).

nnsylvania (parts of Bedford, Cumberland, and Philadelphia counties).

nnessee (all except Rutherford County).

rginia (Cabell, Grayson, Greenbrier, Halifax, Hardy, Henry, James, King William, Lee, Louisa, Mecklenburg, Nansemond, Northampton, Orange, Patrick, Pittsylvania, Russell, and Tazewell counties).

## 1820 Schedules Missing

abama (all).

kansas Territory (all).

eorgia (Franklin, Rabun, and Twiggs counties).

diana (Daviess County).

aine (parts of Penobscot and Washington counties).

issouri (all).

ew Hampshire (Grafton and parts of Rockingham and Strafford counties).

ew Jersey (all).

orth Carolina (Currituck, Franklin, Montgomery, Randolph, and Wake counties).

hio (Franklin and Wood counties).

nnsylvania (parts of Lancaster and Luzerne counties).

nnessee (Anderson, Bledsoe, Blount, Campbell, Carter, Claiborne, Cocke, Grainger, Green, Hamilton, Hawkins, Jefferson, Knox, McMinn, Marion, Monroe, Morgan, Rhea, Roane, Sevier, Sullivan, and Washington counties).

## Note

he following substitutes for the missing census schedules of 1790 ave been compiled from tax lists.

elaware: *Reconstructed 1790 Census of Delaware.* Compiled by Leon DeValinger. Washington, 1954. (National Genealogical Society, Special Publication No. 10.)

entucky: *"First Census" of Kentucky, 1790.* Compiled by Charles B. Heinemann and Gaius Marcus Brumbaugh. Washington [ca. 1940].

entucky: *"Second Census" of Kentucky, 1800.* Compiled by G. Glenn Clift. Frankfort, Ky., 1954.

ermont: *Heads of Families at the Second Census of the United States Taken in the year 1800: Vermont.* Montpelier, Vt., 1938.

**INDEX**

# Index

The names of fictitious people and imaginary places mentioned in the text are not included in this index. Neither are authors, editors, and titles of books listed in the bibliographies in the appendixes. Titles of books mentioned in the text are listed, followed in parentheses by the name of the author or editor. Names of places are not usually included.

## ABOUT THE AUTHOR

GILBERT H. DOANE, who wrote *Searching for Your Ancestors* in 1937, was editor emeritus of *The New England Historical and Genealogical Register* and professor emeritus at the University of Wisconsin. James B. Bell is director of the New England Historic Genealogical Society.

# We Deliver!
## And So Do These Bestsellers.

# RELAX!
## SIT DOWN
### and Catch Up On Your Reading!